Divide, Provide, and Rule

Divide, Provide, and Rule

An Integrative History of Poverty Policy, Social Policy, and Social Reform in Hungary under the Habsburg Monarchy

by

Susan Zimmermann

CEU PRESS

Central European University Press
Budapest–New York

Published in 2011 by

Central European University Press

An imprint of the
Central European University Limited Company
Nádor utca 11, H-1051 Budapest, Hungary
Tel: +36-1-327-3138 or 327-3000
Fax: +36-1-327-3183
E-mail: ceupress@ceu.hu
Website: www.ceupress.com

400 West 59th Street, New York NY 10019, USA
Tel: +1-212-547-6932
Fax: +1-212-548-4607
E-mail: mgreenwald@sorosny.org

ISBN 978-615-5053-19-1

Library of Congress Cataloging-in-Publication Data

Zimmermann, Susan.
Divide, provide, and rule : an integrative history of poverty policy, social policy, and social reform in Hungary under the Habsburg Monarchy / Susan Zimmermann.
p. cm.
"English translation c2011, John Harbord."
Includes bibliographical references and index.
ISBN 978-6155053191 (hbk.)
1. Public welfare–Hungary–History–19th century. 2. Poverty–Government policy–Hungary–History–19th century. 3. Hungary–Social policy. 4. Hungary–Social conditions–19th century. 5. Hungary–Economic conditions–19th century. 6. Hungary–History–1867-1918. I. Title.
HV260.5.Z56 2011
362.5'5610943909034–dc23
2011037329

Printed in Hungary by
Akadémiai Nyomda, Martonvásár

Contents

List of Illustrations

List of Tables

Preface

There are different types of acknowledgements and indebtedness I would like to list here. First of all, the Austrian Academy of Sciences must be mentioned for being so kind as to give permission to use as a basis for some sections of this book a study it commissioned back in—I believe—2007. This study was published as Susan Zimmermann, "Armen- und Sozialpolitik in Ungarn im Vergleich mit Österreich" [Poverty policy and social policy in Hungary compared to Austria], in: Helmut Rumpler, Peter Urbanitsch, eds. *Die Habsburgermonarchie* 1848–1918, vol. 9: Sozialstrukturen, partial vol. 1: Von der feudal-agrarischen zur bürgerlich-industriellen Gesellschaft, partial vol. 1/2: Von der Stände- zur Klassengesellschaft [The Habsburg Monarchy 1848–1918: Social structures: from the feudal-agrarian to the bourgeois-industrial society: from estatal to class society] (Vienna 2010), 1465–1535.

I am most grateful to Tibor Sándor who generously offered his professional knowledge and help in order to identify and assemble the photographs contained in this volume (and many others) as well as the cover photograph; he also provided the information contained in the List of Illustrations at the beginning of this book. Many archivists and librarians in Budapest and elsewhere have been helpful in making my access to and use of the material this book draws on (and my earlier research on which parts of it builds) as smooth, easy and above all enjoyable as possible, and I would like to thank each of them here. Gabriela Dudeková and others drew my attention to important historical facts; Theodora Văcărescu and others helped with organizational matters. Without the imperturbability of my translator, John Harbord, I would surely have been lost amongst all the *főispánok*, *külső cselédek,* and other figures and institutions pertaining to Hungary under the Habsburg Monarchy—figures and institutions who in such a lively manner have populated my own imagination for many years but are so desperately unknown to the English-speaking world.

I hope that this book can achieve more than simply making readers in various countries more familiar with an important dimension of the social and political history of Hungary. I would also like to see this study contribute to an internationalization of historical writing in Europe and beyond that does not simply add—under the banner of "European enlargement"—the history of the less advantageous regions of the continent to the canon. Rather I hope that my "country-study" on Hungary may serve as a point of reference for a new international and transnational history which draws a more realistic picture of the past and present of inequality and exploitation within and between the countries and regions of Europe.

I. Introduction

"Today I visited the Kereskényi family. During the winter time, they live in the 'small house'; the need for heating is less there. I open wide the door and greet the dwellers with hearty goodwill. But the vapor billows out in thick white clouds and causes the words to catch in my throat. As they hear me enter, three children rush to the door. One is the 'sweet', the second the state child, the third a guest." The visitor had come to the village of Hernád in the winter of 1912–1913 to check on the well-being of one of the 54,000 foster children for whom the Hungarian state system of child protection had taken material responsibility. She was well aware that "faultless families" did not exist, "at least not in those circles who take state children into care." Therefore, the visitor confided, the authorities as a rule accepted as foster families those who were "faultless in a relative sense."[1] The Hungarian state system of child protection, starting around the turn of the 20th century, was a remarkable invention among social protection policies nationally and internationally. Children's poverty and "neglect," and the perceived need to do something about it, was a heated topic in Hungary as elsewhere in the period. Yet child protection was only one of a whole range of fields and themes of social reform; social reform itself was, alongside poverty policy and social policy (i.e. labor protection and social insurance), only one of the three large policy areas contemporarily considered destined to deal with social need and social risk. In what follows, all of these policies together will be termed need-related policies. The unstable and blurred boundaries between social inclusion and social exclusion and the scope of unattended need so visible in the state of affairs in Hungarian child protection on the eve of World War I were characteristic of other policies concerned with social need and social risk too. In the Kingdom of Hungary, with its population of 18 million and span-

[1] *A gyermekvédelem lapja* 9 (1913): 77 f. The figure for the number of "state children" refers to 1910. I have not marked the abbreviations in this and the following original quote in the introduction.

ning a territory far larger than present day Hungary, 33 percent of the labor force outside primary production, but less than six percent of the overall population enjoyed state health insurance. Added to this there was also huge variation according to region, gender, occupational status, and other factors. In poverty policy likewise, politics of social inclusion were intimately connected with politics of exclusion. Not only were members of the Roma population[2] subject to particular persecution, for example when forced labor was introduced in 1913. Nor could those who were considered "respectable" among the poor count unconditionally on even minimal support either. In 1887, in the capital city of Budapest, which was economically booming and growing rapidly in the decades before 1914, an aging theater actor who had initially been admitted to the municipal poor house suddenly faced the threat of relocation to a far away community which was considered his "home town" by the authorities. In a letter addressed to the "honored" Budapest authorities, the man explained: "I have been away from my home location for 21 years; I have neither relatives there nor even acquaintances from whose mercy I could expect any pittance." The Budapest authorities therefore "may be as propitious as to grant that I may spend my remaining time, which is anyway short due to my very old age, in the local poor house." The authorities remained firm and ordered relocation. Before this could happen, the actor left the poor house, hiding his neediness from the authorities' eyes and control.[3]

This book is intended as an integrative study of the history of poverty policy, social reform, and social policy in Hungary in the period from 1848 to 1914. In a variety of contexts it compares Hungarian developments with the situation in Austria, the other half of the Habsburg Monar-

---

[2] There were groups other than Roma among the population labeled as "Gypsy" in contemporary language. A special survey conducted by the Hungarian authorities in 1893 found 272.776 "Gypsies" as compared to an overall population in the Kingdom of Hungary of more than 15 million (1891). János Váradi, "A magyarországi cigány népesség számának alakulása 1850–1910" [The development of the Gypsy population 1850–1910]. *Regio. Kisebbség, Politika, Társadalom* 20, no. 4 (2009): 60–81, here 74 f.; *A Magyar Korona Országainak az 1891. év elején végrehajtott népszámlálás eredményei. I. rész. Általános népleírás* [Census of the lands of the Hungarian Crown conducted at the beginning of the year 1891. Part I. General description of the population]. Magyar Statisztikai Közlemények. Új Folyam [Hungarian statistical publications. New sequence] (Budapest 1893), vol. I. beginning of the year 1891. Part I. General description of the population] (Budapest 1893), I.

[3] Budapest Főváros Levéltára [Budapest Capital Archive], Budapest Székesfőváros Tanácsának iratai [Documents of the Administrative Council of the Capital and Royal Seat Budapest] (henceforth BFL-C), IV 1407b 400/1882-IX.

chy into which the Kingdom of Hungary was incorporated and within which the country enjoyed, after 1867, far-reaching political autonomy as to internal affairs. The study also presents and discusses quantitative data, when possible exploring change over time, about provision, coverage, repressive strategies, level of benefits, and so on for core areas of need-related policies, so as to lay the groundwork for systematic comparison with other countries and contexts.

The integrative perspective is pursued on a variety of levels and with a number of intentions. First, I aim to demonstrate that the need-related policies in all three major fields covered by this study simultaneously entailed strategies of inclusion and exclusion. I show how both of these sides of the need-related policies built on particular visions of and aimed at bringing about particular patterns of change in social relations in society. Need-related policies in the 19th and early 20th centuries are thus shown to have not been simply about welfare and social integration—not to mention the prehistory and emergence of the "welfare state." Instead the study demonstrates that need-related policies were aimed at making people—and different groups of people differently—conform to dominant social and economic expectations and interests, and that there was anything but a simply correspondence between need and welfare. In fact, the Hungarian case as explored in this study amply demonstrates that there was, in many instances and on a variety of levels, a tendency according to which greater need resulted in less welfare (and the other way around). While neither exploring the extent nor the reasons for social disintegration as a prominent socio-economic feature that undoubtedly characterized Hungarian society at the time, the following chapters make unmistakably clear that suppression, control, and, importantly, ignorance of manifestations and consequences of need were frequently at the heart of Hungarian policies. This was different only when larger state or municipal goals called for more far-reaching intervention or when the authorities were concerned about social instability and (potential) unrest—the latter attesting to the role the agency of those in need has played for shaping need-related policies.

Second, the integrative perspective is aimed at exploring the ongoing relationship and historical interaction between poverty policy, social reform, and social policy and the key actors in each of these fields. Any evaluation of the overall socio-political effect of need-related policies in a given context needs to be grounded in a parallel investigation of various policy measures and their results, the level and scope of benefits and provision, data about coverage, and so on, in (at least) all three policy areas covered by this study. In addition, the interdependency between developments in these three policy areas needs to be taken into account. Their simultaneous investigation reveals, for example, how developments in the field of health care for the poor in Hungary were influenced by both social insurance and poverty policy, or how the invention of the state childcare system was related to practices in municipal poor relief which were more exclusionary than in neighboring Austria. While the need to integrate the study of all areas of the need-related policies is well known in principle to historians of welfare and the welfare state, few studies have attempted to integrate these dimensions. Welfare in rural contexts and smaller communities, welfare by nonpublic actors, and the very interaction between the different branches of the need-related policies have recently been shown to be some of the most important research *desiderata*.[4] This study takes some steps to integrate some of these and other dimensions.

Third, I explore how in the context of need-related policies the social difference and distance—the difference between diverse social groups, between rural and metropolitan, "developed" and "less developed" areas, as well as between different types of labor relations—was created and transformed, deepened, and occasionally challenged. It is by paying attention to and dissecting these diverse dimensions of difference that this study tries to provide a more inclusive history of need-related policies and some of its socio-political consequences in Hungary. Integrative historical writing, in other words, is achieved by accounting for historical fragmentation. One important device the study employs towards this goal is to focus on how need-related policies constructed legal and social boundaries and distinctions between different groups, areas, and labor and social relations. This focus is complemented by the analysis of the ensuing legal and political struggles over these boundaries amongst the diverse authorities and between the authorities on the one hand, and those groups and peoples targeted by the diverse policies as well as the political movements that aimed to represent some of these groups and their interests, such as the workers' and the tenants' movements, on the other.

---

[4] See the careful overview over recent developments in the study of the multilayered history of welfare in various European states by Inga Brandes, Katrin Marx-Jasulski, "Armut und ländliche Gesellschaften im europäischen Vergleich. Eine Einführung" [Poverty and rural societies in European comparison. An introduction], in: Inga Brandes, Katrin Marx-Jasulski, eds. *Poor Relief and Charity. Rural Societies in Europe, 1850–1930* (English-German) (Frankfurt/M.–Berlin–Berne–Brussels–New York–Oxford–Vienna 2008), 9–45.

Each of the three main chapters of this book discusses one of the major areas of these need-related policies, with the analysis of poverty policy and the subchapter on workplace-related labor protection, covering the whole period under investigation. This is because these were the two policy fields where substantial action developed early on played an important role throughout the period. In discussing poverty policy, I focus on institutional care as well as other forms of provision and benefits for adults as well as children, the role of which grew over time, and mention early housing policy. Equally important were policies related to social phenomena such as begging, vagrancy, and illegal prostitution, as well as to the issue of the "home town" and the relocation of those in need. For all of these fields of action there existed—or were created early on legal frameworks at national level, while the municipalities and a whole variety of local, regional, and national actors played a decisive role in fleshing out what poverty policy meant in practice. However, local variation notwithstanding, low levels of public provision, ignorance of need, and a focus on "doing away" with and criminalizing the visible signs of neediness seem to have prevailed everywhere. Nonpublic welfare played an important role that deserves to be further investigated.

Social reform policies as discussed in chapter III partly grew from inherited poverty policy, while in part they marked historically new beginnings. Aside from the state child protection system, public policies of workers' housing and incipient labor market policies accounted for the three most important fields in which (potentially) far-reaching social reform strategies took root. The capital city, Budapest, took the lead in bringing about change in the latter two fields, yet the state and a few other municipalities and private actors did make a noteworthy contribution too. Within the new state child protection system, the municipalities were forced into a subordinated role, including shouldering the burden of substantial compulsory material contribution. In many respects, the state was hesitant to bring about the legal change that would have been a precondition for more far-reaching social reform to develop countrywide.

Social policy in the shape of labor protection and social insurance as discussed in chapter IV provided for regulation and protection of labor and labor relations in the workplace and the mediation of labor-related social risk. In both subareas, regulations pertaining not only to labor in trade and industry but to the large field of noncommercial, agricultural, and bonded labor played an important role. In labor protection, legal differentiation according to the type of worker went along with differentiation according to the character of the work, with growing emphasis on the former over time. While workers' insurance was to an extent designed along Bismarckian and Austrian lines, Hungary was rather inventive when it came to agrarian social policy. The patterns of economic development and political interest as well as related struggles over the boundaries between the insured and the noninsured gave a particular coloring to developments in the field of social insurance. Social insurance policies also contributed to changing the institutional landscape of the Hungarian state.

What was particular to Hungary amongst all these developments? What was the contribution of Hungary to the development of need-related policies internationally? And what is the contribution of my version of a Hungarian "country-study" to the historiography of welfare and the welfare state? I shall try to provide some answers to these questions in the concluding chapter V.

II. Poverty Policy

Policy on poverty in Hungary under the Habsburg Monarchy developed over the decades against a backdrop of major economic liberalization and hand in hand with a policy of promoting commercial and industrial development. In consequence, it encouraged willingness to undertake wage labor and the acceptance of mobility, the minimalization of state responsibility, and governmental welfare obligations. It also led to suppression of divergent ways of life among the impoverished classes where these disturbed public order or were perceived as socially threatening. Emergency welfare measures and one-off actions in times of crisis, as well as growing emphasis on state intervention and state control of the social sphere completed the picture.

When it came to awareness of municipal welfare obligations in practice, there were marked differences between rural and urban areas, and it was only towards the end of the period that modest steps were taken towards reform aimed at social integration. From the outset, the trend towards minimalism in poor relief—except for the regulations on legal residence status (*községi illetőség*)—was considerably more marked in Hungary than in Austria. New regulations in related areas led over the decades to even more marked ostracism and social exclusion in welfare policy.

While the development of the legislative foundations for this middle-class liberal poverty policy in Hungary occurred mainly from the 1860s onwards, this policy was founded on older traditions of dealing with poverty and welfare that gradually amalgamated with increasing public provision in the years between 1848 and 1914.

II.1. Traditions and Ways of Private and Public Poor Relief in the Context of Limited Civic Self-development (from 1848 to the early 1860s)

The driving political and social forces of the "neoabsolutist" period, namely defeudalization and commercial liberalization, together with creation of a common economic space in the "Austrian Empire," offered limited capacity for major innovations in the area of welfare. It was in this period that the concept of "belonging to the municipality" (*Gemeindezugehörigkeit*) and the related idea of a municipal[1] duty of care first began to enter the Hungarian legal culture. Even the rudiments of a civil communal law and a connected public welfare obligation had hitherto been entirely absent in Hungary; dealing with the problem of poverty had been entirely the business of the police. The Austrian penal code, introduced in 1852,[2] placed provisions against mendicancy, except in special cases, in the hands of the local authorities, in this case the local police.[3] A workhouse serving among other things to accommodate beggars and the "work-shy" had existed in the city of Pest since 1845. Elsewhere this function was fulfilled by general prisons, in which the inmates were obliged to work.[4] In short, care for the poor in Hungary in the neoabsolutist period remained largely in the hands of the police and private charity.

As a result, the neoabsolutist period did not in fact represent any real break with the prerevolutionary period. In Buda and Pest, the two cities that were united (together with Óbuda) into the capital city of Budapest in 1872–73, the Pest and the Buda Women's Charitable Associations (*Pesti jótékony nőegylet* and *Budai jótékony nőegylet* respectively), both founded in 1817, in which upper and middle class, i.e. noble and non-noble women

[1] For the use of the terms "municipal" and "municipality" throughout this study see p. 21, fn. 37.

[2] *Allgemeines Reichs-Gesetz- und Regierungsblatt für das Kaiserthum Österreich*, Kaiserliches Patent vom 27. Mai 1852 [General Imperial legislative and governmental gazette of the Austrian Empire, Imperial patent of 27 May 1852].

[3] Andor Csizmadia, *A magyar közigazgatás fejlődése a XVIII. századtól a tanácsrendszer létrejöttéig* [The development of Hungarian administration from the 18th century to the emergence of the ‹1919› Soviet system] (Budapest 1976), 88–95; Andor Csizmadia, *A szociális gondoskodás változásai Magyarországon* [Changes in social welfare in Hungary] (Budapest 1977), 47 ff.; Act 5/1878, in: *Magyar Törvénytár* [Hungarian corpus juris], fn. 1 to the Act (in the following I give only the Act, except when referring to additional material contained in *Magyar Törvénytár*); *Allgemeines Reichs-Gesetz- und Regierungsblatt für das Kaiserthum Österreich*, Kaiserliches Patent vom 27. Mai 1852 [General Imperial legislative and governmental gazette of the Austrian Empire, Imperial patent of 27 May 1852].

[4] Ferenc Rokken, "A pesti kényszerítő dologház" [The Pest workhouse]. *História* 3 (1930): 82–87, here 83 ff.; Jos. Rózsay, *Sanitätsbericht vom Jahre 1851 über das Zwangsarbeitshaus zu St. Rochus und die Armenversorgungsanstalt der Königlichen Freistadt Pesth* [Sanitary report from 1851 on the Workhouse of St. Rochus and poor relief institute of the Royal City of Pesth] (Pesth 1852), 1; Csizmadia, *Szociális gondoskodás* [Social welfare], 47–52.

worked together, provided institutional continuity.[5] The humble poor houses in the municipalities of Buda and Pest also remained into the neoabsolutist period; in Pest these were replaced in 1856 by the newly built Elizabeth Poor House, designed to accommodate 235 individuals.[6]

In fact, the cities and municipalities of the Kingdom were covered by a relatively tight-knit network of institutions and trusts dedicated to charitable purposes, though perceptive observers such as Moriz von Stubenrauch pointed out that for some of these institutions there is no clear evidence that they performed any kind of activity. The institutions served a wide variety of purposes, both as a whole but often in the case of individual institutions as well. They classified themselves as being for the poor, orphans, foundlings, the sick, the terminally ill, the mad, or various combinations thereof. For example, associations for the support of poor houses also sometimes functioned as institutions of public welfare. Apart from these, there were women's welfare associations concerned with public or private poor relief—such as provision for women in childbed—with orphanages, or those like the Romanian Women's Association, founded in the Transylvanian city of Brassó (Braşov, Kronstadt) in 1849, which undertook the professional training of girls and women. In Temesvár (Timişoara, Temeschwar) in Transylvania, women's associations took the lead in nonpublic welfare for decades with the Israelite Women's Association of the Inner City (*Belvárosi israelita nőegylet*) and Israelite Women's Association of the Factory City (*Gyárvárosi israelita nőegylet*) established in 1846, and the "Benevolent Blessed Virgin" Roman Catholic Women's Association (*"Segítő Boldogasszony" római katholikus nőegylet*) in 1857. Among the Saxons of Transylvania, charitable work was closely and almost exclusively associated with the Evangelical Church of the Transylvanian Saxons. It is also worth mentioning the mutual help institutions, associations for the aid of injured or sick members of various professions, widows' associations, unions for the support of the sick, homes for elderly priests, or the pensioner's home for the musicians of the cathedral of Pécs. Various foundations were concerned with the clothing and industrial training of poor boys and girls, or concerned themselves

[5] Moriz von Stubenrauch, *Statistische Darstellung des Vereinswesens im Kaiserthume Österreich* [Statistical presentation of societies in the Austrian Empire] (Vienna 1857), 83.

[6] Josef von Kőrösy, *Die Armenpflege der Haupt- und Residenzstadt Budapest in den Jahren 1900–1902* [Poor relief in the Capital City and Royal Seat of Budapest in the years 1900–1902] (Berlin 1905), 31 f., 34.

with the so-called "home-poor" who were too ashamed to turn to an institution.

A range of groups, circles, and institutions were involved in the founding and upkeep of these organizations and activities. These included members of the bourgeoisie such as Dorottya Vass, who in 1770 founded an orphanage for 30 children in Sopron County, nobles and affluent landowners such as the Esterházy family, former local officials and clergy, Catholic, Jewish or Evangelical parishes, boroughs, counties, and even the Hungarian estates. The Josephian era of poor relief at the end of the 18th century had led to the founding of a range of such institutions. Examples include the city poor house of Sopron (1787) and the institute for the poor in Pozsony (Bratislava, Pressburg, also in 1787). The latter lacked any financial basis when it was founded and was maintained exclusively by campaigns for donations organized by Count Emmerich Csáky.

The history of benevolent institutions thus goes back to the 18th century and in a few individual cases to the 17th, such as in the case of the poor house for seven men and five women founded by Archbishop György Széchényi in 1687 in Győr. The founding of such establishments in the 19th century was spread across the decades. The period from the 1830s to the 1850s was the heyday for the founding of institutions and associations for the upkeep and sustenance of infants, and women played a central role in this regard. Other individual initiatives also emerged in the neoabsolutist period. Towards the end of the 1850s and early 1860s, several mutual help associations were founded in Vas County that were soon to prosper.[7]

[7] Elek Fényes, *Magyarország ismertetése statisztikai, földirati s történeti szempontból* [Description of Hungary from the statistical, geographical and historical point of view], vols. I-1 and I-2 (Pest 1865, 1866); Elek Fényes, *A magyar birodalom statisticai, geographiai és történeti tekintetben. Részletes és kimerítő leírása Magyar és Erdélyországnak* [The Hungarian Empire in statistical, geographical and historical perspective. Detailed and extensive account of Hungary and Transylvania] (Pest 1848); J.C. von Thiele, *Das Königreich Ungarn. Ein topographisch-historisch-statistisches Rundgemälde, das Ganze dieses Landes in mehr denn 12.400 Artikeln umfassend* [The Kingdom of Hungary. A topographical, historical and statistical overview, capturing the whole of the country in more than 12,400 articles] (Kaschau 1833); Romulus Kácser, *Temesvár emberbaráti intézményei* [The philanthropic institutions of Temesvár] (Temesvár 1906), 58 ff; József Geml, ed. *Temesvár szabad királyi város közállapotai az 1910. évben* [The public conditions in the Royal Free City of Temesvár in 1910] (Temesvár 1910), 89; Hansgeorg von Killyen, "Zur Geschichte der siebenbürgisch-sächsischen Kinderschutzbewegung und der Säuglingspflegerinnen-Schule in Hermannstadt" [On the history of the Transylvanian-Saxon child protection movement and the infant nurse's school in Her-

In sum, then, the scene as regards welfare provision and social care, and as regards the spectrum of providers, founders and supporters in the Hungarian Kingdom, was very similar to that in Cisleithania. The most important contemporary statistical account of associations and institutions, however, mentions an important difference. As Moriz von Stubenrauch pointed out: "The very significant number of such institutions in Hungary must be in part ascribed to the circumstance that there *public* poor relief is not yet organized to the same extent as in the other provinces of the Empire, hence private charity appears to be more urgently required to assist the needy…"[8]

The reemergence of constitutionalism from the beginning of the 1860s and the related legal "Compromise" or dualism between the "Kingdoms and States represented in the Imperial Council" and the Hungarian Kingdom, which was wrapped up in 1867, marked a watershed in poverty policy in both halves of the Empire. Though many of the old public and private institutions and associations remained, inherited ways of operating were preserved and additional ones developed,[9] the unfolding bourgeois state nevertheless created a historically new framework for public and social welfare policy.

II.2. Legal Foundations of Poverty Policy in Flux (from the 1860s to 1914)

During the period of constitutional dualism, with the regaining of an independent legislative competence, developments in the Kingdom of Hungary were characterized by the rapid creation of its own legal framework for all areas connected to poverty policy. This process entailed to a limited extent the preservation of traditions from the period before 1848 and from the era of neoabsolutism that was so heavily dominated by Austria. At the same time, many economically liberal ways of thinking found their way into the new framework for poverty policy. In both halves of the Dual

mannstadt]. *Zeitschrift für Siebenbürgische Landeskunde* 21 (1998): 26–37; Hansgeorg von Killyen, "Zur Geschichte des siebenbürgisch-sächsischen Fürsorgewesens" [On the history of Transylvanian-Saxon welfare]. *Zeitschrift für Siebenbürgische Landeskunde* 8 (1985): 163–172.

[8] Stubenrauch, *Statistische Darstellung* [Statistical presentation], 71 f.

[9] This process and some of the varieties thereof are discussed in some detail for the examples of the Pest and Buda Women's Charitable Associations and the Pest Israelite Women's Association (*Pesti izraelita nőegylet*) established in 1867, by Katalin Pik, *A szociális munka története Magyarországon (1817–1990)* [The history of social work in Hungary (1817–1990)] (Budapest 2001), 19–38.

Monarchy this policy was characterized, in its legal foundations and development at the level of the state and subordinated public authorities, by the fact that the element of provision was systematically linked to the exclusion of the needy from receiving benefits and the repression of unsupported poverty. Basically, four levels of regulation of the problem of poverty were interlinked. In keeping with the principle of municipal responsibility as based in the concept of legal residence status (*községi illetőség*), provision of the poor became a duty of the municipality of origin. As a consequence, due to the liberal regulations regarding the right of domicile in the context of urbanization and (largely internal) migration, there was always a large group of people who were not settled in the municipality that would have been responsible for their welfare. Secondly, the appearance of poverty in the form of—to use the terms of the period—vagabondage as well as illegal begging and prostitution became punishable and pursued by the police. Thirdly, in cases where the legal residence status did not coincide with the actual place of residence (*idegen illetőség*)—if the individual concerned caught the attention of the authorities and the police—the policy of forcible return (known as "the push") to the legally responsible "home" municipality became commonplace. And finally, municipalities were given a great deal of freedom as to how they defined and implemented their poor relief responsibilities on the basis of their general legal obligations as well as local regulations and practice. As a result, the criteria for access to relief provision, as well as the concrete provisions available, varied widely.[10]

In Hungary, the responsibility of municipalities for the core areas of poor relief was set in place by the municipal legislation of 1871–1872 and then definitively established in 1886.[11] The legislators took care thereby to situate municipal care obligations towards those poor who "are simply not able to support themselves without public help," in second place to the aid provided by private "benevolent institutions" and the "alms of individuals." With the exception of the municipal law of Budapest, an additional clause specifying that relief should be provided only "in proportion to local circumstances," served to create an overall restrictive tone. Even in the laws of the capital, there was no specification as to the form or extent of relief that should be provided.

The regulations regarding municipal responsibility—the foundations of which were laid with the first blossoming of pronounced economic liberal-

[10] For the actual development of poor relief, see chapter II.3.

[11] Act 18/1871, Act 36/1872, Act 22/1886.

ism and optimism about modernization in Hungary before 1873—were more flexible in form and encouraged greater mobility than in Cisleithania. After continuous residence in a municipality for two (from 1876 for four) years, together with proof of payment of municipal contributions, which included payment of local taxes levied in addition to profit and income tax, it was possible to apply for legal residence status in the municipality of residence. This was a precondition for—among other things—transferring the responsibility for aid for those concerned from the municipality of origin to that of their present residence. The legal residence status of married women, however, followed that of their husband. To prevent so-called sham marriages for the purposes of applying for legal residence status in the municipality of residence, the legislation and jurisprudence insisted that the right of wives could under no circumstances—for example in the case of divorce—be transformed into an independent right.[12]

In social reality as well as at the legal level, however, there were strong countertendencies against the relatively integrative trend of legislation on the principle of legal residence status. At the heart of this restrictive dynamic was the tax system. The debate continued for decades as to whether, for example, those working in tied service were entitled to apply for legal residence status in their place of residence, given that they did not contribute personally to the costs of the municipality but only through the tax contributions of their employers.[13] Already in 1883 the whole category of day-laborers was also exempted from direct tax liability.[14] For decades these two groups of workers made up a huge proportion of the overall workforce in Hungary. In addition, "broad strata" of the population who were required to pay taxes in reality "escaped" doing so.[15]

In contrast to this restrictive trend, the highest administrative authorities and the minister for the interior strove, especially from the 1890s, for

[12] Susan Zimmermann, *Prächtige Armut. Fürsorge, Kinderschutz und Sozialreform in Budapest. Das "sozialpolitische Laboratorium" der Doppelmonarchie im Vergleich zu Wien 1873–1914* [Splendid poverty. Welfare, child protection and social reform in Budapest. The "socio-political laboratory" of the Dual Monarchy in comparison to Vienna 1873–1914] (Sigmaringen 1997), 33.

[13] *Közigazgatási elvi határozatok egyetemes gyüjteménye* [Universal collection of principle administrative decisions], 3 vols. (Budapest 1895), vol. I, 437 f.

[14] Act 10/1883; *Képviselőház Irományai* [Documents of the House of Representatives] 1884/1887, vol. IX, no. 263, 275.

[15] Walter Löwenfeld, "Die Statistik der direkten Steuern" [Statistics of Direct Taxation]. *Zeitschrift für Volkswirtschaft, Sozialpolitik und Verwaltung* 14 (1905): 299–320, here 307 ff.

an expanded definition of the regulations for applying for legal residence status in the place of residence. These authorities took a clear position against the resolute strategies used by those municipalities that were the main recipients of in-migration to avoid shouldering responsibility for providing aid to larger portions of the urban populations. The minister and the highest administrative authorities now developed a number of strategies to thwart these politics on the part of cities that hosted ever more immigrants from the countryside. These cities, especially the capital, Budapest, were to be obliged to accept social responsibility for larger portions of their inhabitants so as to relieve the strain on the poorer out-migration municipalities. The state had no desire to take over the duty of care in general. Yet at the legal level, the authorities did resort to clear measures aimed at the reform of the existing rights related to the principle of legal residence status only with regard to illegitimate children.[16] These children became henceforth members of the municipality, i.e. they acquired legal residence status, in which their mother had been resident at the time of their birth. In addition, foundlings were from now on, if their municipality of origin could not be determined, also under the jurisdiction of the municipality in which they were found.

Beyond the issue of adjudication of the law and jurisdiction related to the principle of legal residence status, the state made efforts in a number of other policy fields to expand and reform the legal regulations by which administrations could be forced to provide for welfare for the poor.[17] However, major reforms were carried out in only few areas. In accordance with the law of 1898,[18] a State Healthcare Fund (*Országos betegápolási alap*) was created to be financed by the levying of a supplementary tax on direct state income tax. The creation of the Fund and related measures constituted the first significant pre-1914 break with the principle of local responsibility for some of the costs of poor relief. Henceforth the funding of two types of care for the poor would—through the Fund—be nationalized; in other words, the principle of municipal responsibility for poor relief according to the legal residence status of the individual concerned was to be abandoned. Health care for the poor until then had been co-financed from the funds for care of the sick of counties and major cities,[19] whose income came from a locally levied noncompulsory supplementary

[16] Act 5/1876, Act 22/1886.

[17] Zimmermann, *Prächtige Armut* [Splendid Poverty], 36–41.

[18] Act 21/1898.

[19] For this terminology see p. 21, fn. 37.

tax.[20] First, with the goal of covering and "distributing equally" the costs of public healthcare, responsibility for the expenses of the destitute sick was thus shifted, insofar as it concerned accommodation in healthcare institutions or costs for medicine. Second, "costs of care, maintenance, and education for foundlings and children declared abandoned by the public authority up to the age of seven years" were to be covered from the newly established State Healthcare Fund.[21]

The state also made efforts to force the municipalities to better discharge their preexisting duties of care towards those for whom they were locally responsible, that is, those whose legal status of residence was identical with their actual place of residence. A few months after the entry into effect of the new regulations related to the State Healthcare Fund, the minister for the interior issued a follow-up directive on the "type and extent of public aid" as regards how it was henceforth to be practiced by municipalities.[22] Besides specifying the legal regulations regarding welfare obligations for various groups of the sick and the disabled, the directive exerted palpable political pressure from the minister towards the municipalities. The larger cities were required to increase their provisions for the institutional care for the poor, specifically in the creation of "poor houses, houses for the sick and disabled and similar institutions." Besides keeping general records of all those needy persons residing in the municipality, the directive unconditionally required the enactment of local statutes on poverty in all municipalities within one year. In keeping with international policy trends, also followed in Austria, of increasing "individualization" of poor relief, the directive for the first time required that

[20] The justification for the new law explained—in so far as health care for the destitute sick was concerned—exactly the situation which had led to the passage of the new bill. Because of the principle of costs of hospital stays being borne according to the legal residence status of the poor who had fallen ill, the in-migration major cities and counties were largely relieved of the burden of covering the cost for the hospitalization of the poor. In contrast, some out-migration counties found themselves compelled to levy particularly high local additional taxes to cover the costs incurred elsewhere by the hospitalization of those who had migrated to other counties and major cities (where industrialization was rapidly progressing) and who had fallen ill at their new place of residence. Act 3/1874, §§2, 3; László Pomogyi, *Szegényügy és községi illetőség a polgári Magyarországon* [Poverty policy and legal residence status in bourgeois Hungary] (Budapest 2001), 103 f.

[21] For the change in child protection policy that had its beginnings here, see chapter III.1.

[22] Ordinance 51.000/1899, Minister for the interior, in: *Magyarországi rendeletek tára* [Collection of Hungarian ordinances]; in the following I quote all ordinances from this official collection unless otherwise indicated.

the personal circumstances and the "condition" of needy individuals should be the measure used in establishing the type of welfare to be provided. At the same time, however, the minister kept to the old formulation of the municipal law whereby the establishment of rules in enacting the new municipal statutes on poverty had to take into account the "local circumstances"—a provision that left ample space for the local authorities to minimalize provision. Finally the minister's decree specified that those counties that chose to create a common poor relief fund for all municipalities in their district were also obliged to establish a statute regulating the use of monies collected in this fund.

State efforts above and beyond this decree to change the circumstances related to poverty in Hungary through countrywide reorganization or legislation failed to get any further than the formulation of a "proposal for a legislative bill" in 1908.[23]

As a result of these developments, numerous constraints continued to exist in the field of welfare provision and the allocation of benefits. Regardless of these constraints, over the decades both policy and governance persisted in the illusion that needy individuals who—in the short or long term—had no possibility to support themselves would be provided for, if not in the municipality of their residence then at least, in the municipality of origin. In this way, the problem of poverty to all intents and purposes officially disappeared. If poverty should then nonetheless become apparent in the public eye, a specific machinery of police and public authorities was activated in order to ensure that the offending social phenomena disappeared or were at least brought under control. The phenomena that this machinery was typically concerned with were first and foremost survival strategies that clashed with the principle according to which those of the poor who were capable of (in reality frequently unavailable) work were expected to do so, and that were seen as disturbing the public order. These notably included "vagabondage" and those forms of "begging" and "prostitution" as were classified as illegal. These sorts of social behavior had in common that they made the problem of poverty publicly visible, and were perceived as deviant and prosecuted accordingly.

After the Austrian penal code in 1852 placed the agenda regarding mendicancy in Hungary in the hands of the municipal police, it took an-

[23] *A Magyar Királyi Kormány 1908. évi működéséről és az ország közállapotairól szóló jelentés és statisztikai évkönyv* [Report and statistical yearbook on the activities of the Hungarian Royal Government and the public conditions in the country in 1908] (Budapest 1909), 30.

other decade after the constitutional "Compromise" till 1879 before independent Hungarian regulation was established. The provisions of the penal law thereby enacted regarding minor offences[24] were to remain in effect until 1913. Against the background of ongoing efforts to liberalize economic conditions and the freedom of movement of the workforce, begging and vagabondage (except in severe cases, such as the formation of gangs or possession of arms and the like) received relatively mild punishments. It was explicitly stated that those arrested could not be compelled into forced labor.[25] It was clear just how closely connected the new regulations were with efforts to enforce (availability for) wage labor, from the fact that in 1882 the minister for the interior allowed the major cities to issue permission for the collection of alms—a circumlocution for begging permission—only in those cases where these were given to severely disabled individuals. At the same time, it was obvious that the by-laws of 1879 were explicitly not aimed at the suppression of begging with official permission and at particular times. The category of authorized begging, that is, begging as a way of ensuring the survival of those otherwise unable to work remained widespread throughout Hungary until 1914.[26]

From the late 1880s on, there began to appear an organized opposition to the relatively mild and liberal rules dealing with mendicancy and vagabondage by those able to work. Representatives of a very different thinking on poverty policy and spokespersons of the "Reform school" of Hungarian criminal law, which mixed a range of approaches to the issue, were at the core of the group demanding change. Individualization, an active fight against criminality and protection of society against "threats to public safety" were some of the main ideas of the Reform school.[27] There was consensus among those who advocated reforms that among beggars and vagabonds who were able to work, a distinction could be made between those who were also willing to do so and the work-shy.[28]

[24] Act 40/1879.

[25] The Pest workhouse was closed after the new law had been issued. Rokken, "Kényszerítő dologház" [The workhouse], 83 ff.; Csizmadia, *Szociális gondoskodás* [Social welfare], 50.

[26] Zimmermann, *Prächtige Armut* [Splendid poverty], 61 f., and chapters II.3.2. and II.3.3.

[27] Kinga Beliznay and others, *Magyar jogtörténet* [Hungarian legal history] (Budapest 1996), 298–302.

[28] Ferencz Finkey, *A csavargás és koldulás szabályozása kriminálpolitikai szempontból* [The regulation of vagabondage and mendicancy from the point of view of criminal policy] (Budapest 1909), 6; *Képviselőház Irományai* [Documents of the House of Representatives] 1910/1915, vol. XXVI, no. 771; *Magyar közigazgatás* 17, no. 47 (1899): 4.

The threat of forced labor was presented as a solution to the perceived problem that possible welfare benefits for those able to work but temporarily unemployed might be "misused" by the work-shy. Forced labor was also seen as a means of disciplining those groups of the population who no longer had a chance to survive based on more traditional ways of subsistence, and still were not integrated into the world of (modern) wage work. Racist assumptions that "itinerant Gypsies" were an important element of this group also appeared in the relevant drafts of the new legal regulation.[29] However, partly due to financial straits, it took until 1913 before the long discussed and desired law regarding "the threat of the work-shy to public safety"[30] became reality. Those capable of work who nonetheless repeatedly pursued a "work-shy way of life" or exposed their families to "moral decadence" could be punished with one to five years of forced labor. The clauses of the law referring to forced labor first came into effect in 1916. Critics of the new regulations stressed that any meaningful distinction between the work-shy and the unemployed in general could only be possible when the Hungarian labor market as a whole had reached an appropriate level of organization, and the increasingly discussed institutions of support for the unemployed were finally put into practice.[31]

In contemporary discourse and legislation, prostitution was not addressed in the context of maintaining public safety or of poor relief, but rather in separate categories of "morality," "vice," the "vice squad," and protection of public health. Against the backdrop of the so-called "double morality" whereby men enjoyed a wide range of sexual freedoms, none of which were extended to women, prostitution in general was tolerated and regulated. However, those women suspected of prostitution who did not conform to these regulations were subject to persecution by the police and the vice squad. According to state and local regulations, offences included "loitering" and "streetwalking" on the part of registered prostitutes, and "secret" prostitutes "caught in the act of fornication" in public or private places faced persecution too. Like beggars and

[29] As stated in the draft of 1907, reprinted in Ferencz Finkey, *A csavargás, koldulás és iszákosság törvényhozási szabályozáshoz* [On the legal regulation of vagabondage, begging and drunkenness] (Budapest 1910).

[30] Act 21/1913.

[31] Pap, Géza. "Törvény (1913. évi XXI. törvénycikk) a közveszélyes munkakerülőkről" [Law (21st Law of 1913) on the publicly dangerous work-shy] *A munkanélküliség elleni küzdelem*, no 1. (1913), 5–13, here 10 f., 13.

vagabonds, prostitutes who did not keep closely to the regulations ran the constant risk of ending up in police custody.[32]

The openly repressive side of poverty policy described here did not dwindle in importance in Hungary over the decades, anymore than it did in Cisleithania; on the contrary, it was developed further. This was also true for the relocation measure known as the "push," another key element in the edifice of classical poverty policy as a policy of exclusion and marginalization. The fundamental freedom of movement of citizens in both halves of the empire was only guaranteed to the extent that the right to settle or to stay in any part of the empire—with the exception of the home or assigned municipality—was dependent on the ability to survive in the municipality of residence "without placing any burden on the community."[33] Those residing in a place other than their home municipality who fell into penury, or in ignorance of the legal situation turned to the local authorities for help, could as a rule expect to be forcibly returned to their home municipality. In Hungary, forced relocation was, until 1885, based on a regulation issued in 1851 by the gubernator installed on the part of the Austrian side to govern Hungary.[34] In 1867 the Hungarian minister for the interior called on the authorities to strictly implement the existing by-laws and to immediately relocate unauthorized beggars to their home municipality.[35] The "relocation directive" enacted in 1885[36] was created in order to standardize relocation policy for the whole territory of the Kingdom of Hungary. The threat of relocation was directed at illegal prostitutes, vagabonds, unauthorized beggars, the "habitual work-shy," and those "persons fundamentally suspicious with regard to public safety" who were "unable to provide evidence of regular accommodation, employment or income for their upkeep." Those individuals who were imprisoned as a result of various offenses under the minor offences act of 1879 were also to be relocated at the end of their sentence if they had been taken into custody in a place other than their home municipality. Those

[32] Susan Zimmermann, "'Making a Living from Disgrace'. The Politics of Prostitution, Female Poverty and Urban Gender Codes in Budapest and Vienna, 1860s–1920s," in: Malcolm Gee, Tim Kirk, Jill Steward, eds. *The City in Central Europe: Culture and Society in Central Europe since 1800* (London 1999), 175–195.

[33] In Hungary Act 18/1871, §12.

[34] *Budapest Fő- és Székesvárosi Állami Rendőrség 1895. évi működése* [The activities of the State Police in the Capital City and Royal Seat of Budapest in 1895] (Budapest 1896), 224.

[35] Ordinance 177/1867, Minister for the interior, 512.

[36] Ordinance 9389/1885, Minister for the interior.

relocatees who were considered to present no public hazard, as well as illegal prostitutes, were provided with a "compulsory pass" and sent on their way without an escort, while those classed as dangerous were accompanied by a "relocation escort." The home municipalities were then to deal with relocatees who were unable to work according to their usual procedures, while every effort was to be made to get the work-shy to work.

II.3. The Development and Practice of Poverty Policy (from the 1860s to 1914)

The fact that the legal regulations in practice only imposed the duty of poor relief—in the sense of the obligation to provide welfare for the poor—on cities, towns and villages to a very minimal extent, led to practices that while limited in coverage were very varied in form. Besides the main agenda of institutional and non-institutional provision, i.e. indoor and outdoor relief for adults and children, classical welfare as provided by the smaller and larger municipalities included special categories such as welfare for the homeless. This welfare policy, however, was accompanied over the decades by a policy of rendering poverty wherever possible invisible, and by socio-political oppression and marginalization of the poor.

Below, I present an overall picture based on available quantitative and qualitative data, of structure and development of both major fields of poverty policy in Hungary: welfare provision on the one hand and repressive measures on the other. In the second and the third subchapter I then analyse how within both fields the responsible authorities put existing regulations into practice and how they dealt with the poor on a day-to-day level.

II.3.1. The two sides of poverty policy: general trends

The main indicators that provide a picture of the structure and significance of poor relief as a part of municipal policy include the share of welfare expenditure as a part of the overall expenditure of the municipalities, the level of welfare expenditure per capita (expenditure per inhabitant of the municipality), per person receiving care, and a range of information about the distribution of welfare expenditure according to sector, type of benefit, etc.

For the Hungarian Kingdom, due to the organization of municipal budgets into numerous overlapping accounts, it is impossible to have a systematic overview of the level of welfare expenditure for Hungarian municipalities.[37] Analyses permitting a relatively coherent picture of the welfare expenses both for smaller municipalities and for major and secondary cities are available for the year 1908. Longitudinal studies of the development of welfare expenditure and welfare policy for the capital, Budapest, and comparatively for the three industrial metropolises Budapest, Vienna, and Prague complete the picture.

For the Hungarian smaller communities in 1908, 2.2 percent of the overall "regular expenditure," or 1.99 million crowns were spent on the welfare sector. This share—if we exclude the very small villages with less than 100 and the somewhat larger communities (albeit still classified as "smaller community") with more than 10,000 inhabitants (which devoted 4.1 percent and 3.4 percent of their "regular expenditure" respectively to welfare)—varied little between the smaller and larger among these communities (1.9 percent to 3.0 percent). Comparing different counties, however, noticeable variations appear, from 6.8 percent in Vas County on the border with Austria where the large number of poor-houses contributed to the high expenses, to 0.2 percent in Fogaras County in Transylvania.[38] In general, the

---

[37] The Hungarian term *törvényhatóság* in Hungarian administrative terminology referred both to the counties (*megye*), the highest level regional administrative unit, and also mostly larger cities which enjoyed a special administrative status, that of the *törvényhatóság* and thus were not administratively subordinate to the counties. There were certainly cases where smaller towns that had declined historically in importance enjoyed the status of *törvényhatóság*, while rapidly expanding new cities had not yet acquired that status. Urban settlements that did not hold the rank of *törvényhatóság* were classified as cities of secondary status (*rendezett tanácsú város*). In this study I refer to those *törvényhatóság* that were not cities as counties, and to urban *törvényhatóság* as major cities. Cities of secondary status I refer to as secondary cities, and all other communities (*község*) as smaller communities (including villages). Some of these last may have had a relatively urban character but lacked the status of *rendezett tanácsú város*. I use "municipality" and "municipal" in this study as general cover-all terms for all communities except the counties.

[38] A part of the overall welfare expenditures flowed from the municipal treasury (the so-called municipal account or fund) in various other accounts, notably the "poor fund" and in some counties the "fund for officially abandoned children." Transfers from the municipal treasury to various welfare funds, of which the poor fund used to be by far the largest, constituted only about a quarter of the total monies flowing into these funds. The funds themselves also applied money to welfare purposes that because of the flow of monies between the municipal treasury and the welfare fund cannot simply be added to the welfare expenses the municipality transacted through the municipal treasury. In the present and subsequent discussion of overall expenditures of municipalities in 1908, transfers from the municipal treasury to the welfare fund are included, while the expenditures of the welfare fund itself are not. The municipal poor funds themselves in 1908 spent (for their proper, i.e. various welfare purposes) 0.86 million crowns. All municipal welfare funds taken together (i.e. the poor funds and the various minor or special funds who were maintained in

fact that a smaller community devoted a relatively higher percentage of its overall expenditures to welfare—if contemporary analyses are to be believed, setting aside for a moment the not inconsiderable influence of poorhouses—was only in small part due to the fact that the community in question "took welfare provision… more seriously." Rather in some cases, the reason for the high proportion of welfare expenditure can be found in the low level of the overall budget of the smaller communities located in the poorest counties. Contemporary analysis identified "liability to recourse" as another reason. According to this principle, any municipality where costs incurred for welfare provision for an individual whose legal residence status tied him or her to another, i.e. the home municipality, was entitled to request from the home municipality a refund of the costs incurred. This created a particular burden for the territories near the Austrian border, due to the high level of emigration to Cisleithania. Finally, a particularly important factor was the obligation to pay for children between 7 and 14 years of age who were officially declared as "abandoned" and were cared for within the state system for the protection of children developed since the turn of the century.[39] Not only was the number of children cared for within this system constantly increasing, but among these children, the share who had reached the age of seven was also on the rise. The municipalities had no right to terminate state care for these children, yet they were required to pay for their care. This laid a particular burden on the smaller communities of those counties that were more seriously affected by emigration to the USA. But even taken as an average across the country, 44.2 percent of welfare expenditures by the smaller communities were incurred in this category, almost as much as the expenditure for the so-called "community poor." A further 9.8 percent went on the care of those poor who were terminally ill and the physically and mentally handicapped poor.[40]

The system of poor relief and welfare in the Hungarian major and secondary cities was characterized by features that were in part similar, in part different. In 1908, the 137 major and secondary cities (excluding Budapest) spent 2.1 million crowns on institutional and non-institutional provision, not including the care of orphans and abandoned children from the age of 7.

the same way as the poor funds) spent 0.95 million crowns. László Buday, *Magyarország községeinek háztartása az 1908. évben* [The budget of the smaller communities in Hungary in 1908] (Budapest 1913), 86 ff., 97 f., 218 f., 229; own calculations.

39 For this system, see chapter III.1.

40 Buday, *Magyarország községeinek háztartása* [Budget of the smaller communities], 86–89.

The overall budget of these cities amounted to 75 million crowns. The figures for major cities (without Budapest) alone amounted to 1.1 million crowns (welfare expenditures) and 42.9 million crowns (overall costs). Of these welfare expenditures, for cities as a whole, 44.6 percent went on institutional care and 55.4 percent on non-institutional care.[41]

As regards the institutional welfare provisions represented in this data, these included the accommodation of 3,600 individuals in 116 poorhouses and more specialized institutions for the elderly poor, 3,419 children and adolescents in 83 orphanages, children's homes, and houses of correction, and 1,103 individuals in 36 other institutions. In addition, in Budapest there were four institutions for the care of adults, with 1,489 inhabitants, 16 institutions for the care of children and adolescents, with 1,427 inhabitants, and three other institutions housing 559 individuals. Around 44 percent of these in total, 258 institutions were run by the major and secondary cities themselves, while some 48 percent were in private hands, but as a rule supported in some form or other by the municipality. The data also include other institutions which operated on the territory of major and secondary cities, specifically two state-run houses of correction, as well as institutions run by the county (this was the case in only two counties; in other counties the county institutions were located outside the cities), and 17 state-run children's homes. The last served to gather and distribute children under the auspices of the state system for the protection of chil-

[41] A small number of cities that provided no or incomplete figures for their welfare expenditures are excluded from my calculations. The welfare expenditures here include both those incurred directly by the municipal treasury and also those incurred by poor funds and other funds. There is no double accounting here, and the actual expenditures are—in included areas—more comprehensively recorded than in the case of the smaller communities. On the other hand, welfare expenditures calculated in this way cannot be related in a meaningful manner to figures for the overall expenditure from the municipal treasury proper. The poor funds were kept within the overall municipal budget as independent accounts, i.e. with their total revenue and expenditure kept separate from other funds and the municipal treasury. A large part of the poor funds' income in many places was made up of fines paid by the inhabitants of the municipality for particular offences, and the municipal councils also directed certain revenues (such as in Temesvár, revenues from the issue of permits for entertainment events or official identity cards or certificate) into the poor fund. Legally the counties had the right to levy an additional local tax (*pótadó*) of up to three percent on certain general taxes in order to finance the poor fund, among other matters. Gusztáv Thirring, ed. *A magyar városok statisztikai évkönyve* [Statistical yearbook of Hungarian cities] (Budapest 1912), 548 f., 555 f., 590–597; Geml, *Temesvár szabad királyi város* [Royal Free City of Temesvár], 79; Act 15/1883, §9; own calculations.

dren and accounted for around one fifth of the children and adolescents in care institutions mentioned above.[42]

As regards the information about non-institutional welfare, i.e. outdoor relief, from these data, the average figure for aid in major cities in this sector including all types of non-institutional aid—financial, sickness and burial aid as well as other types—amounted to 52.4 crowns per person per year; for secondary cities, the figure was 35.6 crowns. In total, major cities supported 9,412 individuals, secondary cities 12,017. Smaller communities supported a total of 16,914 so-called "community poor" from the funds of the local treasury and the poor fund to the tune of 54.8 crowns per person per year. According to these combined data, in all Hungarian major and secondary cities as well as smaller communities combined (excepting Budapest) in the year 1908 on average, at most[43] one in 453 individuals enjoyed—in some form or at some time—support within the category of outdoor relief for adults, often in kind.[44]

The approximate value of welfare assistance provided by the Hungarian municipalities can be assessed for example in comparison to the regulations about contributions to and sickness benefits granted by the national health insurance scheme for workers. Here the upper limit for income to be covered by compulsory insurance was a daily (!) wage of eight crowns, and in the case of illness the national health insurance paid up to 20 weeks sick

---

[42] Thirring, *A magyar városok statisztikai évkönyve* [Statistical yearbook of Hungarian cities], 548 f., 553 f.; *Jelentés az állami gyermekmenhelyek 1907–1910 évi munkásságáról* [Report on the work of the state children's asylums from 1907–1910] (Budapest 1913); own calculations.

[43] It cannot be ruled out that individuals who received more than one form of non-institutional aid from cities may appear more than once in the statistics.

[44] Population figures from 1910. A small number of cities are not included as they did not provide (full) figures. Thirring, *A magyar városok statisztikai évkönyve* [Statistical yearbook of Hungarian cities], 555 f.; Buday, *Magyarország községeinek háztartása* [Budget of the smaller communities], 86 f., 238 f.; *A Magyar Szent Korona Országainak 1910. évi népszámlálása. Második rész. A népesség foglalkozása* [Census of the Lands of the Holy Hungarian Crown, 1910. Part Two. The Occupation of the Population]. Magyar Statisztikai Közlemények. Új Sorozat [Hungarian statistical publications. New series] (Budapest 1913), vol. XLVIII; *A Magyar Szent Korona Országainak 1910. évi népszámlálása. Negyedik rész. A népesség foglalkozása a főbb demográfiai adatokkal egybevetve s a népesség ház- és földbirtok-viszonyai* [Results of the census in the lands of the Holy Hungarian Crown in 1910. The occupations of the population compared with the most important demographic figures and conditions of property and land ownership of the population]. Magyar Statisztikai Közlemények. Új Sorozat [Hungarian statistical publications. New series] (Budapest 1915), vol. LVI; and own calculations.

pay at 50 percent of wages.[45] The wages of "unskilled day laborers" who performed the simplest type of hard physical work in the city of Temesvár and earned around 30–40 crowns a month at the beginning of the 20th century, may serve as another point of reference.[46] The system of non-institutional poor aid (for adults) was and remained throughout the period before World War I a system of minimal support for marginal groups.

Comprehensive figures for the expenditure of secondary and major cities on officially abandoned children between 7 and 14 are not available. However, one can assume with some confidence that they too showed the same trends of growth as was the case for the smaller communities discussed above.

The data discussed thus far does not include the capital city and major center of urban growth, Budapest. The analysis of long-term trends in welfare expenditure and provision in Budapest as compared to the other two main industrial metropolises of the Habsburg Monarchy, Prague and Vienna, makes visible not only the limits of public assistance for the poor in conditions of increasingly universal wage labor, but also those factors that explain the variations in welfare policy development.

The data presented in Tables 1 and 2 show clearly that the three metropolises of the Habsburg Monarchy succeeded in avoiding responsibility for a significant part of the social costs of industrialization. While the population and communal budget of the cities increased, and the share of social expenditures in the overall budget did show a slight increase, the share of welfare expenditures in the budget of Budapest, setting aside the new area of communal housing, [47] actually decreased. In the Hungarian capital, the level of welfare expenditure per capita as a whole was considerably lower than in Vienna. The expenditures per inhabitant in the two capital cities of the empire, however, were clearly increasing, while in Prague they stagnated. As a whole, the average welfare expenditures per capita in the three cities over the period reached a level that could at best be described as extremely modest. In these three industrial metropolises, as elsewhere, the policy of providing for those in need, in comparison to the development of areas such as education or healthcare,[48] failed to show any significant increase or improvement.

[45] Act 19/1907, §§24, 50.

[46] József Geml, *Temesvár lakáspolitikája. Tanulmány a munkáslakások kérdéséhez* [The housing policy of Temesvár. A study on the question of workers' housing] (Temesvár 1906), 105 f., 117.

[47] See chapter III.2.

[48] Melinz, Zimmermann, "Die aktive Stadt" [The Active City], Tables 1/I-III.

Table 1: Municipal Budget in Budapest, Prague and Vienna: Overall Expenditure and Social Expenditure [(a)]

Year	Budapest			Prague			Vienna		
	Total expenditures	Social sector[(b)]	Welfare alone	Total expenditures	Social sector[(b)]	Welfare alone	Total expenditures	Social sector[(b)]	Welfare alone
	(1000 crowns)	*(% of overall budget)*		*(1000 crowns)*	*(% of overall budget)*		*(1000 crowns)*	*(% of overall budget)*	
1892	29,000	22.9	4.5				61,309	34.8	10.5
1902	46,395	27.3	3.0	36,059	13.7	3.4	102,112	32.9	11.5
1912[(c)]	116,196	38.7	3.5 (+5.1)[(d)]	48,752	17.0	3.0	170,173	37.9	12.3

(a) Figures for Prague are not fully comparable, although as far as possible, as in the case of Budapest, the figures regarding internal flows between budget categories have been adjusted (for Prague a few estimates have been made in order to achieve this goal). In Budapest and Prague in the period under investigation there was no incorporation of formerly independent outside municipalities; Budapest had a comparatively extensive administrative area from the beginning while Prague had only a very small city territory as compared to the overall size of the agglomeration. In Vienna there were important incorporations of formerly independent municipalities in 1904.

(b) The social sector includes the areas of education (schools and kindergartens) healthcare and welfare in all three cities.

(c) For Prague 1911.

(d) In brackets the share of total expenditures for communal housing, which is included in the category of the social sector.

Source: Gerhard Melinz, Susan Zimmermann. “Die aktive Stadt. Kommunale Politik zur Gestaltung städtischer Lebensbedingungen in Budapest, Prag und Wien (1867–1914)” [The Active City. Municipal Policy and the Shaping of Urban Living Conditions in Budapest, Prague and Vienna (1867–1914)], in: Gerhard Melinz, Susan Zimmermann, eds. *Wien, Prag, Budapest. Blütezeit der Habsburgermetropolen. Urbanisierung, Kommunalpolitik, gesellschaftliche Konflikte (1867– 1918)* [*Vienna, Prague, Budapest. Heyday of the Habsburg Metropolises. Urbanization, Communal Policy and Social Conflict* (1867–1918)] (Vienna 1996), 140–176, 263–276, figures taken from Tables 1/I-III.

Table 2: Welfare Expenditures Per Inhabitant (in Crowns) in Budapest, Prague and Vienna

Year	Budapest		Prague (= Prague +4 suburbs)[(a)]		Vienna	
	Total	Non-institutonal aid	Total	Non-institutional aid	Total	Non-institutional aid
1900	1.67	0.50	6.56 (3.71) [(b)]	2.04 (1.38) [(b)]	5.01	3.11
1910	3.04	0.52	6.36 [(c)]	-	9.20	4.82 (4.33[(d)])

(a) The figures for Prague are not strictly comparable with Budapest and Vienna.
(b) Welfare expenditures for 1902.
(c) Welfare expenditures for 1911; population figures based on census results and estimated upwards.
(d) "Other public aid" excluded.

Source: Melinz, Zimmermann, "Die aktive Stadt" [The Active City], data from Table 2.

As a whole, then, public poor relief in the Hungarian Kingdom was characterized by very limited quality and quantitative development. For decades, the policies pursued by public authorities in the field reflected classical liberal social-political thinking. At the same time, however, mention should be made of features of the development of care for those in need that lie beyond the bounds of poor relief as pursued by public policy. These include, on the one hand, the policies of social reform as well as the national health insurance scheme for workers (which also covered work-related accidents) first established in the 1890s. These developments, which will be addressed in subsequent chapters, unquestionably alleviated the material and social pressure the municipal authorities must have experienced as people in need of social assistance turned to the classical public poor relief administration for help. On the other hand, private welfare, i.e. denominational and nondenominational charity and benevolent activities of the churches also played a role. An accurate estimate of the material contributions of actors in this area of welfare provision for the needy is not possible on the basis of existing research. A statistical census of societies and associations in Hungary in 1878 reveals no more than 225 benevolent societies, including 148 women's societies and many Jewish organizations, whose annual expenditures add up to 434,000 guilders (217,000 crowns).[49] At the beginning of the 20th century, "300–400 asso-

[49] Elena Mannová, "Charitable Societies and the Construction of Collective Identities," in: Moritz Csáky, Elena Mannová, eds. *Collective Identities in Central Europe in Modern Times* (Bratislava 1999), 197–216, here 204.

ciations," both denominational and secular, engaged in outdoor relief.[50] A study on the activity of legal registered associations (i.e. excluding the churches as such but including denominational associations established according to the requirements of civil law and sponsored by the churches) in Somogy County in southwestern Hungary in the period between 1867 and 1918, including all those founded and active in the county, shows a lively development of new associations in (among others) the area of charity and welfare. The findings of this study confirm the considerable influence of women's societies, particularly the especially large number of Jewish women's societies and somewhat later Catholic and nondenominational women's societies. After the turn of the century, societies of the Christian social movement and workers' unions were added, the latter being especially concerned with meeting the needs of disabled and elderly workers. As regards the extent of the activities of all these associations, the study does not offer quantitative details or allow for generalization.[51] In contrast, contemporary experts, who were concerned with extending the public welfare system, limited themselves to the general complaint that private charity and welfare in Hungary was no more than "a casual affair."[52] All these details and figures, however, exclude the charitable activities of churches and parishes—except those cases when duly constituted civil associations were supported by and closely collaborated with the churches, a feature that became more significant in later decades—or only touch upon a few minor areas of these actors' contributions must have been significant.[53]

As regards the reverse side of—limited—public welfare policy, the repressive aspect of poverty policy, classical liberal socio-political thinking

---

[50] Gábor Gyáni, *A szociálpolitika múltja Magyarországon* [The past of social policy in Hungary] (Budapest 1994), 19 f.

[51] The study includes a detailed list of societies. Sándor Bősze, *"Az egyesületi élet a polgári szabadság ..." Somogy megye egyesületei a dualizmus korában* ["The life of associations is civic freedom"... The societies of Somogy County under the Dual Monarchy] (Kaposvár 1997), 162–166, 211–246. Regarding the significant development of Jewish charitable activities, figures for Pozsony (Bratislava) and Budapest are also available. Mannová, "Charitable Societies," 212 f.; Julia Richers, "Johanna Bischitz," in: Francisca de Haan, Krassimira Daskalova, Anna Loutfi, eds. *A Biographical Dictionary of Women's Movements and Feminisms: Central, Eastern and South Eastern Europe, 19th and 20th Centuries* (Budapest – New York 2006), 58–61.

[52] Tivadar Forbáth, *A magyar szegényügy rendezése* [The regulation of the poor relief system in Hungary] (Budapest 1910), 129.

[53] My thanks to Gabriela Dudeková, Bratislava, for underlining this important insight. See also chapter II.3.2.

and action, combined with new and gradually stronger policies of social control, persisted for decades. In this area, the authorities strove to suppress, eliminate, and persecute those symptoms of poverty that were publicly visible in disturbing ways and sought to eliminate those survival strategies amongst the poor which were perceived as subverting the virtues of industriousness, respectability, and modernization. This was clearly reflected in the long-term trends in forced relocation and policies against unauthorized begging and prostitution.

In the capital, Budapest, alone from the 1890s to the start of the World War I, yearly between 4,000 and 8,000 individuals were placed in the police prison and relocation house under suspicion of a variety of related offences, namely vagabondage, repeated vagabondage, begging, repeated begging, "qualified begging," or unauthorized prostitution. Added to this, there were annually well over 1,000 (in the two years displaying the most extreme figures over 2,500) cases of "forbidden return" related to the offences mentioned above and others. The level of committals (not including "forbidden return") in 1910 was 6.4 per 1,000 inhabitants, after—with the rapid growth of the city population—it had peaked at 11 committals per 1,000 inhabitants in earlier years. Shortly before the World War I, it was scarcely lower than in 1893, when it had been 7.5 per 1,000.[54]

The fact that unauthorized prostitution played an important role amongst the undesired survival strategies practiced by women, or put differently: that the authorities perceived and dealt with the undesired survival strategies of poor women in large part from a gender-specific moralizing perspective, is also confirmed by the statistics. Amongst those held in the Budapest police prison and relocation house for begging and vagabondage, women made up around one fifth. If those women held for infringement of the regulations on prostitution are included in the calculation, the overall percentage rises to 30 and even 40 percent. In Vienna the number of charges of prostitution as a fraction of overall charges for infringement of the regulations with regard to §5 of the so-called "Vagabond law" of 1885[55] by the beginning of the 1890s was between a quarter and a third.[56]

---

[54] Zimmermann, *Prächtige Armut* [Splendid poverty], Table 4; population figures for 1893 estimated on the basis of figures for 1890 and 1900.

[55] Act 89/1885.

[56] The latter category did not include the less serious charges of infringement of the police ban on immoral behavior, the number of which was at least as high. Zimmermann, "Making a Living," 184 f.

Countrywide statistics for Hungary do not exist for the activities of either the civil authorities or the police against begging and vagabondage, nor yet regarding forced relocation. There are figures, however, about the proportion of the population living in communities other than those to which they belonged according to their legal residence status. It was these individuals who, if they breached poverty-related regulations, were in danger of forced relocation. As early as 1891, before a new wave of industrialization and urbanization took shape in the Kingdom of Hungary, 26.6 percent of the population belonged to this group on national average, with women representing 48.7 percent of these individuals. In major cities, the overall proportion of those who according to their legal residence status belonged elsewhere was much higher, reaching 46.6 percent.[57]

No real decline in relocation as a method employed by the police in cooperation with the local authorities of "sweeping away" poverty can be seen over the decades. Statistics for Heves County, for example, show (in absolute figures) comparing the second half of the 1880s with the early years of the new century, no clear reduction in the number of relocations.[58] In the County capital of Temesvár, which in 1910 had 73,000 inhabitants, a total of 986 individuals were held for vagabondage in city police station in 1909, to which can be added 418 "transitory relocatees" and 342 admitted for other offences. Of these taken together, 986 were expelled or relocated, a rate of 1.4 relocations per inhabitant.[59] In Budapest the number of relocations from the 1890s to the start of the World War I showed an overall pattern of growth, reaching a peak with nearly 9,000 individuals in 1909 and 1913. Over the decades the ratio of relocations to population decreased only slowly. In 1890 it was 13.21 and in 1910 had dropped to 9.54 per 1,000 inhabitants, thus markedly higher than in the County capital of Temesvár, which would have been a center for immigration and development. Added to this in Budapest (like Temesvár above), there were the transitory relocatees who passed through the city on the way from the place of their arrest to their home municipality. From

[57] *1891. évi népszámlálás* [Census results 1891], vol. I, 57* f., 47.

[58] The (in part estimated) number of relocations per inhabitant was far lower than in Budapest. Pomogyi, *Szegényügy és községi illetőség* [Poverty Policy and Legal Residence Status], 80; own calculations.

[59] The figures on relocation also include those for transitory relocatees being moved further on. The population of the rapidly growing County capital for 1909 is calculated on the basis of figures for 1900 and 1910. Geml, *Temesvár szabad királyi város* [Royal Free City of Temesvár], 65; *Magyar Statisztikai Évkönyv. Új folyam* [Hungarian Statististical Yearbook. New Series], vol. XVIII, 1910, 13.

the mid-1890s on, over 1,000 individuals from this category passed through the capital every year, peaking at 2,464 in 1901 and 3,990 in 1913. If the number of transitory relocatees is added to the other figures for relocations, far higher and increasing figures for expulsions from the capital result, with 5,509 individuals in 1893, 6,934 in 1900, 10,454 in 1910 and finally 12,771 in 1913. That the imperial capital Vienna was less exclusionary in its poverty policy than Budapest, with the gap between the two increasing further in the new century, can be seen from the development of relocation ratios. In the imperial capital, the figure for relocations per 1,000 inhabitants was 3.84 in 1890, or 4.26 if those held in workhouses and correctional institutions under the "Vagabond law" of 1885[60] are included. This number fell dramatically after the turn of the century, particularly due to a reform of the legislation on the legal status of residence that applied throughout Cisleithania, and in 1910 was only 1.43 per 1,000. In Prague, the relocation ratios also dropped dramatically in the new century and in 1907 were slightly lower than in Budapest in the same period.[61]

As a whole, Hungarian poverty policy over the decades, both in the area of poor relief as well as in that of the aggressive suppression of poverty, was more characterized by continuity than by change. Besides the motivation of the state and the municipalities to minimize their responsibility for poor relief, there were at least two other factors that contributed to this stagnant tendency. First, the basic functioning, the "logic" of classical poverty policy as the suppression of poverty and minimal poor relief provided little opportunity for the development of new solutions to the main symptoms, problems, and consequences of contemporary social change. The partial lifting of the burden through growing initiatives for state and municipal social reform from the 1890s and the rise of state social policy[62] reduced the acute need to take action, and thus contributed indirectly to the fossilization of this inherited pattern of poverty policy.

Second, the legal and administrative construction and the practical application of the existing national legislation as well as local statutes on poverty contributed to the preservation of the status quo and the restrictive character of Hungarian poverty policy over the decades. It is to these patterns of poverty policy as put into practice that we now turn.

---

[60] Acts 89/1885 and 90/1885.

[61] Zimmermann, *Prächtige Armut* [Splendid poverty], Tables 5 and 9; Melinz, Zimmermann, "Die aktive Stadt" [The Active City], 169.

[62] See chapters III and IV.

II.3.2. The practice of poor relief as provision

The fact that poor relief as provided by secondary and major cities and smaller communities (including villages) in Hungary was "sketchy and inadequate," and "many urgent and important issues of poverty unresolved" was even admitted by the minister for the interior.[63] Experts spoke of the "utter disorganization and aimlessness" of the system of poverty policy in Hungary.[64] What was in many cases the first register of municipally supported poor, which occurred as a consequence of the ministerial decree of 1899, cast a harsh light on the practice of poor relief, which remained invisible both in the official documents about poverty policy in general and in the contemporary expert discourse. The conditions in the rural district of Igal,[65] situated south of Lake Balaton and north of the seat of Somogy County, Kaposvár, serves as a vivid example of this reality. In this district 33,807 individuals lived in numerous small communities, none larger than 3,000, only three having a population of over 2,000. 82 percent of the population lived—as part of the labor force or family members—from agriculture, scarcely 10% from business and trade; an additional 2 percent belonged to the nonagricultural category of day laborers and 1.6 percent to the group of the household servants.[66] Amongst households living from agriculture, 41percent were managed as households of agricultural laborers or servants. The register of the poor compiled on the orders of the Chief District Administrator (*főszolgabíró*) from 25 January 1900, reveals for the whole district of Igal 45 paupers who received some form of support, including two children, five under 50, 14 between 50 and 60, and 21 over 60 years old. These were typically either heads of families or widows with several young children, or—in large numbers—persons who had no relatives or whose only child worked, for example, in service.

---

[63] *A Magyar Királyi Kormány* [The Royal Hungarian Government] 1908, 30.

[64] Forbáth, *A szegényügy rendezése* [The regulation of the poor relief system], 11.

[65] *A Magyar Szent Korona Országainak 1900. évi népszámlálása. Második rész. A népesség foglalkozása községenként* [Census for the Lands of the Holy Hungarian Crown for the year 1900. Employment of the population by municipality]. Magyar Statisztikai Közlemények. Új Sorozat [Hungarian statistical publications. New series], vol. II (Budapest, 1904). For details of the very similar conditions in the 1890s in what is today Szabolcs-Szatmár-Bereg County, see Ibolya Gaál, *A szegényügy- és felnőttvédelmi szociálpolitika története Szabolcs-Szatmár megyében 1867–1989* [History of poverty policy and the social policy of the protection of adults in Szabolcs-Szatmár County], 2 vols. (Nyíregyháza 1997), vol. I, 15–29, and annexes nos. 3, 6.

[66] The contemporary data on occupational structure were calculated with reference to the individuals and their family members in all cases.

Amongst the adult poor, there were almost as many women as men. In 32 cases, permission to beg, registered as one of the possible forms of support, constituted the only or principal form of income. These permits were issued either in the form of the right to beg "from house to house," or a generally formulated permission, partly limited to certain days, to beg "within the community." In a further seven cases rather than issuing a begging permit, the authorities had obliged the inhabitants of the community feed the poor in a "house to house" system. Four of the 45 paupers received an allocation of firewood, four a modest financial payment, in one instance 1.50 crowns per month for two; in the latter case it was also mentioned that the payment was financed from the interest from the poor fund. Eight recognized paupers were provided with accommodation. In some cases, two of the above-mentioned forms of provision were combined, but only few of those who were reduced to a begging permit received extra material support. One pauper was supported in exchange for performing work for a farmer.[67] If the poor register of Igal for 1900 shows only the actual "community poor" who received some form of support, a similar document from the district of Fehérgyarmat in the then County of Szatmár, today in the far northeast of Hungary, from the year 1891 shows that numerous persons who applied for help in individual smaller communities were turned away.[68]

The issuing of begging permits as a form of poor relief was in no way limited to the countryside. Indeed according to a decree of the minister for the interior from 1882, begging permits were only to be issued by counties and major cities[69] and only for their own territory and for the permanent inhabitants of the same. Individuals in possession of such permits could present themselves in the individual municipalities of the relevant county and request a begging permit, which could be issued by the municipality for the period they saw fit to determine.[70] Major cities thus had the freedom in the decades to come, according to the degree of 1882, to use local begging permits as a means of poor relief. In cities of different legal status as well, begging permits issued in large number played a significant role. In the County seat (from 1876), Nyíregyháza, in different years of the last

---

[67] Somogy Megyei Levéltár [Somogy County Archive] (henceforth SML). Igali Járás. Közigazgatási ügyek [District of Igal. Administrative business] no. 876, 1900. Községi ellátásra utalt községi szegények összeirása [Register of municipal paupers reliant on community provision].

[68] Gaál, *Szegényügyi politika* [Poverty policy], vol. I, Table 2.

[69] S. fn. 41.

[70] Ordinance 18613/1882, Minister for the interior.

quarter of the 19th century, there were between 39 and 87 persons in possession of such permits. Of the 48 persons registered in 1882, 13—including four women—were allowed to beg in front of the Evangelical and Calvinist churches. These included four blind individuals, two without legs and one without hands, one with only one leg and suffering from gout, a further (female) gout sufferer, two individuals with "sick hands," a man with a stroke, and a woman "in rags."[71] On top of the continued legality of begging by permit it was well known and the subject of official complaints at the highest level that in the issuing of the permits the relevant by-laws were regularly ignored, and particularly many smaller communities issued permits on their own criteria.[72]

At the same time, more financial aid was given in cities than in small communities. For example, the 16 registered recipients of financial aid in the County seat, Kaposvár, in 1908—with 24,000 inhabitants (1910)—received an average sum of 32.8 crowns per capita per year. In this regard Kaposvár was 25 percent lower than the countrywide average for both major and secondary cities (not including Budapest), which was 43.5 crown per recipient per year, although the average sums paid per capita and per year between individual cities varied very considerably.[73] In Temesvár, altogether 600 recipients received 76.9 crowns on average per year, this figure including one-time, monthly, childcare and medications benefits.[74]

The modest level of municipal financial aid for the poor obviously served, among other things, to emphasize one important social distinction. The number of worthy paupers whom the authorities in Kaposvár and other municipalities had to recognize as belonging to the municipality according to their legal residence status, and with reference to public knowledge about their continued residence in the given municipality during past decades, was very small. Yet these paupers were to constitute a social class clearly distinct from ordinary respectable townsfolk. A good illustration of this is the example of a former police constable who had served the city of Kaposvár for 24 years. In the light of "the present difficult living conditions," the city council decided in 1913 in favor of his application for an increase in his monthly (!) "mercy money" (*kegydíj*)

[71] Gaál, *Szegényügyi politika* [Poverty policy], vol. I, Tables 9 and 10.
[72] Gaál, *Szegényügyi politika* [Poverty policy], vol. I, 41 f.
[73] Thirring, *A magyar városok statisztikai évkönyve* [Statistical yearbook of Hungarian cities], 555 f., *1910. évi népszámlálás* [Census results 1910], vol. XLVIII; own calculations.
[74] Kácser, *Temesvár emberbaráti intézményei* [The philantropic institutions of Temesvár], 45.

from 24 to 30 crowns. The city of Kaposvár thus granted János Császár, even before the requested increase, charity nine times as high as the average amount received by the "municipal poor."[75]

In his decree of 1899, the minister for the interior had, as mentioned in chapter II.2. above, insisted that the municipalities create (new) statutes on poverty within the year. This obligation was not met everywhere, and where it was, the new statutes differed by and large very little with regard to regulations for welfare provision from the old ones, or perpetuated the existing local practice. In Nyíregyháza, the capital of then Szabolcs County, like elsewhere, the ministerial decree gave the debate about the problems of poverty a certain impetus. On 4 November 1901 the county introduced a new poor statute, resolved still in 1899, and on the same day the newly built municipal asylum for the poor and the sick was officially opened. But as regards non-institutional care, everything remained unchanged. Only those needy persons who had no relatives to support them, could not be supported by private charity, and were completely destitute and unable to work or earn an income by any other means had a chance of receiving financial aid. The amount of money issued (0.5 to 2.5 crowns per month) also changed very little: in 1891 adult paupers had received 1.0 to 2.0 crowns and in 1896 1.0 to 1.5. Although in reality from 1896 emergency aid (i.e. one off) payments were also made, the authorities were wary of including this category as a possible form of aid in the new poor statute. Begging within the municipality was forbidden (which did not prevent the issuing of begging permits), and those among the poor who were capable of such were to be put to work.[76]

In the major cities and counties several years elapsed after the ministerial decree of 1899 before the minister was able to report positive results. In 1906 the point was finally reached where "more municipalities[77] [had] established by statute poverty policy on a new footing, in keeping with the expectations of the modern age."[78] This statement reflected among other things the satisfaction that the capital, Budapest, under pressure from the ministerial decree of 1899 had finally in 1905, after prolonged birth

[75] Thirring, *A magyar városok statisztikai évkönyve* [Statistical yearbook of Hungarian cities], 238; SML. Kaposvár rtv. Képviselő testület. Jegyzőkönyvek [Secondary City of Kaposvár. Council minutes] 1913, Box 2. Közgyűlés [Municipal Council] no. 141. 17.994/1913.

[76] Gaál, *Szegényügyi politika* [Poverty policy], vol. I, 26 ff., and supplement no. 10.

[77] The official term covered major cities and counties.

[78] *A Magyar Királyi Kormány* [The Royal Hungarian Government] 1906 (Budapest 1907), 27.

pangs, passed a new poor statute, which entered into force in 1906.[79] In the regulations of the new statute, there is clear evidence on the one hand of the impact of the winter of hardship and unemployment at the beginning of the century. On the other hand, the new regulations were marked by an aspiration to make certain central elements of the debate on the reform of non-institutional care or outdoor relief—a debate that had continued since the 1890s, and not just regarding the capital—into the foundations of the new approach. Both overtly and covertly, these debates and plans about reform were first and foremost concerned with the limitation of costs through increased efficiency in the distribution of aid. Accordingly, the Budapest reform was primarily concerned with using all available means to push those amongst the needy who were capable of work back into (often not available) employment. Support in kind rather than with money, workshops providing employment, and the allocation of work tools to those requesting aid—all these strategies appeared at least on the paper of the new statute. Against a backdrop of a recovery of the labor market, even as the new regulations were coming into force, it is not surprising that little more remained of the policy of work promotion than the consistent refusal of poor aid to those fit for work.

A second key feature of the innovation was the attempt to constantly and individually supervise and keep check on aid recipients. Efficient forms of administration were planned, private charity or civil welfare activity was to be more closely connected to public welfare, under the supervision of the authorities, the randomness and haphazardness of aid given by private charity was to be reduced and multiple provision prevented. None of these efforts, however, got beyond the initial stages, confirming for Budapest the assessment of the expert of the time, Tivadar Forbáth, who lamented the "total disorganization" of "Hungarian private charity."

A third planned innovation, targeted at the stabilization of social circumstances of those aid recipients who would be more accurately identified on the basis of the first two reform strategies, was the increased focus on the family in the system of aid. To this end, the increase in the maximum monthly aid from 10 to 15 crowns was accompanied by additional gradated payments for family members of the recipient. The analysis of individual cases of the application of this regulation shows that married men who were unable to work and whose wives' earnings were low or

[79] Important industrial cities such as Temesvár were still occupied with preparatory work at this point. Kácser, *Temesvár emberbaráti intézményei* [The philantropic institutions of Temesvár], 43 f.

erratic had chances of receiving monthly support, while on the other hand married women who were unable to work and whose husbands earned very little were refused such support.

As a whole, the actual changes in non-institutional poor aid (outdoor relief) in Budapest, due to the new statute lagged far behind the very ambitious expectations, though a certain increase in levels of aid issued per capita of the population was perceptible. In the area of municipal welfare for poor children as well, the issuing of the new poor statute in Budapest brought little substantial change. As a state system of provision for "abandoned" children within the state system for the protection of children was put in place, the much criticized municipal practice of placing orphans and children of parents unable to work to be fed in foster families began to lose importance. Yet the problems connected with the lack of official supervision of those children who were placed by their parents or relatives, as well as by public authorities, in outdoor foster care did not go away. The focus of public attention on the new state system for the protection of children meant that less attention was paid to these problems. At the same time, authorities and public discourse for decades clung to the very shortsighted perspective according to which the catastrophic fate of many foster children was caused by a lack of official supervision alone. The new poor statute also failed to introduce the allocation of educational allowances for children of parents in need or of single mothers. Last but not least, the creation of a modern and effective protection system for mothers and infants remained a pipe dream for municipal policy in the capital city of Budapest.[80]

Conditions in institutional poor relief in the Hungarian capital were similarly characterized by stagnation. Representatives of the division of the municipal administration responsible for the poverty agenda made desperate efforts over the decades to get the construction of a new large-scale poorhouse under way, so as to take control of the "ignominious" conditions in the existing institutions. The "unsustainable" conditions in these institutions persisted, however, in spite of the marked differentiation between individual groups of residents and the improvement of technical equipment, as well as in personnel and levels of care that took place in the years before the war.[81]

At least in the larger cities, provision for the homeless formed a separate part of communal welfare provisions. A private shelter for the homeless had

---

[80] Zimmermann, *Prächtige Armut* [Splendid poverty], 118–126, 142–157, Table 2. Forbáth, *A szegényügy rendezése* [The regulation of the poor relief system], 129.

[81] Zimmermann, *Prächtige Armut* [Splendid poverty], 126–129, including the original quotations.

existed in Budapest since 1876, and since 1880 the society responsible for it was supported by the municipality. Prompted in part by the cholera epidemics of 1886 and 1892, which permitted the "discovery" of "unsatisfactory" living conditions under which particularly in the capital those of the "temporarily resident working class suffered," the municipality resorted to increased support for the now rapidly multiplying shelters provided by private societies. In 1895 these counted a total of 387,000 overnight stays. In a direct response to the two cholera epidemics, the municipality undertook for the first time the construction of emergency housing out of its own funds. In 1893, this amounted to 1,800 living and sleeping spaces, which in spite of the best efforts of the authorities, promptly turned into permanent accommodation for the poorest strata of the population.[82]

While it is impossible at the present state of research to give a substantial overall evaluation of the role of nonpublic welfare in supporting those in need, one example may be mentioned. In the "multilingual and multidenominational" city of Temesvár in Transylvania women's philanthropic associations based in religious denominations and representing at once the major national and language groups were the major agents of private welfare even in the early 20th century. To the Jewish and the Roman Catholic associations established from the middle of the 19th century two protestant associations were added in 1889 and 1901 respectively, while Serb women became active in the Greek Orthodox Serbian Philanthropic Women's Association (*Görög keleti szerb nők jótékony egylete*) from 1900 and Romanian women in the Greek Orthodox Romanian Women's Association (*Görög keleti román nők egylete*) from 1905. These organizations spent more than 21,000 crowns annually on the needy, as compared to 46,000 crowns spent by the municipal poor fund. On top of this, a number of philanthropic funds distributed part of their rather modest revenue to the poor, mostly on a given day of the year. Last but not least, aid given by the "denominations" —that is aid distributed directly by the churches and other purely denominational bodies—has to be mentioned, which amounted to "thousands [of crowns] annually" for each denomination.[83]

---

[82] Zimmermann, *Prächtige Armut* [Splendid poverty], 130–141.

[83] This last, in the case of the Greek Orthodox denomination, included a monthly benefit of "40–60 crowns" for "numerous impoverished Serbian families," and it seems rather likely that the foundation providing these benefits was duly established according to civil law. Kácser, *Temesvár emberbaráti intézményei* [The philantropic institutions of Temesvár], 45–61.

II.3.3. The practice of poverty policy as suppression of poverty

Poverty policy as a policy of the suppression of poverty targeted principally the elimination of the visible public symptoms of poverty. It was concerned first and foremost with the suppression and punishment of the so-called vagabondage, as well as unauthorized begging and prostitution, and with the relocation of these conspicuous individuals who did not enjoy legal residency status in the municipality where they had attracted the authorities' attention back to the municipality of their origin. In some cases the individuals concerned had never resided in this municipality of origin; in some cases they did not even know the name of the village or town to which, for example, their grandfather had been legally tied and which legally still counted as their "home." Added to the in itself purely administrative process of official establishment of the home municipality of persons in need, in practice poverty policy clearly used the legal residency clause as a strategy for avoiding the welfare obligations of the municipality. A further element of repressive poverty policy was forced labor, although in the years before the World War I, the relevant Hungarian law of 1913 on the "publicly dangerous work-shy," unlike the Austria "Vagabond law" of 1885, was not fully enforced. Its paragraphs on forced labor only entered into effect in 1916.[84]

The local and regional authorities took the policy against vagabondage and unauthorized begging very seriously. In many places in Hungary from the 1870s, relevant by-laws were passed or revised. For decades these constituted—if differentiated according to legal residence status—a form of aggressive pressure on those who did not pursue a respectable means of living. The existence and lifestyle of these people were considered tantamount to a threat to "public safety" and local authorities tended to automatically make them the principal suspects for robbery, theft, and other forms of criminality occurring in a given locality. Accordingly, the County of Veszprém passed a "County statute on relocation" in 1876 in which the relevant authorities throughout the county were called upon to expel all "itinerant Gypsies" and other "suspicious vagrants who could not prove their identity." Moreover, the dwellings of herdsmen and "other suspicious buildings" should be regularly checked and any "strangers" found therein

---

[84] Pál Angyal, Gyula Isaák, *A Kihágási Büntető Törvénykönyv. Jegyzetekkel, utalásokkal, magyarázatokkal és bírói gyakorlattal* [Criminal Code for Minor Offences. With comments, indications, explanations and judicial practice], 2 vols. (Budapest, third edition, 1937), vol. II, 319.

arrested and brought before the authorities. Various types of decrees aimed at preventing the wandering of "foreign" as well as locally resident and registered "Gypsies" were commonplace in other districts too, though it was certainly not this social group alone against that repressive poverty policy was directed.[85] Nagykálló, a farming town with a population of just under 6,000 a few kilometers from the city of Nyíregyháza, which in 1876 became the seat of Szabolcs County (in present-day Szabolcs–Szatmár–Bereg County) passed a local statute in 1872. As a result, the municipality of Nagykálló had the right and the obligation to imprison "unlawful beggars" for up to six hours. "Work-shy, vagrant individuals coming from elsewhere are to be banished, and in the case of contumacy to be punished." In the case of "grave" extenuating reasons, strangers to the municipality might be granted a begging permit for not longer than 48 hours.[86]

In the local statutes on matters of poverty policy, such by-laws were regularly combined with those others described earlier that in however minimal fashion were nonetheless aimed at welfare provision. This combination of the two faces of local poverty policy was discursively maintained by the illusion that every man or woman could, in so far as he or she wished to do so, hold down a "respectable occupation." If the authorities had questioned this vision that "respectable" occupations and lifestyles were indeed an available option for everybody, this would have severely undermined their customary repressive approach to dealing with poverty. Local poverty policy thus held fast to its combination of repression and minimal welfare provisions and as a result struggled fruitlessly for decades, with constant new statutes and decrees, against the despised figures of the work-shy vagrant (including illegal prostitutes) and the unauthorized beggar. The County seat, Kaposvár, for example, felt the need once again in 1911 to forbid "begging from house to house" and to require the head of the police to "enforce this ban."[87] When in November 1901 the above-mentioned new poor statute of the County seat, Nyíregyháza, came into force, the head of the local police posted an official announcement in all the surrounding settlements and hamlets administratively be-

[85] The Veszprém statute is reprinted in Barna Mezey, ed. *A magyarországi cigánykérdés dokumentumokban 1422–1985* [The Hungarian Gypsy question in documents 1422–1985] (Budapest 1986), 219 f.; László Pomogyi, *Cigánykérdés és cigányügyi igazgatás a polgári Magyarországon* [The Gypsy question and management of Gypsy affairs in bourgeois Hungary] (Budapest 1995), 117–125, 222–230.

[86] Original text of the statute in Gaál, *Szegényügyi politika* [Poverty policy], vol. I, 15 f.

[87] SML. Kaposvár rtv. Képviselő testület. Jegyzőkönyvek [Secondary City of Kaposvár. Municipal Council. Minutes] 1911, no. 240. 14064/1911.

longing to Nyíregyháza. He ordered the official organs to ban all beggars, and if they should persist in begging, to deliver them to his police station at the expense of the city of Nyíregyháza. To any "stray foreign Wallachian Gypsies" this requirement applied even "if they are not begging."[88] As regards relocation, the authorities also made enthusiastic efforts, via administrative reform, to give the struggle against itinerants without any fixed means of income somewhat less of the appearance of tilting against windmills. Thus in 1901 there occurred a reform in the practical handling of relocation to, from and through the in-migration metropolis Budapest. By decree of the minister for the interior, a regular rail transport system was introduced for relocatees and so-called "transit relocatees" who were being expelled from or via Budapest to the provinces. Those concerned were henceforth to be regularly gathered together in groups and removed from Budapest in early trains, separated from regular travelers, on established "relocation routes."[89]

The windmill-tilting struggle against vagabondage, unauthorized begging, and prostitution by those from within and beyond the municipality was not only pursued (in vain) in the dry phrases of statutes, decrees, and administrative reforms. Across the country, but particularly in the capital, the problem was for decades the subject of endless debates. In Budapest these debates remained acrimonious even after the enactment of the new poor statute, which in the spirit of the above-described ostensible illusion had been dreamt of as leading to the final disappearance of poverty. Before the end of 1906, the year in which the new statute finally entered into force, an interpellation was raised in the municipal council, the political decision making body of the capital. Still, it was stated with great disappointment and abhorrence, "the same beggars… every kind of old, blind or crippled individual… [were to be seen] all over the streets." "Jocularity" appeared only once within the debate on the interpellation, on the occasion when someone interjected, "They should go to the County State Officials [*főispánok*]."[90]

[88] Gaál, *Szegényügyi politika* [Poverty policy], vol. I, supplement no. 10.

[89] Mihály Szaplonczay, *A toloncz-ügy közigazgatása. A tolonczügyre vonatkozó összes rendeletek és szabályok gyüjteménye és magyarázata* [The administration of relocation. Collection and explanation of all decrees and directives related to relocation] (Budapest 1903), 8 ff.

[90] The County State Officials (*főispánok*) were the representatives of the state in the county administration. The interjection played on the principle of decentralized responsibility for the administration of the poor including the principle of legal residence status. *Fővárosi Közlöny. Budapest székesfőváros hivatalos lapja* 17 (1906): 377.

As the practice of repressive poverty policy against the poor unfolded, both the class- and gender-specific prejudice and partiality of the authorities, as well as the survival strategies, and the resistance of those affected became clearly apparent. In matters of relocation, for example, the minister for the interior had to repeatedly restrain the excessive zeal of the authorities, such as when a woman was relocated for the sole reason that she could demonstrate no regular occupation and by her own admission "on one occasion went to a hotel with a Guard from the Financial Authority [*pénzügyőr*] to abandon herself to lust."[91] Many of those affected used all means at their disposal to avoid the actual relocation, often to the entirely unknown and far-distant provincial municipality deemed responsible for them. The authorities complained about those who provided false names or false home municipalities so as to postpone the relocation, and they complained likewise about the "regular" escapes of relocatees on their way "home," often already in the suburbs of the urban area where they were arrested.[92] Although contemporary discussion focused almost exclusively on this as an organizational problem, at the latest the return to the home municipality revealed ruthlessly the reasons that forced people to leave again. Not only was there no provision for the new arrivals if they were unable to work, and no work available if they were able to, but if they were classified as work-shy, "supervision" by the local authorities as was legally requested was not provided. Rather, in the provinces even the relocated poor for whom the respective communities were responsible according to the principle of legal residence status were often "simply not tolerated" by the authorities, and the local people considered even "escaped prisoners… as better than relocatees." The local authorities, according to those in the capital concerned with relocation agendas, attempted in this way to "free" themselves as quickly as possible from the relocatees,

[91] In contemporary discourse, songs, etc. the "Guard from the Financial Authority" (*pénzügyőr*) served as a well-known figure that symbolized both the upward-mobility hopes of lower class girls and female servants and the sexual exploitation of such hopes; the *pénzügyőr* also symbolized the fact that these women were at the mercy of those representing the local authorities. *Közigazgatási elvi határozatok egyetemes gyüjteménye. Új-folyam* [Universal collection of principal administrative decisions. New series], 3 vols. (Budapest 1900, 1906, 1910), vol. II, 332.

[92] *Budapest Állami Rendőrség* [Budapest State Police] 1895, 260; *Budapest fő- és székváros közigazgatási bizottságának jelentése a közigazgatás összes ágainak állapotáról az 1891. év II-ik felében* [Report of the administrative committee of the Capital City and Royal Seat of Budapest on the state of all branches of the administration in the second half of the year 1891] (Budapest 1892), 43.

and abetted their earliest possible disappearance by providing begging permits for larger regions or even by providing them funds with which to travel.[93] In this way, relocation as a whole came to resemble a kind of system of interconnected tubes for the transportation of individuals who were unable to work or had no fixed occupation.

The prejudice of the authorities was perhaps most apparent in their everyday dealings with the ways of living and survival strategies of individuals of working age with no fixed employment. In the Igal district, for example, the activities of the official organs in this regard ranged from active pursuit of a group of "itinerant Gypsies," to the relocation of a female stove fitter who amused herself in the local tavern, to proceedings against a butcher in search of work. In the first case, the police pursued the already departing "itinerant Gypsies" and seized two of the three wagons. Those involved had, according to the record, while claiming to be "hail damaged" or "wood-carvers," been begging in various places in the area. "Yet they understand nothing of wood carving, they simply tramp and beg under this pretence." The two family men concerned were accordingly sentenced to pay a fine. Like the delinquents in the other two cases, because of indigency or inability to pay the same, they were instead placed under arrest, in this case for twelve hours, and "to provide their own sustenance," and were subsequently packed off in the direction of their home municipality. In the case of the stove fitter, this was a 45-year-old divorced day laborer, who declared that she had been working for some time in the area, had already built two stoves, and had accordingly left her employment book with her employer. In contrast, the district notary of Magyaratád, thanks to whom the woman was arrested, claimed that she had "been roaming around here for days without any form of identification or employment" and had "displayed improper parts of her body" in the local tavern. This last accusation was also contested by the woman in question. "It is true," according to the record of the interrogation, said the woman, who like the "itinerant Gypsies" was illiterate, "that on the evening of the 27th of the month, in the tavern of M[agyar]atád … I flirted [literally: engaged in amorous adventuring] in a drunken state with the individuals gathered there and out of pure cheek lifted my skirt to the knee, but it is not true that I displayed improper parts of my body in ex-

93 *Budapest fő- és székváros közigazgatási bizottsága 1891/II* [Report of the administrative committee of the Capital City and Royal Seat of Budapest 1891/II], 40; *Budapest Állami Rendőrség* [Budapest State Police] 1897 (Budapest 1898), 227 f.; 1908 (Budapest 1909), 229.

change for money." Katalin Kovács was also sentenced to twelve hours arrest and sent back to her home municipality. In the case of the skilled butcher's assistant, the required arrest prior to relocation on the grounds of "unemployed vagrancy" was in fact 24 hours. The 40-year-old skilled butcher spoke Hungarian and German, was "moderately" well-dressed and could read and write. There had been no entries in his employment book for almost three months because, he stated, steady work was nowhere to be found, and for the last two months he had "worked here and there for one or two days on a daily wage, and that is why nothing was entered in my book ... Now I was heading for Kaposvár, because I had heard that there was work to be had there with the railway. I haven't stolen anything or robbed anyone, and when my food and money ran out and I couldn't find any work, I got by from begging."[94]

Besides punishment and relocation, as a part of the everyday efforts to suppress poverty, the battle of papers between different authorities and municipalities to establish the legal residence status, and thus the municipality responsible for the person concerned also played an important role. Where the establishment of the responsible municipality was delayed, this meant not only that the assertion of liability to recourse for subsequent welfare provisions[95] between municipalities was also delayed, but in addition that the person concerned was denied even the most minimal poor aid for a longer period of time. In this way, the principle of municipal responsibility for poor aid was in practice transformed into a means of avoiding welfare obligations altogether. For example, there were official complaints from the municipal council of Budapest that in the course of the authorities' deliberations in attempting to establish the municipal responsibility in certain, not so rare cases "files covering 4–5 years, absolute tomes"[96] were produced. "If across the country the insoluble case-files on establishing the legal residence status were to be gathered together and set alight, such a cloud of smoke would arise as would cover seven counties... That would be a true bonfire to the glorification of the institution of

[94] SML. Igali járás. Kihágási ügyek [District of Igal. Administrative offences], 1900, nos. 124, 126 and 24.

[95] See above pp. 14 f.

[96] *Fővárosi Közlöny* 12, no. 75 (1901), supplement: 2. Indeed the fat case files on documenting the procedure of establishing legal residence status still exist today in the archives, as do the many complex high-level administrative decisions, printed in the relevant specialist publications of the time, offering eloquent testimony to the conditions and strategies summarized here and in subsequent chapters.

public administration."[97] Even the administrative procedure for winding up of contentious issues regarding legal residence status were inconsistent, unclear, and to a large extent characterized by imponderability and uncertainty.[98] And finally the legislation itself, with its combination of prolonged residence and contribution to the municipal costs as a prerequisite for the application for legal residence status in the place of residence, contributed significantly to increasing the inertia of the administrative procedure in establishing the legal residence status of people in need. Registers existed neither for the documentation of actual residence status nor for legal residence status, tax details had to be checked in folios from various years, and in principle all these data had to be gathered together. "Hundreds of thousands of those on small incomes pay no direct taxes, and when it comes to establishing legal residence status, extracts from the register of taxes follow fast upon one another and tedious habitual clauses from the minutes of the municipal authorities, '... though he resided here 10 years, 20 years etc., he paid no taxes, thus legal residence status in this municipality cannot be recognized'."[99]

In a country in which freedom of trade and commerce was a guiding star of economic thinking and politics and the workforce had the right to look for work and livelihood wherever they might find it, local responsibility for poor relief, though it served exclusionary poverty policy well, also created gross budgetary imbalances and awkward administrative circumstances. This was one of the reasons why around the turn of the century the state and some municipalities turned to new socio-political horizons. It is to this new chapter in Hungarian need-related policies that we turn now.

[97] György Szeglethy, "A községi illetőség és a szegényügy országos rendezése" [Legal residence status and the countrywide regulation of poverty policy]. *Városok Lapja* 1 (1906): 2.

[98] *Magyar közigazgatás* 5, no. 11 (1887): 2 f.; *Közigazgatási elvi határozatok. Új-folyam* [Principle administrative decisions. New series], vol. III, 276 ff.

[99] Ferencz Nagy, "A községi illetőség" [Legal residence status]. *Magyar közigazgatás* 33, no. 27 (1905): 1 f., here 2.

III. Social Reform and State Intervention (from 1898 to 1914)

At the latest by the 1890s it was increasingly felt that political action on what contemporaries called "the social question" in its many diverse branches and aspects could no longer be avoided. Hungarian society seemed in some regards to have gone off the rails; new social problems and conflicts loomed, and existing social relations and problems began to be perceived in new ways. The central intersection of the novel efforts for social reform was undoubtedly the capital, Budapest, where the "social question" began to take the center stage in the most intense and visible manner. Against this background, in 1906 a new generation of reformers came to the fore in the Budapest city hall. Driven in part by the wave of social tensions that was growing in the city, the professionally minded group around Mayor István Bárczy pushed through a number of reform projects in the final years before World War I. It was with a focus exclusively on the most extreme "hubs" of material and political tension that the economically liberal-dominated municipal council—in which the old encrusted and highly elitist political structures dragged on—accepted these reforms carried out by the otherwise at best tolerated reformers. Mayor Bárczy canvassed a few highly motivated professional into the municipal administration, and this group transformed Budapest into a municipality which tried out a number of new and, in contemporary international context, progressive socio-political reforms.[1] In national politics a similar rejuvenation did not take place, yet between 1906 and 1910 there was a marked change of government on this level too. In the era of the national liberal coalition government under Sándor Wekerle (April 1906–January 1910), social-conservative and paternalistic forces in the interests of controlling some aspects of the "social question" and some consequences of economic liberalism—via a combination of social-integrative and law-and order-based reforms—played a bigger role than before or hereafter.

[1] According to Imre Ferenczi, who can be considered as a key figure of the social reform efforts in the capital. Imre Ferenczi, "A főváros szociálpolitikai programmja" [The socio-political program of the Capital]. *Munkásügyi Szemle* 2 (1911): 3–7, here 7.

Against this backdrop, new social reforms and policies began to be pushed through. Partly these became only possible due to new state legislation, partly it was the capital city, Budapest alone, and to a much smaller extent municipalities elsewhere in the country, who took the lead, and in some policy fields new forms of cooperation between state and local government unfolded across the country. While Budapest's municipal policies on unemployment, and even more so with regard to public housing, led the field in social reform and innovation throughout the country, in the area of child welfare and child protection, due to the powerful grasp of the state, the capital city played a complementary role at best.

III.1. Child Protection

The new regulations introduced in connection with the establishment of the State Healthcare Fund, by which the funding of institutional healthcare for the poor and (in part) the care for "abandoned" children was nationalized in 1898[2], were preceded by many years of debate. With regard to child protection, at the heart of these discussions was the system of care for "foundlings" and the possible establishment of a state home for foundlings, together with the problem of children born out of wedlock and abandoned (especially in the capital). From 1898 the costs incurred for the care for children under the age of 7 declared "abandoned by the public authorities were covered by the State Healthcare Fund. At first the authorities tried to bypass the construction of state institutions caring for these children. Any institutional involvement of the state in solving the "social question" was a highly controversial issue in general. In this case it was feared that parents would exploit such institutions and that their sheer existence would damage the sexual morals, especially of women, i.e. stimulating sexual relations that were not sanctioned by the law and were socially inacceptable. Against the backdrop of these fears and related debates, private associations were entrusted with the institutional care of what became known as "state children." But as the related costs exploded and municipalities succeeded in gradually extending further and further the circle of children under the age of seven classified as abandoned, so as to ensure that the state would reimburse costs, the minister decided on a radical change of approach. In 1901 two laws were passed transforming child protection on the national level into a socio-political institution that not only was financed by the state but was the direct responsibility of the

[2] See chapter II.2.

ministry for the interior. As a result, construction began on a network of state children's homes that were to form the core of a new state child protection policy.[3] The term "abandoned" was defined more loosely in the new regulations than hitherto, so as to increase the authorities' room for maneuver and to give some leeway in future with children who did not strictly count as foundlings but still needed to be taken care of.[4] At the same time, the new regulations[5] seriously limited the freedom of action of municipalities regarding provisions for "abandoned" children from the age of 7 to 14. The financial responsibility of the municipalities for this group remained unchanged, and they were at the same time obliged to leave these children in state asylums and pay for them if they could not be accommodated by another institution or association belonging to or under the supervision of the municipality concerned. A decree from the minister for the interior in 1907[6] heralded a further extension and partly novel orientation of the state child protection system in Hungary. Henceforth, even "minors who have been hitherto exposed to moral decay, morally abandoned or neglected"—including delinquent minors—were to be included in state child protection. In this way the category of the deviant child and child neglect entered Hungarian law. This new category considerably enhanced the options available to the relevant authorities. Now even children whose parents were materially well off enough to be able to care for the child could be declared "abandoned," and through the medium of the state children's homes could be passed on to foster parents for strict upbringing or placed in other special homes. The decree was complemented by an amendment to criminal law,[7] the clauses of which relating to young offenders entered into force in 1910. For children and minors under the age of criminal responsibility—henceforth 18 years—who had been "exposed to moral decay in their surroundings hitherto," the amendment, like the minister's decree, allowed them to be committed to a state corrective institution. There were also a variety of possibilities for children to be placed under the supervision of various, in part newly created, committees or authorities outside the walls of corrective institutions or prisons.[8]

[3] Act 8/1901; Ordinance 79.1/1903, Minister for the interior; Zimmermann, *Prächtige Armut* [Splendid poverty], 152–157, 303–307.

[4] Ordinance 79.1/1903, Minister for the interior, 535 f.

[5] Act 21/1901; Ordinance 79.1/1903, Minister for the interior.

[6] Ordinance 60.000/1907, Minister for the interior.

[7] Act 36/1908.

[8] Zimmermann, *Prächtige Armut* [Splendid poverty], 360–364.

On the basis of these remarkable legislative reforms to the organizational and institutional framework of child protection and child welfare, Hungary developed an extensive new system of state child protection that obligatorily included the municipalities. The rapidly created state children's homes, which numbered 17 scattered across the country (for a certain period 18), accepted on a permanent basis only sick, weak children and those in particular need of care. In addition they functioned as organizational and supervision centers for the "child colonies" in individual villages where children were cared for in foster families.[9] By 1902 there were already 22,139 children in care under the state child protection system, and by 1913 the figure had risen to 56,535.[10] In addition, further state correction institutions were established and numerous private institutions created or extended, most notably by the highly active National Child Protection League (*Országos Gyermekvédő Liga*), which cooperated closely with the public child protection authorities. These institutions pursued corrective child and juvenile care and education on the basis of the legal changes of 1907 and 1910, which aimed at including new groups of "abandonded" children by expanding the legal definition of entitlement to state child protection. Between 1910 and 1913 three new corrective institutions operated by the state were established, two of them in Budapest, and capacity rose from 940 to 2,605 places. This expansion focused particularly on deviant boys, and as a result the share of places available for girls decreased to 12 percent.[11]

Hungarian state child protection avoided locating homes in centers with non-Hungarian-speaking nationalities—thus for example, there was no state home in Pozsony—and blatantly pursued a policy of Magyarization of the next generation. When the number of children in care in state homes dropped noticeably from 1902 to 1903, the minister for the interior made no secret of the fact that the "main cause" was the Magyarization strategies of the state child protection authorities. Specifically, children were "regularly placed with foreign [Hungarian] speaking foster parents; in consequence a very large number of parents resisted their child being placed in state care."[12] Unlike in the case of the Magyarization of the set-

---

[9] *Jelentés az állami gyermekmenhelyek 1907–1910 évi munkásságáról* [Report on the work of the state children's asylums].

[10] *A Magyar Királyi Kormány* [The Royal Hungarian Government] 1903 (Budapest 1904), 23; 1914 (Budapest 1916), 31.

[11] Zimmermann, *Prächtige Armut* [Splendid poverty], 363.

[12] *A Magyar Királyi Kormány* [The Royal Hungarian Government] 1903, 23.

tled non-Hungarian population, however, the child protection authorities did not feel under any obligation to intervene in the "Gypsy problem" through the state child protection system. The minister made this very clear in connection with one particular case. The children of "itinerant Gypsies" were not to be declared "abandoned" so long as their mother was willing and able to take care of them. Accordingly, the minister reversed the decision on the part of the County Guardianship Authority (*árvaszék*) to place in a state home 15 "itinerant Gypsy" children. The minister obviously rejected the idea that taking children away from their parents and educating them at the state's expense might or should contribute to settling at least the next generation of "Gypsies." Instead, the necessary future child protection measures for the "solution" to the "Gypsy question" were rather to "be closely fitted to the quintessential character of the Gypsy race."[13]

The range of problems that the new system faced in practice were connected to the continuity and associations that linked it back to traditional poor care. For one, it had to deal with the same phenomena that had long plagued privately organized foster care. These included the often inadequate quality of foster parents, problems with the organization of medical and other supervision of the conditions of foster care, problems with wet nurses, and so on. A second and new kind of problem appeared as a result of the institutional isolation of the state child protection system. The authorities made every effort to prevent the "abuse" of the socially inclusive child protection system to compensate for the lack of comparable structures and system of social care in other policy fields, such as, for example, poor relief for adults. The system was to be concerned with only those children who had "reached the door of the [state-run children's] home as it went through the Calvary of life." This isolation was consistently defended; the ministry did not respond positively even to the repeated demands for state homes to take over the supervision of children privately placed in foster care. Third, headaches were also caused by the fact that it was often impossible to implement the regulation stating that the parents of children in state care, if materially able, were obliged to contribute to the costs of care. The state child protection authorities had originally assumed that a significant share of those parents who were able to work and had been freed of the duties of childcare would be in a position to contribute. But soon complaints arose that "recalcitrant parents" could not be

[13] The ordinance, issued in 1916, is reprinted in Mezey, *Magyarországi cigánykérdés* [Hungarian Gypsy question], 211 f.

forced by any "legal means" to fulfill their obligations as regards payment. They lived "here today, there tomorrow" and evaded every attempt to trace them.[14]

There was one crucial point, however, in which the new system differed fundamentally from the old poor relief: it was not based on the principle of minimizing costs. And precisely for this reason, and because poverty was widespread and children's homes were one of the few places where those in need could turn in hope of being relieved of at least a small part of their material burdens, the gates of state homes, as the above figures show, were taken by storm. Given the resulting explosion in costs, specialists soon started to discuss reforms and alternatives. They agreed that the financial support of children within their original family was not feasible, as benefits of this type, given the lack of any other substantial system of support, would be sure to be spent on family needs or indeed on "amusement at the tavern," while the "child would stay hungry." The situation came to a head after the decree from the ministry for the interior in 1907 added to the materially defined term "abandonment" the category "neglect" as an additional ground for acceptance. The sudden rapid increase in admissions from 1907 led to budgets being exceeded and growing debts on the part of the municipalities, which were obliged to reimburse the costs of state care for the older children. This state of affairs soon cleared the way for "far-reaching economies." For the years 1910 to 1912 the budget of state child protection was frozen and the number of admissions dropped dramatically. At the same time, however, the battle against "neglect" initiated by the ministerial decree of 1907 and the amendment to the penal law of 1908 got under way. As a result, forced intervention into the affected families, strict educational measures, extensive pedagogical and police supervision, as well as referral of "neglected" children—whom one of those responsible had forwarded to a state children's home —to various institutions of corrective education became a prominent part of the new system of child protection. The number of children accepted into state children's homes under the diagnosis of "neglect" rose sharply. In 1912 nearly twice as many "60,000ers"—the name taken from the number of the by-law of 1907—were admitted as in 1910, and the share of "60,000ers" amongst those admitted increased countrywide from 4.2 to 9.2 percent.[15]

---

[14] Zimmermann, *Prächtige Armut* [Splendid poverty], 310–317, including both original quotes.

[15] Zimmermann, *Prächtige Armut* [Splendid poverty], 317–322, 359–369.

The new child protection system was systematically built on cooperation between state and municipal authorities, and the relationship between these two exhibited a number of important features. For one, cities and smaller communities suddenly found themselves under enormous pressure due to the obligation to pay for those children between the age of 7 and 14 admitted into state homes.[16] In order to support the smaller municipalities and those affected by emigration in particular, the state resorted to various measures. The second child protection law of 1901 permitted the use of the available part of the reserve fund for orphans kept by the counties and major cities as a means of covering a part of the expenses. Added to this, from 1902, there was to be an annual contribution from the ministry for the interior principally for covering the costs of those abandoned children who according to their legal residence status belonged to municipalities that possessed no funds or assets. The last resort, and one that in fact was used not infrequently, was the levying or increasing of a compensatory tax at county level.[17]

All in all, the emigration municipalities generally remained in the passive role of financially burdened and insufficiently supported local authorities in the new state-communal child protection system, having next to no influence on regulations or practice. In contrast, municipal policy in the capital in particular developed a range of innovative solutions, partly in cooperation with the state, partly circumventing a visibly resisting state. One of these was the first tentative attempt on the part of the capital's poor relief authority—i.e. the responsible section within the central municipal administration—to provide supplementary support for children raised in families who otherwise would have had no other choice than to hand over their children into state care. This solution was in any case less cost-intensive for the municipality.[18]

A more far-reaching innovation, however, was the introduction of the institution of professional guardianship under the direct control of the Budapest municipality in 1910. This meant that the possibilities for raising funds for the financial support for children born out of wedlock were to include officially enforced paternal alimony, rather than ever increasing extensions to the municipal (and state) budget. Initially the minister and the capital's poor relief authority had been resistant to this innovation, but those traditional male-centered attitudes which placed responsibility for

[16] Figures for costs in chapter II.3.1., information on payment obligation in chapter II.2.
[17] Zimmermann, *Prächtige Armut* [Splendid poverty], 309 f.
[18] Zimmermann, *Prächtige Armut* [Splendid poverty], 325 f.

illegitimate children at the door of "fallen" women were too dominant. If public authorities established and implemented a legal obligation for care on the part of the father of the illegitimate child, the old male prerogative of not taking responsibility for offspring stemming from extramarital sexual relationships would be seriously challenged. Only after the Budapest municipal council appointed a new chair of the municipal Guardianship Authority (*árvaszék*), who cooperated closely with the reformers who controlled the Budapest city hall from 1906, was there a U-turn in the thinking of this official body responsible for deciding on matters of guardianship. Immediately following the appointment of the new chair, Béla Melly, a separate section for child protection was created within the municipal Guardianship Authority. Working closely with progressive lawyers and other agents of change, this body pursued, as far as was possible within the limits of the law, a policy of exacting alimony from "natural," i.e. illegitimate fathers. For mothers who were not of full age—in Hungary 24 years—a professional guardian was appointed for the child automatically, while for mothers from the age of 24 years official pressure was applied—given that the law did not permit other alternatives—to persuade the mothers themselves to sue for alimony. The aim was either that the mother should acquire the means to care for the child herself or through private arrangements, so that it should not be declared "abandoned" in the first place and placed in state care, or alternatively, that the costs of state care should at least in part be offset by paternal alimony. Thus the municipality of Budapest advocated and as far as possible put in practice on the local level a reform that allowed the state-municipal child protection system to be developed further without this leading automatically to an increase in expenses.[19] Social reform in the capital city as pursued by its municipal authorities thus expanded on the Hungarian system of child protection in a particular way. The introduction of professional guardianship added a new element to the system, an element which came closer to modern forms of social policy that would combine provision systematically and effectively with policies of preventing need and creating a close nexus between contribution and benefit.

Unlike in the case of professional guardianship, the new policy on "neglect" of minors, particularly in the capital, developed out of the close cooperation of various authorities, including non-municipal and non-public ones. It was a policy that was designed first and foremost in response to the new forms of neglect that emerged from the "specific living

[19] Zimmermann, *Prächtige Armut* [Splendid poverty], 186 f., 322–337.

conditions of the metropolis." This concerned children who were largely left to their own resources, went to school irregularly or not at all, grew up largely on the streets, whose exhausted parents only returned home after they were asleep, and who lived in apartments where bed lodgers came and went. The consequences were, at least in the eyes of contemporary observers, a lack of moral and social control. In their view this led in the case of boys and to some extent girls to the formation of gangs and theft, while for girls "neglect" in addition or instead "typically" meant "love affairs for money." In 1912, neglect was cited as the grounds for admission for 22.3 percent of all children admitted to state care; for the provinces, in contrast, the figure was only 5.5 percent. Even before the reform-minded change at the top of the Budapest municipal Guardianship Authority, this body had shown itself to be a hard-core proponent of drastic measures against parents who themselves did nothing to prevent the "moral neglect" of their children. The Budapest police, in a prominent about-face, fell into line with the new state approach to child protection, adopting for the first time preventive if still repressive intervention measures. With the creation of its own "Children's Police" (*gyermekrendőrség*) within the Danube district police commission, the police judicial authorities of the capital became one of the front-runners in supporting the institutional independence of youth jurisdiction. This tendency was driven further and nationalized by a decree issued by the minister for justice in 1909. The "child court" of the Budapest police dealt with and tried all transgressions by minors, and worked in close collaboration with the old and new child protection authorities. Only in the area of the fight against child prostitution was there a clearly visible difference in understanding between the authorities in the capital and the minister for justice. The latter continued to hold fast to the traditional position that those women and girls who were perceived as prostituting themselves were to be left to their fate, without exception. Such a stance ruled out any kind of child protection intervention.[20]

As a whole, state-municipal child protection occupied a highly particular and in a sense ambivalent position within the Hungarian system of poverty and social policy. On the one hand, the child protection system can be considered as a unique, and uniquely expansive, state response to the phenomenon of poverty and "neglect" of minors. The legislation that provided those children officially classified as "abandoned" or "ne-

[20] *Budapest Állami Rendőrség* [Budapest State Police] 1908, 206; Zimmermann, *Prächtige Armut* [Splendid poverty], 346–369.

glected" with "the right to be admitted into a state children's home"[21] was a far-reaching intervention and social reform initiative even by international standards. The new system involved a constant fight with the problems of separating child poverty from poverty as a whole. The broad social responsibility which public authorities assumed by creating the child protection system rapidly led to what was perceived as a critical situation or crisis of the system, mainly due to the lack of comparable arrangements in other areas of social and poverty policy.

At the same time, the new child protection system remained restricted by the philanthropic and charitable *modus operandi* of traditional poverty policy. A preventive approach that would have focused on preventing children from getting into a situation where they needed to be taken into state care in the first place, as well as the principles rapidly gaining ground in social policy of reciprocity or shared risk, were absent. The combination of the isolation of the child protection system in the social field as a whole and the "social unproductiveness"[22] already criticized by contemporary reform-oriented professionals and discourses made the state-municipal child protection system a bottomless pit. The consequence, from 1907 onwards, was a double strategy of restricting numbers admitted on grounds of material "abandonment," i.e., material poverty, and repressive policies against "neglect."

III.2. Housing Policy

From the perspective of the lower classes, the "housing question," regardless of important differences between the cities and the countryside, was of central importance, when it came to organizing their own survival and daily life. Their most important concerns were essentially the unavailability of (adequate) housing and the often unaffordable rents. From the point of view of the authorities, in contrast, the main concerns, initially at least, were only for the immediate consequences of the housing problem, namely homelessness (as mentioned earlier) and the health-related consequences of inadequate living conditions, whereby epidemics spread quickly in the miserable living quarters of the lower classes and endangering the urban population as a whole. In the years after 1900, however, a new approach of public intervention emerged in the area of housing pol-

[21] Ordinance 79.1/1903, Minister for the interior, 535.

[22] Kálmán Csorna, "Az állami gyermekvédelem és a főváros" [State child protection and the Capital]. *Városi Szemle* 12 (1926): 78–90, here 81.

icy, which particularly addressed the problems of homelessness and workers' housing in the Budapest metropolitan area, as well as the living conditions among the lower classes in rural areas as part of the changes in agrarian social policy.

The proponents of the new housing policy, which took the form of social-reform-oriented intervention, had at their disposal three basic ways of influencing the housing conditions of the lower classes: first, sociopolitically motivated intervention in the regulation of rent contracts, second, public or publicly assisted building activities, and finally, public intervention into the economic factors influencing private apartment building and rent price formation.[23]

Policies aimed at the last of these areas impacting on the building of housing in Hungary, like in Austria, were initially limited to tax relief on incomes accruing from the ownership of housing. Then from 1906 on, the reform-minded Budapest municipal administration sought new directions in communal land policy and other cities began to make similar efforts towards reform.[24] But these attempts of the authorities to influence the general conditions for the utilization of capital in the housing sector to the benefit of tenants met with sharp resistance from opposing forces in the Budapest municipal council. Specific plans for the introduction of a land value tax (and a real estate value tax), both aimed at taxing appreciation in value, did not even make it to the council, failing to get past the finance committee at the end of 1907. Subsequent related attempts also failed in the early stages. The reformers met with somewhat more success, however, in their efforts to change the municipal land policy itself.[25] In the final years before the war, similar modest changes occurred in the land policy of several other Hungarian cities as well, many of which owned a considerable amount of land, often outside the actual administrative area of the city. Already in 1907 the Hungarian Congress of Cities spoke out in favor of reforms in land taxation, and from 1912 several cities passed

[23] Gerhard Melinz, Susan Zimmermann, "Mit den Waffen der Sozialpolitik? Wohnungspolitischer Interventionismus in Österreich und Ungarn von 1890 bis in die 1930er Jahre" [With the weapons of social policy? Housing policy interventionism in Austria and Hungary from 1890 to the 1930s], in: Clemens Zimmermann, ed. *Europäische Wohnungspolitik in vergleichender Perspektive* (1900–1939) [European housing policy in comparative perspective (1900–1939)] (Stuttgart 1997), 85–129, here 85–93.

[24] Emerich Ferenczi, *Die kommunale Wohnungspolitik in Ungarn, namentlich in Budapest 1910* [Municipal housing policy in Hungary, specifically in Budapest 1910] (no place, year given), 11 f., 17 f.

[25] Zimmermann, *Prächtige Armut* [Splendid poverty], 284–293.

statutes on land taxes that took appreciation in value into account, or took steps towards passing such regulations.[26]

On the question of tenancy law, both major cities and cities of secondary status possessed the right—albeit to be confirmed by the minister for the interior—to enact legally binding tenancy law regulations.[27] Other than this, there were no general regulations that could directly influence the conditions of tenancy and letting. The statute concerned with the letting of housing issued by the Budapest municipality in 1885 was based on legal thinking that obviously saw no reason or opportunity for intervention in the free play of market forces on the housing market. It contained no binding regulations on the amount of rent the owner could ask for a flat, or on the protection and rights of tenants. It was only once that the generation of reformers in the Budapest city hall took things in hand that a new direction in policy could be seen, also influenced by a well organized and partly militant tenants' movement, supported by but not identical with the Hungarian Social Democratic Party (*Magyarországi Szociáldemokrata Párt*). In 1906 a demonstration of 40,000 demanded that the municipal authorities should decree an upper limit for rent fees and called for a rent boycott if by February 1907 this demand was not fulfilled.[28] In 1907 the leadership of the city administration presented a proposal for a new statute on tenancy that contained regulations—for certain housing—aimed at the protection against rent increases and termination of tenancy in the first year. The draft statute encountered stiff and at first successful opposition in the municipal council and only finally became effective with the energetic support of the minister for the interior. In this and other important issues regarding the protection of tenants from the worst impositions of house owners, the municipal council received support in these years from the national liberal coalition government under Sándor Wekerle (April 1906 – January 1910).[29] A similar innovation in policy regarding the protection of tenants occurred neither in Vienna and Austria nor yet in other Hungarian cities before 1914.

---

[26] György Schulpe, *Munkásügyi reformok. Állámügyi, törvényhatósági és társadalmi szocializmus* [Reforms to workers' affairs. State, municipal and social socialism], 2 vols. (Pozsony 1908), vol. I, 42 ff.; Imre Ferenczi, *A lakásügy állása és haladása Magyarországon az utolsó három évben* [The situation and progress of housing in Hungary in the last three years] (Budapest 1913), 51 ff.

[27] Act 59/1881, §93.

[28] *A magyarországi szocziálisztikus munkásmozgalmak az 1906. évben* [The socialist workers' movements of Hungary in the year 1906] (Budapest 1907), 246 ff.

[29] Zimmermann, *Prächtige Armut* [Splendid poverty], 132 f., 260–269.

While there was negligible change in terms of intervention into the economic conditions of residential building activities and piecemeal (though important) reform in the field of tenant protection, the country underwent far-reaching changes in the area of public or publicly assisted building activities. With regard to the problem of workers' housing in urban industrial zones, from 1908 on an entirely new kind of public intervention was to be seen.

One of its key features was an extensive municipal program in Budapest for the construction of small apartments, started in 1909, which soon attracted international attention. This turnabout in municipal policy became possible not only because the reformers around Mayor István Bárczy (1906–1918) were determined early on to bring about a decision to engage in municipal house building, but also as a result of massive pressure on the part of the tenants' movement and the Social Democratic Party. While, at least during the political process leading up to the adoption of the famous municipal bill on public housing in 1909, the interaction between the reformers in the city hall and the Social Democratic Party at times appears to have been politically carefully orchestrated,[30] the same cannot be said of some of the activities of the tenants' movement. Organized resistance against "rent usury" had been recorded already from 1895, and from 1904 there were organized demonstrations, resistance against the usual eviction practices and occurrences of militant and violent resistance. From 1907 organized "rent strikes," i.e. refusal to pay the rent and active resistance against the ensuing eviction, were on the agenda and supported by the Social Democratic Party. In the same year violent incidents between tenants on the one hand and landlords and facility managers on the other, the public threat to systematically adopt this and other types of *action directe*, and multifaceted manifestations of solidarity became key features of the movement. The controversies between landlords and tenants reached a peak in 1910, the year after the municipal council adopted the famous municipal bill on public housing.[31]

---

[30] Zimmermann, *Prächtige Armut* [Splendid poverty], 249–258.

[31] Albert Lichtblau, "Boykott, Krawall, Gewalt, Demonstration. Die Budapester Mieterbewegung 1906 bis 1912 und exkursive Vergleiche zu ähnlichen Vorgängen in Wien" [Boycott, riot, violence, demonstration. The Budapest tenants' movement 1906 to 1912 and some elements of comparison to similar events in Vienna], in: *Archiv. Jahrbuch des Vereins für Geschichte der Arbeiterbewegung* 8 (1992), 65–82; Albert Lichtblau, Budapester Mieterbewegung. Dokumentation [The Budapest tenants' movement. Documentation] (unpublished research report); Michael John, *Hausherrenmacht und Mieterelend 1890–1923* [Landlord power, tenants' misery 1890–1923] (Vienna 1982), 44 ff.; Fe-

Against this background, the approval of the bill in the Budapest municipal council by those political forces—in part direct representatives of the construction business sector and/or landlords themselves—that pursued undamped liberalism appears less astonishing. Approval for the grandiose municipal housing project in 1909 was primarily thanks to the fact that accepting the construction program was considered by the majority of these political forces in the municipal council as a lesser evil than the escalation of the housing crisis and the accompanying social conflicts.

Without the municipal reformers who had captured the top ranks of the municipal administration, however, the reform could never have taken place. Yet the reformers could come up with their famous draft bill only after, under the coalition government, the national legislation had passed in 1908 a special law on the "development" of the capital city. This law formed part of a series passed in 1908 and 1909 which also laid the legal foundations for the change in the construction of workers' housing countrywide. These provided for example the necessary financing by credit and freedom from housing tax for the erection of state workers' housing in Budapest and the surroundings. One law contained a paragraph referring to companies of the Budapest city government, ensuring the exemption of the already planned municipal housing program from tax on condition that the apartments were let at cost price. The construction of workers' housing in other cities was also granted tax relief, albeit to a lesser extent than in Budapest, so long as the houses concerned remained property of the municipality.[32]

Already in 1908 the state authorities decided that they themselves would take direct responsibility for public construction of apartments for the laboring classes in the suburbs of the capital. The "Wekerle estate"—soon to be so called after the prime minister Sándor Wekerle—comprised

renczi, *Die kommunale Wohnungspolitik* [The municipal housing policy], 22; *Források Budapest történetéhez* [Sources on the history of Budapest], 4 vols. (Budapest 1971–1973), vol. II, 1873–1919, 251.

32 Act 48/190; Schulpe, *Munkásügyi reformok* [Reforms to Workers' Affairs], vol. I, 42 ff.; Imre Ferenczi, "A magyar lakásügy haladása az utolsó öt évben" [The progress of Hungarian housing affairs in the last five years]. *Városi Szemle* 3 (1910): 351–364, here 353; Ferenczi, *A lakásügy az utolsó három évben* [Housing affairs in the last three years], 33; Géza von Geyr, "Die Wekerlesiedlung in Budapest. Staatliche Arbeitersiedlung und Gartenstadt" [The Wekerle-settlement in Budapest. State workers' housing and garden city], in: *Ungarn Jahrbuch* 17 (1989), 71–94, here 74; Árpád Schmelhegger, "Városépítés" [Building the City], in: *A negyvenéves Budapest. Értekezések a városi közigazgatás köréből* [Budapest forty years. Studies on municipal administration] [Budapest 1914], 378–437, here 397 f.

close to 3,000 workers' apartments, most of them inhabited by employees of large state enterprises such as the railways and the post office. A paradigmatic example of social paternalism formed from stone and wood, the estate was designed as a garden city, including a provincial town type main square, churches, schools, and kindergartens. The buildings were decorated with numerous motifs representing or evocative of Hungarian historical (people's) architecture.[33]

Altogether, by 1913 more than 10,000 new apartments had been built by public authorities in the metropolitan region of and surrounding Budapest, by far more than half of which were constructed by the municipality. Some two fifths of the housing built by the Budapest municipality came into being through the construction of regular apartment blocks. Three fifths of the new municipal apartments, however, were constructed in the simplest possible manner, at ground level, or with a single storey as "small apartment colonies," an approach reminiscent of the construction of emergency housing from the days of the old poverty policy. Yet the municipality made stringent efforts to distinguish its new housing policy from the old poor relief and to stress the respectability of the occupants—not least by giving preference to families with a male head and children. The fact that the new municipal housing policy was based on a thoroughly masculinist attitude became even more apparent when it came to those important additional building projects which formed part of the 1909 reform package. Besides the apartment blocks and the "colonies" themselves a "People's Hotel" (*népszálló*) with 396 beds was built as a hostel for male workers temporarily without accommodation. The original plan was to offer accommodation for women and men in the people's hotel. Yet it soon became clear that women would simply not be able to afford the rent for a bed because of their lower wages. With reference to the "failure" of women's homes abroad due mainly to "morality"-related problems—"fortunately"—it was decided in the last moment to go for a

[33] Albert Werkner, *Der Kleinwohnungsbau in Budapest* [The construction of small apartments in Budapest] (Weida 1913), 51–57; Dezső Schuler, *A hajléktalanság kérdése a székesfővárosban* [The question of homelessness in the Capital City and Royal Seat of Budapest] (Budapest 1935), 47 f.; Ferenczi, *A lakásügy az utolsó három évben* [Housing affairs in the last three years], 55–59; Geyr, "Die Wekerlesiedlung" [The Wekerle-settlement], esp. 80 f., 83. Its paternalistic integrationist attitude notwithstanding the coalition government pursued uncompromising policies of repression against the workers' movement. Péter Hanák, "Das Zeitalter des Dualismus" [The dualist period], in: I. Barta et.al., *Geschichte Ungarns* [A history of Hungary] (Budapest 1971), 379–495, here 465 ff.

male-only "hotel." Besides the "People's Hotel" there was a second institution, the settlement type "People's Home" (*népház*) equipped with 150 beds (in four dormitories, one of them for women), a people's kitchen (*népkonyha*) serving food to the local poor, a children's home, a popular library, and a workshop offering employment on behalf of the public authorities (instead of cash or other forms of material support) for the able-bodied poor who had asked for benefits from the municipal poor relief authorities.[34]

Among the other Hungarian cities, only a few—Temesvár, Nagyvárad (Oradea) and Sopron—took advantage of the improved conditions since 1909 facilitating the construction of municipal housing. In Pozsony (Bratislava, Preßburg), ten municipal workers' housing blocks with 120 apartments had been built earlier, shortly after the turn of the century, and the authorities planned for additional activities which, however, did not materialize. Instead, Pozsony developed into a center of social housing for industrial workers promoted and brought about not by the public authorities but by the propertied classes themselves. By 1908 around 700 flats had been erected by social reformer György Schulpe and other "factory owners, independent gentlemen etc.," with Schulpe including a whole range of social institutions in his own "spotless" settlement. In Temesvár the shift to a partly state-aided municipal policy for own construction and advancement of housing construction as a part of the industrial worker and agricultural programs got under way from 1905. The change had been preceded by a considerable "illicit" settlement movement of those directly affected by the lack of adequate housing for the growing workers' population of the city.[35]

---

[34] Zimmermann, *Prächtige Armut* [Splendid Poverty], 259 f., 270–279, including all original quotes.

[35] Quote "spotless" in italics in the original. *Magyar Hirlap 18*, 7 June (1908): 44 f.; Gabriela Dudeková, "Das soziale Wohnmodell für Arbeiter in Preßburg am Ende des 19. Jahrhunderts" [The social housing model for workers in Bratislava at the end of the 19th century], in: Viliam Čičaj, Othmar Pickl, eds. *Städtisches Alltagsleben vom Mittelalter bis zum Ende 19. Jahrhunderts. Die Referate des Internationalen Symposions in Častá-Píla vom 11. bis 14. September 1995* [Urban every-day life from the medieval age to the end of the 19th century. The presentations given at the International Symposium in Častá-Píla, 11 to 14 September 1995] (Bratislava 1998), 339–346; Kácser, *Temesvár emberbaráti intézményei* [The philantropic institutions of Temesvár], 67; Geml, *Temesvár lakáspolitikája* [The housing policy of Temesvár], 36–39; Geml, *Temesvár szabad királyi város* [Royal Free City of Temesvár], 74–78; Ferenczi, *Die kommunale Wohnungspolitik* [The municipal housing policy], 25 f.

Even earlier than was the case for urban housing, new attitudes made themselves felt in Hungary with regard to accommodation for rural workers. Large-scale agricultural production, which employed huge numbers of unskilled workers and agricultural laborers, was of central importance in the Hungarian economy. After pronounced social conflicts in the 1890s, which brought about innovations in the regulation of labor relations in the agrarian sector,[36] the beginning of the century marked the beginning of a new, if strongly paternalistic agricultural social policy.[37] This policy found no equivalent in Austria, where peasant agriculture dominated in many territories. Measures for state responsibility for the accommodation of the agricultural workforce were already introduced under the liberals in 1901, and these were provided with an independent legal foundation[38] and further extended by the coalition government in 1907 in the form of state support for the construction of so-called "economic workers' housing," that is of individual dwelling houses rather than apartment blocks, for agricultural laborers. From 1907 on, the state systematically supported the construction of these houses—principally by financing credit and providing support in the repayment of loans—and the sale of property or workers' housing built by the local authorities. Yet by the beginning of the war only some six to seven thousand agricultural workers' houses had been completed while the construction of a significantly larger number had been approved and started. Support for the construction of housing for pick and shovel men (*kubikosok*)—the expression "*kubikos*" stood and stands in Hungarian even today for rural poverty, extreme exploitation, and social marginalization—was rejected by the minister on the grounds that this group could not be classed as agricultural workers.[39]

All in all, social reform in the area of housing policy enjoyed limited success, not least because of the dominance of the interests of (the construction) industry and property owners in political representative bodies in both urban and rural areas regarding intervention in the shaping of tenancy and the economic factors of housing construction. As to public and publicly assisted construction for the lower classes, strong resistance had

---

[36] See chapter IV.1.3.

[37] See chapter IV.2.

[38] Act 46/1907.

[39] Geml, *Temesvár lakáspolitikája* [The housing policy of Temesvár], 32–35, 110; Ferenczi, "A lakásügy az utolsó öt évben" [Housing affairs in the last five years], 354–358; Jenő Czettler, *Magyar mezőgazdasági szociálpolitika* [Hungarian agricultural social policy] (Budapest 1914), 1035 f.; Schulpe, *Munkásügyi reformok* [Reforms to workers' affairs], vol. I, 31–49.

to be overcome. Nevertheless, precisely because public construction of workers' housing neither constituted a direct intervention into matters of rent setting and terms of contract in the housing sector nor an interference into economic determinants of housing production, a real change in this sector towards state—and through state intervention also municipal—reform was possible. While in other industrial centers of Hungary such as Pozsony and Temesvár the municipal authorities took only limited advantage of new opportunities for public engagement with the construction of workers' housing, the capital city of Budapest took a clear lead in this field.

III.3. Unemployment and Labor Market Policy

Policies regarding the "beggar and vagabond question" and the growing conflicts over this issue since the 1880s involved, as we have seen, the question of unemployment of those willing and able to work. However, initially there were no new visions on how to handle and no new measures targeted at this problem. Instead it was addressed with the same age-old recipes of poverty policy. New, more strongly socio-politically directed initiatives in dealing with what was increasingly conceived of as unemployment first appeared with the economic downturn that started in 1896, accompanied in Budapest by strikes, and between 1900 and 1903 by mass unemployment, and particularly in winter by mass suffering. In 1896 the ministry of commerce was galvanized into seriously studying the problem of unemployment and the lack of any policy aimed at organizing for labor exchanges or employment agencies (*munkaközvetítés*). This study was the first to officially link unemployment to the question of the organization of the labor market, i.e. with a vision of organized socio-political intervention into the functioning of the labor market. In 1898 the well-known social reformer, György Schulpe, who was also practically active in many areas, particularly in Pozsony, presented with a complete legislative proposal for establishing a system of labor exchanges, though according to the proposal the management of these exchanges would have been left in the hands of the existing local authorities. The Budapest poor relief administration for its part initially dealt with the crisis in an entirely traditional manner, increasing its already well-known efforts for the creation of workhouses and forced labor at municipal level, as well as collaborating with the National Industrial Union (*Országos Iparegyesület*). The organized workers' movement and the trade unions continuously exerted pressure on the authorities to finally engage with the establishment of public labor exchanges and other measures of relief for those "100,000 unemployed individuals who are vagabonding, starving, and devoid all means of survival" everywhere in the country.[40]

Ultimately it was the National Industrial Union which headed a "movement" that was to address the question of "elimination of rapidly growing unemployment in the capital" in a much broader sense. The idea first and foremost was to establish a public job-creation scheme and to place the rudimentary system of job exchanges as hitherto operated by the Trade Corporations (*ipartestületek*),[41] private agencies, and trades unions on a new footing. Eventually, the National Industrial Union turned to the minister for commerce with its own petition "in the interests of the creation of a central labor exchange institute in Budapest." A particularly important task of the proposed institute was seen to be the removal—in particular in the period of economic crisis—of surplus labor from the capital. Collaboration with the existing employment agencies was planned. This also meant that the inherited mechanisms and policies of the suppression of the workers' movement, which drew attention to itself with meetings and demands for solutions to the unemployment problem, should in part be complemented by monitored socio-political integration. With the dawn of the new century, the minister for commerce finally passed the charter for the new institute. The costs were to be shared equally between the capital, the Budapest chamber of trade and commerce and the ministry, though in reality the contribution of the ministry rapidly became the largest. The institute was to persist in its activities in the case of strikes and lockouts. It was headed by a director with full and broad powers, with a board composed of three equal parts, i.e. representatives of the employers,

[40] *Budapest Állami Rendőrség* [Budapest State Police] 1899 (Budapest 1900), 290 ff.; Schulpe, *Munkásügyi reformok* [Reforms to workers' affairs], vol. II, 73–90; Dudeková, "Das soziale Wohnmodell" [The social housing model], 342 f.; Zimmermann, *Prächtige Armut* [Splendid poverty], 193–200, provides details also on the earlier history and involvement of the workers' movement.

[41] The term Trade Corporation (*ipartestület*) referred to the association of those practicing a trade or craft which required a proof of competence in that trade. These Trade Corporations had to be founded (except in smaller communities) when at least two thirds of those practicing this trade wished to do so. They were, among other things, to serve the regulation of relations between employers on the one hand and workers and apprentices on the other, and provide mechanisms to resolve conflicts between these parties. Commercial and industrial enterprises of the factory type as well as shareholding companies could not be forced to join, but individual employers with large-scale businesses who employed apprentices could. The Trade Corporations are not to be confused with chambers of trade and commerce. Act 17/1884, section IV.

the trade unions and other representative organizations of employees and workers, and "impartial" experts. The latter were to be delegated in equal numbers from the ministry and the capital city of Budapest. Strong protests on the part of the workers' movement—which had always demanded parity between employers and workers on the board and administration of any future public institution in the service of social or (as it was called at the time) workers' policy—over the composition of this new body were of no avail. In spite of this, the new institute was very popular from the outset with those in search of work, even if the number of placements, after a sharp upswing in 1903 thanks to restructuring, as a whole increased only slowly. Placement of job applicants (back) into the "provinces" did indeed play a certain role in the activities of the institute. The share of women amongst those placed never exceeded 16 percent.[42]

Once the Budapest central labor exchange institute started operating, the ministry began negotiations with the chambers of trade and commerce for a "nationwide organization" of labor exchanges. Despite initial concerns about "financial coverage" as an impediment to their realization, in 1905 two further labor exchange institutes were opened in Pozsony and Temesvár. Both were modeled on the Budapest institution, the one in Pozsony being headed by György Schulpe.[43] In subsequent years the competition between public labor exchange institutes on the one hand and those run by trades unions on the other steadily accompanied the expansion of the public labor exchange system.[44] Contemporary Hungarian experts assessed the services provided by the state-created labor exchange institutions as cumbersome and not truly impartial, and complained that with regard to the scope and results of labor exchange activities there was scarcely another country "in such backward circumstances" as Hungary.[45]

These debates and conflicts notwithstanding, it was beyond doubt for contemporary expert opinion that the expansion of the system of public

---

[42] BFL-C IV 1407b 132/1897-IX, Petition of the National Industial Union; Schulpe, *Munkásügyi reformok* [Reforms to workers' affairs], vol. II, 73–90; *A Magyar Királyi Kormány* [The Royal Hungarian Government] 1903, 60; Zimmermann, *Prächtige Armut* [Splendid poverty], 200 ff.

[43] *A Magyar Királyi Kormány* [The Royal Hungarian Government] 1901 (Budapest 1902), 73; 1905 (Budapest 1906), 53 f.; Dudeková, "Das soziale Wohnmodell." [The social housing model].

[44] *A Magyar Királyi Kormány* [The Royal Hungarian Government] 1906, 67; 1909 (Budapest 1910), 62.

[45] Emerich Ferenczi, *Die behördliche Organisation des Arbeitsmarktes in Ungarn* [The official organization of the labor market in Hungary] (Vienna 1917), 160 f.

labor exchanges alone was no solution for the hardship of the unemployed. It was all too clear that the local authorities and poor relief administration continued to shoulder the burden of dealing with the hardship of the unemployed.

In Budapest, the winters of hardship and suffering at the beginning of the century saw sometimes militant protests on the part of the organized movement of the unemployed. Yet the response of the municipal authorities remained closely tied to traditional poverty policy. Limited public relief work and additional financial aid were provided, and the municipality repeatedly voiced the demand that the state authorities should bring forward public works they had planned for the future. At the same time, these crises and social tensions at the beginning of the new century, together with the first broader debates about the necessity of an independent municipal workers' policy were to pave the way for a variety of separate workers'-policy-related projects. In 1906 a plan for a municipal unemployment insurance scheme was finally tabled. By this time, however, the economy was back on track again, and the—partly related—dramatically increasing housing shortage thrust the issue of workers' housing into the foreground. It was only with a new unemployment crisis looming in 1913 that the department for social policy and culture, which had been formed as a new section within the central municipal administration in early 1912 and was highly professionally oriented, turned words into deeds. At the same time, the social reformers in the municipal government had long made it clear that modern unemployment policy limited to local level without the cooperation of the state was only possible to a very limited extent. Yet despite all odds, the Budapest municipality now attempted a cleverly devised experiment in the payment of unemployment benefits. From a material point of view, this action, which was carried out in two waves, remained very limited. It succeeded, however, for the first time in developing a form of benefits for the unemployed that was distinct from the old poor relief and municipal policy made every effort to emphasize this intention and publicly present the action as such by highly symbolic means. Only those who were not listed in the register of the poor, not permanently unfit for work, liable for health and accident insurance payments through an employment relationship in keeping with the law on health and accident insurance of workers of 1907, and not in receipt of sick benefits from the national workers' insurance, were eligible for benefit. Like in the case of state social insurance policy, these measures on the part of the Hungarian capital further emphasized the distance between insured and uninsured employment, as well as the distance between the sexes on the labor market.[46]

At the same time, this experiment laid bare, at least in the eyes of the reformers in the capital, the "inadequacy of Hungarian social policy arrangements in all their desolation." This was demonstrated by the fact that, as the authorities "proclaimed the availability of [municipal unemployment] benefits ... misery of every kind knocked at the door," misery and need that clearly could not be dealt with in labor-market-oriented unemployment policy on the municipal level.[47] Workers' policy at municipal level could replace neither an integrative poverty policy nor an extensive state social policy. It is to the developments in the later sphere of need-related policies that we turn in the following chapter.

---

[46] Zimmermann, *Prächtige Armut* [Splendid poverty], 187–191, 205–244. See also chapter IV.2.3.

[47] Imre Ferenczi, "A főváros első munkanélküliségi akciója" [The first action of the Capital against unemployment]. *Városi Szemle* 6 (1913): 503–538, here 531 f.

IV. State Social Policy

The growing commodification of employment relations in Hungary, like in many other European countries in the second half of the 19th century was increasingly accompanied by state efforts to regulate and organize these relations and to intervene into problems that arose for employers, employees, the state, and society in connection with the ongoing changes in the world of work. In what follows, those efforts on the part of the state will be presented that at least in part, for whatever reasons, were concerned with the protection and betterment of the workforce. At the center of this stood, on the one hand, worker protection, focused on the working relationship and working conditions, and on the other the system of social security, which was basically geared to protecting the workforce in cases of inability to work, however caused, whether permanent or temporary. These two areas of policy together will be considered as state social policy.

IV.1. Labor Protection (from 1848 to 1914)

Labor protection policy in Hungary, like in other European countries, can be divided into three broad areas. The first of these was general labor protection in commerce and industry, which prescribed the various regulations or protective measures for working conditions in these sectors. Where distinctions were made here, these were tied to the labor condition or, for example, to the size of the business or the status of workers within it. In addition to this, there existed a second area referred to as special protection regulations in the area of commercial or industrial work that were—exclusively or additionally—connected to some personal characteristics of the worker, notably age or sex. Regarding the regulations for learning a trade or for commercial apprenticeship, which will be considered here as part of the special protection regulations, the two areas overlapped in that particular special protections for young workers were tied to the status of apprentice. A third group of labor protection measures were related to working conditions that did not fall into the category of commerce and industry, this covering, among other employment sectors, the broad category of agricultural labor.

At the beginning of the period under investigation here, the relevant trade regulations and laws were of key importance for the whole area of labor protection. The Austrian trade regulation of 1859 remained valid in Hungary as well until after the Compromise of 1867.[1] With the trade law of 1872[2] an independent legal foundation was created in Hungary for the regulation of commercial and industrial working conditions. However, even the second Hungarian trade law of 1884,[3] promulgated 12 years later, remained very much a matter of *laissez faire*, at least as far as labor protection was concerned. The reform of this law was added to agendas again and again over the decades, but was never realized even up to the outbreak of World War I. In spite of this, over the decades certain individual questions of relevance to labor protection were indeed newly regulated or re-regulated. The enactment of three laws covering individual areas of worker protection namely on Sunday rest in 1891, on the special protection of women in 1911, and finally the ban on the production of matches using white and yellow phosphorus in 1911, which entered into force in 1913, were each closely connected with international efforts at labor protection. The fact that Hungary was inextricably teamed in an unequal relationship with Austria on the international stage was a significant factor in shaping developments within the country.

Work in preparation for a complete overhaul of the Hungarian 1884 trade law had existed at ministerial level since the late 1890s. But there were always references to the complexity of the material, the huge extent of the revision, or the need to give space for "the influence of interest groups in the preparatory work" to hold out and justify further delays.[4] After the turn of the century, the fruits of all the preparatory work were made public in the form of a collection of materials. The coalition government of Sándor Wekerle (April 1906 – January 1910) then made serious attempts to bring the elaboration of a new law forward. In 1908 the minister for commerce released a comprehensive plan penned by the secretary of state for the ministry, the internationally recognized specialist in trade and commercial policy, labor protection and social insurance policy,

---

[1] Act 17/1884, fn.1.

[2] Act 8/1872.

[3] Act 17/1884.

[4] *A Magyar Királyi Kormány* [The Royal Hungarian Government] 1899 (Budapest 1900), 55; 1901, 60; 1902 (Budapest 1904), 66 f. (incl. quotation).

József Szterényi. The following year, three weighty tomes appeared containing the comments and responses of the "parties concerned," namely the guilds or Trade Corporations, chambers of trade and commerce, municipalities, labor authorities (of the first and second instance), organizations of employers and employees, and "circles and associations of scientific character." The views of other groups that had proactively involved themselves were also included.[5] The draft bill devoted a separate section to the "protection of those employed in trade and industry," and the author, Szterényi, granted this area a place of special importance in his foreword as being one of three key lines of innovation suggested by the project. The "Protection of Those Employed in Trade and Industry"—"in keeping with the demands of the age of progress"—enjoyed equal importance with "Protection of Trades and the Consolidation of the Foundations of Their Development" on the "basis of compulsory associations" as the second pillar of the reform. This protection was intended to be as extensive as possible "without artificial restrictions to future development." The third pillar was the "Assurance of the Status of Large-scale Industry," "to the extent capital may expect such assurances in the present day economic and production relations."[6]

After the parliamentary elections of 1910, where the liberals, now in the form of the National Labor Party (*Nemzeti Munkapárt*), celebrated an unprecedented victory, the efforts for revision of the trade law did not peter out; however, the preparations for the reform of the trade law in the ministry now changed to the extent that in the end there were a whole series of proposed bills in preparation. This division of the material into various different individual laws was not something that József Szterényi had ruled out at the time of publishing his draft bill in 1908 either. From 1910 individual laws were under discussion for example for labor jurisdic-

---

5 *A Magyar Királyi Kormány* [The Royal Hungarian Government] 1907 (Budapest 1909), 68; 1908, 70; 1909 (Budapest 1910), 61; *Az ipartörvény módosítása. Negyedik rész. Törvényjavaslat az ipar gyakorlásáról, valamint az ipari és kereskedelmi alkalmazottak védelméről. Előadói tervezet* [Modification of the trade law. Part four. Legislative proposal for the practice of trade and the protection of employees in commerce and trade. Preliminary draft], vol. IX (Budapest, 1908); *Az ipartörvény módosítása. Vélemények az ipar gyakorlásáról, valamint az ipari és kereskedelmi alkalmazottak védelméről szóló törvényjavaslat előadói tervezetére* [Modification of the trade law. Responses to the Preliminary preliminary draft of the legislative proposal for the practice of trade and the protection of employees in commerce and trade.], vols. XII-XIV, (Budapest 1909), quotations from vol. XII, 7.

6 *Az ipartörvény módosítása* [Modification of the trade law], vol. XI, 4 f.; the three headlines in italics in the original.

tion or the prevention of the use of poisonous materials. In reality, however, as we will see, in the years before World War I, there was no real progress in any of these areas.[7]

IV.1.1. Protection in industry and trade as differentiated according to the character of the work

The key areas of the incipient general worker protection between 1848 and 1914 were first of all questions related to the equipment and technical configuration of industrial enterprises, particularly as regards to occupational health protection; secondly, the regulation of working conditions at the workplace with a view to protect workers against abuses, and particularly the question of the regulation of working hours; and thirdly the supervision of the relevant regulations by the public authorities.

As regards the matter of occupational health protection in relation to the technical equipment of industrial enterprises, the trade law (*ipartörvény*) from 1872, blessed by the spirit of free trade and liberalism, only contained one vague provision. The relevant trade authorities (*iparhatóság*) should, in the planning of a place of business, take care to ensure such measures as "are necessary for the protection of the lives and health of the workers."[8] The law of 1875 on the coverage of costs of public healthcare[9] obliged owners and employers—at least on paper—to cover the costs of permanently employed workers without means for up to 30 days of hospital or post-natal care.[10] The new trade law of 1884 contained for the first time an—albeit again vague—provision, according to which the operators of factories were obliged to fulfill certain requirements regarding the creation of adequate working conditions. They were to take care to ensure the "greatest possible safeguarding of the lives and health of the workers … at their own expense."[11]

Already during the parliamentary debate on the new trade law, however, major criticisms had been expressed regarding the continued mini-

---

[7] *A Magyar Királyi Kormány* [The Royal Hungarian Government] 1910 (Budapest 1911), 61 f.; 1912 (Budapest 1913), 84; 1913, 80f.; *Az ipartörvény módosítása* [Modification of the trade law], vol. XI, 6 f.

[8] Act 8/1872, §12.

[9] Act 3/1875.

[10] The clauses of Act 3/1875 were extended to the city and district of Fiume (Rijeka) shortly before the creation of the State Healthcare Fund by Act 21/1898. Act 3/1875 was quickly overridden thereafter.

[11] Act 17/1884, §114.

malist approach of the bill concerning workers' protection. The moderately reform-oriented opposition representative, Dániel Irányi,[12] played a key role here. On the 21 and 23 April 1884, he tabled two motions, proposing that parliament call on the government to create a law introducing workers' accident insurance and another to regulate Sunday rest. Both motions were accepted.[13] When efforts to create compulsory accident insurance ground to a halt after the introduction of a law only on health insurance in 1891,[14] a first more comprehensive law on accident prevention was created in 1893.[15] The general formulation of the trade law of 1884 regarding the "greatest possible safeguarding" was taken almost unchanged. However, the new regulations now at least referred to all employers. In addition, the obligations of employers were laid out in some detail in nine points and the minister for commerce empowered to pass further ordinances and regulations for specific branches of industry.

In the final years before the war, the influence of internationalization efforts in the area of occupational health protection made itself felt in Hungary. Although Austria–Hungary had not ratified the international (Berne) Convention of 26 September 1906 regarding the ban on the use of white (yellow) phosphorus in the match industry,[16] the agreement nonetheless had an impact in the Habsburg Monarchy. In Hungary, the relevant law of 1911 finally came into effect in 1913.[17]

With regard to the regulation of working conditions in the workplace to protect employees against abuses, the issue of working hours played a key role. In principle, working hours for adult workers in trade and indus-

[12] In the course of his long career, Irányi was also an advocate of universal male suffrage, of freedom of belief and of civil marriage.

[13] *Országgyűlési Képviselőház Naplói* [Chronicle of the House of Parliamentary Representatives] 1881/1884, vol. XVI, 287 f., 294 f.; 334f., 338; *Országgyűlési Képviselőház Jegyzőkönyvei* [Minutes of the House of Parliamentary Representatives] 1881/1884, vol. III, 310 f.

[14] For further discussion, see chapter IV.2.1.

[15] Act 28/1893.

[16] Both states ratified—separately, of course—only in the 1920s. Apart from the original eight signatory states, a further four states ratified the agreement before the outbreak of the First World War; there were also ratifications by dependencies of these states. Internationales Übereinkommen vom 26. September 1906 betreffend das Verbot der Verwendung von weissem (gelbem) Phosphor in der Zündholzindustrie [International convention as of 26 September 1906 on the abolition of the use of white (yellow) phosphorus in the matchstick industry], contains the law and all additional information.

[17] Act 5/1911; *A Magyar Királyi Kormány* [The Royal Hungarian Government] 1913 (Budapest 1915), 80.

try in Hungary were a "matter of free agreement."[18] According to the trade law of 1872 in factories, the employer was required to post a bulletin of work rules, including specification of the lengths of working hours. These work rules were also to be approved by the trade authorities. In factories where shifts were worked, the factory owner was to ensure "suitable relief" for night-shift workers. The day shift was not to commence before five o'clock in the morning and not to finish later than nine in the evening, and several breaks were to be provided.[19] The trade law of 1884 preserved these regulations unchanged. The only new addition was that workers in trade and industry must have the possibility to attend worship on the relevant official holidays for their religion.[20]

Various ministerial decrees from the 1890s and the period after the turn of the century offer eloquent testimony to the reality of working conditions in Hungarian companies, particularly concerning the question of working hours. In those enterprises where the working times, not counting a lunch break, did not exceed ten hours, the legally prescribed thirty-minute morning and afternoon breaks were in reality canceled—they were "to be considered as occurring before the beginning and after the end of work." In this case, factory owners or overseers were not permitted to prevent employees from consuming food they had brought with them during their work. In factories where work started at seven in the morning, the time when "normally the morning break is given," only an afternoon break was provided. Workers whose job entailed the supervision of spinning and weaving machines were to "enjoy" breaks for food "during their work." In paper mills, where day and night shifts were worked, it was permitted if "the workers so wished" to arrange the change of shift so that alternately they had a full day's rest and a 24-hour shift.[21]

Reform efforts concerned with general regulations on daytime working hours played a subordinate role in political debate and struggle during the decades of the Dual Monarchy. In contrast, individual areas were all the more fought over. The most prominent of these were the questions of Sunday rest and that of evening closing time in the retail trade. With regard to Sunday rest, resistance to the untrammeled liberalism of the bill

---

[18] *Az ipartörvény módosítása. Hazai anyag két részben. Első rész: Joganyag. (Az iparra vonatkozó törvények, rendeletek és határozatok gyüjteménye)* [Modification of the trade law. Domestic material in two parts. Part one: Juridical material. (Collection of laws, regulations and decisions on trade)], 2 vols. (Budapest 1904), vol. II, 131.

[19] Act 8/1872, §§68, 71.

[20] Act 17/1884, §§62, 111, 113, 117.

[21] *Az ipartörvény módosítása* [Modification of the trade law], vol. II, 90 f.

became visible as early as the parliamentary debate on the revision of the trade law in 1884. The motion of the reform-minded representative Dániel Irányi, by which parliament was to instruct the government to create regulations for Sunday rest, was, as mentioned above, in fact accepted. However, it was to take several more years before actual legislative action was to follow. Only when representatives of Austria–Hungary gathered together with those of many other countries at the International Conference on Labor Protection in Berlin in 1890 did the legislative bodies in Hungary actually become active. The responsible official for the trade inspectorate in the ministry for commerce, Szterényi, who represented Hungary in Berlin on the committee for Sunday rest, stated for the record, "that in these matters the conditions in Hungary are the same as those in Austria"—a claim that in no way corresponded to the reality—"and that in Hungary a special law [was] in preparation" that was shortly to be presented in parliament. For this reason, he stated, Hungary would certainly be able to conform with recommendations for compliance in the matter of Sunday rest.[22] Then in 1891 a law on Sunday rest in industry and trade—including the retail trade—was indeed passed.[23] It stipulated a break from work on Sundays of at least 24 hours, however, it left open to the minister for commerce the responsibility and the possibility of granting broad exceptions to this rule. In the same year, there indeed appeared an act authorizing a wide range of exceptions, particularly in the retail trade. In subsequent years the minister for commerce passed a variety of further exceptions. In 1903, the most important clauses regarding the enforcement of the law on Sunday rest were overwritten by a new general act, which for the first time introduced more progressive limitations to Sunday work in the retail trade. Now in Budapest and shortly after also in Zagreb, Sunday opening was to be limited to the sale of basic foodstuffs until ten o'clock in the morning. In the remaining parts of the country, all shops were allowed to open on Sundays until ten in the morning. At the same time, the new act again contained page-long lists of those businesses that were still allowed to continue working for the whole of Sunday or for parts of what was supposed to be a day of rest. The grounds given by en-

[22] The conference was not officially diplomatic in character, however, delegates were sent by governments. From the Habsburg Monarchy high-ranking representatives from the responsible ministries of both Austria and Hungary were present. Protokolle der Internationalen Arbeiterschutzkonferenz. Im amtlichen Auftrag [Minutes of the International Labor Protection Conference. Officially commissioned] (Leipzig 1890), 5 f., 53 f., 221, 223 f.; Meyers Großes Konversations-Lexikon (1907).

[23] Act 13/1891.

trepreneurs or the minister justifying the exception might be that an interruption of the business was not possible. Alternatively, it was possible to call upon the "needs of the consumer," transportation, or military needs.[24] All in all, the issue of Sunday rest in the first decade of the new century was the subject of heated political debates and marked by "great contradictions" caused by "conflicting interests." In 1907 and 1908, concrete steps were made towards a draft proposal for new regulations on Sunday rest in trade and industry. However, with the fall of the coalition government, this proposal disappeared.[25]

Another bone of contention was the matter of closing times in the retail trade. The proposal for a new trade law of 1908 attempted to limit opening hours to the period between six in the morning and eight in the evening, with exceptions, as usual. But it was only with the law of 1913 on "closing times in the retail trade" the validity of which was limited until further notice to the agglomeration of Budapest, that genuine limitations were introduced above and beyond Sunday rest.[26] Henceforth, shops were to remain closed between the hours of eight in the evening and six in the morning on weekdays, and on Saturdays from half past nine in the evening, and employees could not be required to work during this night rest period. Once again, there were exceptions to this law, both with regard to the type of business involved as well as the employment ban.[27]

Efforts to regulate normal working hours became visible in the ministry draft of a law regulating the employment status of employees—that is clerks as opposed to workers—in trade and commerce in 1901. The proposal suggested limiting the working hours of this group of employees to twelve hours a day, including breaks. Although significant exemptions were envisaged, the initiative taken by the ministry nevertheless encountered a united front of resistance from chambers of trade and commerce. For retailers in the countryside, it was argued, the proposed regulation

---

[24] Ordinance 28559/1903, Minister for commerce, reproduced in *Az ipartörvény módosítása* [Modification of the trade law], vol. II, 93–104, 112–130; Farkas Heller, *Magyarország szociálpolitikája* [Social policy of Hungary] (Budapest 1923), 16–22; *A Magyar Királyi Kormány* [The Royal Hungarian Government] 1901, 61; 1902, 67 (incl. quotation); 1903, 59.

[25] *A Magyar Királyi Kormány* [The Royal Hungarian Government] 1905, 53; 1907, 69; 1908, 72; 1910, 62; 1911 (Budapest 1912), 64.

[26] Act 36/1913.

[27] *Az ipartörvény módosítása* [Modification of the trade law], vol. XI, 196 f.; *A Magyar Királyi Kormány* [The Royal Hungarian Government] 1913, 80; Act 36/1913, §§1, 3; Heller, *Magyarország szociálpolitikája* [Social Policy of Hungary], 136 f.

would be "ruinous," a standard regulation was unacceptable and unfeasible, and the maximum working time must be set at 14 hours a day.[28] The draft of the new trade law of 1908 anticipated only one unprotected area: it contained no clauses about the principle limitation of the working hours of adult male workers in trade and commerce.[29] The draft sought to stipulate exceptions—that is protective measures that included adult male workers—for particularly dangerous or harmful branches of industry. Only for private employees and those in trade were no sex-specific limitations to working hours stipulated.[30]

An official monitoring system for the implementation of regulations regarding worker protection at the workplace in Hungary—the institution of a factory inspectorate—developed very slowly, and in practice remained in its infancy for decades. Regarding this institution, the liberal trade law of 1872 *de facto* constituted negligible improvement on the Austrian trade regulation of 1859. The law now required no more than that the trade authority of the first instance must "ensure the factories are inspected by its emissaries from time to time."[31] The second trade law of 1884—thanks once again to the intervention in parliament of Dániel Irányi[32] —required the trade authorities more specifically to ensure adherence to the legal regulations in factories via quarterly inspections. The authorities were required to submit a "detailed report" summarizing the results of these inspections to the minister concerned on an annual basis. In addition, the law gave the minister the right, for the capital and other developed industrial areas, to employ "separate agencies" for factory inspection at the state's expense.[33]

In practice the activities of the factory inspectorate were limited, by these regulations and an additional provision, to tasks connected with the

---

[28] *Az ipartörvény módosítása. Hazai anyag két részben. Második rész: Kivánságok és javaslatok. (Az ipartörvény módósítására nézve felmerült kivánságok és javalatok, valamint törvény- és szabályrendelet-tervezetek gyüjteménye)* [Modification of the trade law. Domestic material in two parts. Part two: Wishes and suggestions (Collection of wishes and suggestions on Modification of the trade law as well as drafts of the law and statutes)], vol. III (Budapest 1904), 419–424.

[29] For the regulations of the draft which were aimed at protection relating to personal characteristics of the worker, see chapter IV.1.2.

[30] *Az ipartörvény módosítása* [Modification of the trade law], vol. XI, 94 f., 196 f.

[31] Act 8/1872, §75.

[32] *Országgyűlési Képviselőház Naplói* [Chronicle of the House of Parliamentary Representatives] 1881/1884, vol. XVI, 338.

[33] Act 17/1884, §121.

policies of the advancement of trades and industries.[34] Then in 1893, a specific law on factory inspection was finally passed.[35] According to this law, the duties of the inspectorate included in particular enforcing regulations for accident prevention and the protection of the life and health of the workers. The powers of the factory inspectorate extended to all businesses that employed more than 20 workers, as well as businesses that operated machines, and—independent of all other requirements—to a range of individually listed types of business, such as chemical factories, for example. In addition, the inspector responsible was to make a personal inspection as part of the approval procedure for the issuing of business licenses, so as to ensure that the relevant worker protection requirements had been adhered to.

Administrative reforms of the newly created factory inspectorate occurred in the next few years. The amalgamation of the factory and the steam boiler inspectorate and a new division of districts of the inspectorate in accordance with the districts of the chambers of trade and commerce in 1901 led to a marked increase in the number of inspections carried out, amounting to 6,224 factories in this year alone. State-owned factories and the building industry continued, however, to have separate systems of supervision. In the building sector no more than 150 inspections were carried out, for example, in 1901. Until World War I, regardless of further administrative reforms, including the creation of smaller factory inspection districts, there were no significant changes in the practices of the factory inspectorate. In the final year before the war, 11,435 factories, 339 building sites, and 32 state factories were inspected.[36] One professional with an interest in labor policy delivered a damning indictment about the organization and activities of the factory inspectorate in Hungary. Local trade authorities, he commented, simply ignored the inspectors' reports about problems identified in the factories. "Without doubt it should be the task of the two chief trade inspectors [in Budapest and Pozsony] to try to pressure the trade authorities to carry out those meas-

---

[34] Sándor Halász, Gyula Mandello, eds. *Közgazdasági Lexikon* [Encyclopedia of economics], 3 vols. (Budapest 1898-1901), vol. II, 74.

[35] Act 28/1893. This law also contained the regulations on accident prevention mentioned earlier.

[36] *A Magyar Királyi Kormány* [The Royal Hungarian Government] 1901, 71; 1905, 55; 1913, 81 f.; Ernő Lőrincz, *A munkaviszonyok szabályozása Magyarországon a kapitalizmus kezdeteitől az első világháború végéig 1840–1918* [Labor relations in Hungary from the beginnings of capitalism until the end of the First World War 1840–1918] (Budapest 1974), 150 f.

ures which the factory inspectors have requested in vain. If no result was achieved, this should be reported to the minister for commerce. We looked for such cases in the [1909] report, but found none. The Budapest chief factory inspector contented himself with stating that there are some trade inspectors who are unable to implement the law properly." Final decisions on the matter of breach of existing regulations in individual factories were often arrived at only after four or more years and even then the employer had still means at his disposal to postpone change.[37]

IV.1.2. Protection for children, juveniles and women as groups defined according to their personal characteristics

Group-specific special regulations for young workers continuously played a certain though limited role in Hungarian labor protection policy over the decades. For female workers, aside from childbed protection, there were for many years no special protective regulations. Only in the last decade before the war were the basic principles of Hungarian policy to shift, partly swayed by the growing international movement for labor and social policy, of which Austria, and the Habsburg Monarchy as a whole, was a part. In Austria the branch of labor protection policy connected to personal characteristics of specific groups of workers was the object of much more pronounced socio-political thought and action than in Hungary, and thus the development of such measures was more dynamic.

Independent Hungarian trade legislation in the form of the first and second trade laws of 1872 and 1884 was very limited regarding the special protection of apprentices and young workers. The employment of apprentices and child factory workers between the ages of 10 and 12 was only permitted by special exception, to be granted by the relevant authorities. Employers were required to observe the general regulations on compulsory education, however, factory owners were allowed to use the notorious factory schools for this purpose. Apprentices under the age of 14 were permitted to work up to ten hours a day, and from 14 not more than twelve hours a day, with an upper limit of ten hours a day for juvenile factory workers. A decree issued by the minister for commerce more than a decade and a half after the passing of the second trade law of 1884 reveals the

[37] Kornél Hlavács, "Az iparfelügyelők tevékenysége az 1909. évben" [The activity of the trade inspectors in the year 1909] (third sequence). *Munkásügyi Szemle* 1 (1910): 718–721, here 718 f., 721.

Hungarian reality behind these legal regulations. Given that "it was customary until now in some factories" to permit juvenile factory workers between 14 and 16 to work 11 hours, the decree simply urged adherence to the existing legal regulations. Apprentices and juvenile factory workers up to the age of 16 were "normally not to be included" in night shifts between nine in the evening and five in the morning. There were exceptions, however, with the permission of the authorities, allowing those over the age of 14 to work up to half of the maximum daily working hours. Only in the matter of the employment of juvenile workers under 16 "in factories or branches of industry declared to be unhealthy or dangerous" did the trade law of 1884 offer hesitant beginnings of more rigorous restriction. The text of the law was of course quick, however, besides employment restrictions, to mention those particular conditions under which employment should be allowed after all. In addition, the register of the "dangerous" or "unhealthy" branches of industry which was to be officially drawn up by the minister responsible, still had not materialized by the turn of the century. Both trade laws also contained vague general directions for taking into account the state of health and physical development of juvenile workers when employing them. Employers were to protect their apprentices from abuses by members of the household and other workers, and not require them to do household work.[38] The professional literature of the time, which for sure did not pursue a collision course in relation to government and employers—mentioning the absence of the register of dangerous industries as a typical example—assessed the "question of enforcement" as the "most serious problem" or "the true Achilles heel of Hungarian labor protection."[39]

Calls for an increase in the minimum age for hiring apprentices—to 14 years—had already been voiced in the parliamentary debate on the new trade law of 1884.[40] Years before the proposal for a new trade law was finally presented in 1908, the ministry and the public were well aware that particularly numerous Trade Corporations, as well as other groups with an interest in the reorganization of working conditions for apprentices, agreed on two basic principles. They wanted, in one way or another, to see the minimum age of apprentices increased and their preparatory training

---

[38] Act 8/1872, §§40, 43, 44, 45, 70; Act 17/1884, §§60, 62, 64, 65, 115, 116; *Az ipartörvény módosítása* [Modification of the trade law], vol. II, 88 f.

[39] Heller, *Magyarország szociálpolitikája* [Social policy of Hungary], 13 ff.

[40] *Országgyűlési Képviselőház Jegyzőkönyvei* [Minutes of the House of Parliamentary Representatives] 1881/1884, vol. XVI, 295.

improved. In comparison, calls for a change in the regulations on working hours played a negligible role.[41] With regard to the minimum employment age of juvenile workers, the draft of the new trade law of 1908 did envisage certain limitations in comparison to the existing legislation. The employment of children under the age of 12 was to be forbidden without exception. For earth workers and miners there was to be a minimum age of 14, while for the repair and cleaning of machines during operation, and for work related to the production and sale of illustrations that "threaten to offend moral sentiments" there was to be a minimum age of 16. In addition, the employment of children under 16 was in future to occur only within the context of an apprenticeship to a trade. Those falling into this category should "generally" be employed only during the daytime, specifically between six in the morning and eight in the evening. For children under 14, the working day was limited to eight hours, while for the 14- and 15-year olds, nine hours was to be the maximum, in each case to include one hour's break. In the case of night work, the working hours were to be shortened by one hour. Numerous exceptions were provided for all of these regulations. No distinction was made between girls and boys.[42]

The draft of the new trade law did then indeed contain concrete and relatively extensive reform proposals for the protection minors at work which clearly were in line with the overall principles discussed above.[43] These shaped the plan for the new trade law, which entailed the introduction of certain limits to the freedom of big business to exploit the workforce, and some degree of support for the crafts and trades. However, plans for an independent law on child labor got no further than a resolution of the lower house in 1910, calling on the minister for commerce to develop and submit a suitable bill as soon as possible.[44]

As regards the matter of female labor, the Hungarian legislation refused for decades to contemplate virtually any form of special protection. The trade law of 1872 contained no regulations of this sort whatsoever. In the process of the debates over the formation of the 1884 trade law, however, the question of special provisions for female labor finally reached parliamentary level. The original draft of the law, like the trade law of 1872, contained no relevant provisions at all. The motion of the national-liberal repre-

[41] *Az ipartörvény módosítása* [Modification of the trade law], vol. III, 319–323, 326.

[42] *Az ipartörvény módosítása* [Modification of the trade law], vol. XI, 119 f., 185–191, 198 f.

[43] See p. 70 f.

[44] Heller, *Magyarország szociálpolitikája* [Social Policy of Hungary], 126.

sentative Count Albert Apponyi, however, who with reference to the German, Swiss and British legislation called for the insertion of an "urgent" clause ensuring at least four weeks childbed rest, encountered very little opposition.[45] In its final version, the second trade law of 1884 thus required factories to provide women in childbed with four weeks unpaid maternity leave.[46] The first health insurance law of 1891 subsequently introduced, in tandem with the introduction of sick benefit, a minimum four-week maternity benefit for all women possessing health insurance of between 50 percent and 75 percent of their income. The reform of 1907 then increased this period to six weeks, without any other changes.[47]

There were already altercations about further special regulations regarding female labor in the parliamentary proceedings on the second trade law. Once again it was Dániel Irányi who presented the relevant motion. Irányi called for an across-the-board establishment of maximum working hours, given that there were "from the perspective of public interest certain limits to individual freedom," by which he meant the complete freedom of factory owners to determine the length of working hours. As a part of this argumentation, however, he moved for a sex-specific differentiation in the extension of labor protection measures for women. Irányi wanted women to have a working day two hours shorter than that of men, namely eleven hours, including breaks, and in addition he called for a general ban on night work for women. He justified his request on the grounds that woman "is by her nature not so strong" as man, and in addition "when married, must not only concern herself with cooking dinner for her husband and family, but with many other household affairs." The minister for agriculture, trade and commerce flatly rejected Irányi's proposal and his justification. It was true that women, being weaker, could not work so long as men. But experience showed "that the weaker woman undertakes lighter work and she completes this lighter work just as easily or otherwise as a man does heavier work." Irányi's motion was thus disposed with.[48]

---

[45] *Képviselőház Irományai* [Documents of the House of Representatives] 1881/1884, vol. XIX, no. 730; *Országgyűlési Képviselőház Jegyzőkönyvei* [Minutes of the House of Parliamentary Representatives] 1881/1884, vol. XVI, 328 ff.; vol. XVII, 32 ff.

[46] Act 17/1884, §116.

[47] On social insurance, see chapter IV.2.3. Childbed aid (according to the law of 1891) was distinguished from other sickness benefits only insofar as it was paid not from the fourth but the first day of "sickness. Act 14/1891, §§7c, d, 8a; Act 19/1907, §§50.3, 4, 51.1.

[48] *Országgyűlési Képviselőház Naplói* [Chronicle of the House of Parliamentary Representatives] 1881/1884, vol. XVI, 330 f.

The opposition to any kind of (extensive) special protection for women that typified this parliamentary debate was to be a feature of official Hungarian labor policy for many years to come. At the international labor protection conference in Berlin, Hungarian delegates, unlike those of Austria, who supported the idea of a universal ban on night and Sunday work for women and girls over sixteen, opposed the extension of this ban to women who had reached the age of 21.[49]

The Hungarian Social Democratic Party generally took a positive view of special regulations protecting women.[50] Around the turn of the century there were frequent calls, especially from the trade unions, but also from the Social Democratic Party, for the creation of special protective regulations for women workers. In the course of the discussion about the revision of the trade law at the beginning of the new century, the relevant groups of the organized workers and trade union movement devoted almost all their attention to the matter of special protection for female labor. The unions were partly concerned with the fact that female labor was relatively cheaper than male. In this regard, their calls for equal pay for the equal work were colored by the perception of the need to protect men's work from cheaper competition. The second concern, and here they were in line with the Social Democratic Party, was the demand for special protection of the "feminine organism" and the "morality" of women, specifically in the form of a ban on women working in particular branches of industry and commerce, and a ban on night work.[51]

The first real political movement for special labor protection measures for women that can be considered a clear break with the existing base line of Hungarian policy in this question only appeared in response to internationally organized labor protection initiatives. Austria–Hungary was one of the thirteen original signatories of the agreement on the 1906 ban on night work for female industrial workers, the Berne Convention. Hungary ratified the Berne Convention in 1908 (Act 53/1908), starting the process for its translation into national law. The Convention stipulated a universal ban on women's night work in industrial businesses with more than ten employees. The definition of "night-time," during which work must not

[49] Protokolle der Internationalen Arbeiterschutzkonferenz [Minutes of the International Labor Protection Conference], 83 f.

[50] In 1880 for example there was a call for a ban on women working in areas that were damaging to health. Katalin Petrák, *A szervezett munkásság küzdelme a korszerű társadalombiztosításért* [The fight of the organized workforce for modern social insurance] (Budapest 1978), 39.

[51] *Az ipartörvény módosítása* [Modification of the trade law], vol. III, 466 ff.

occur, should be from at least ten in the evening to five in the morning and was to comprise at least eleven hours, in some specific cases ten. Exceptions were permitted for businesses that worked with highly perishable raw materials or unfinished goods, and the regulations could be relaxed for non-European states and dependencies outside Europe.[52]

Initially, key clauses of the Convention—with, as to be expected, a great number of exceptions—were incorporated in the draft of a new trade law, which first saw the light of day in 1908. The national liberal coalition government of 1906–1910, during whose period of office the Berne Convention was ratified, and which acted paternalistically in questions of social policy, looked far more favorably on the idea of special labor protection for women than the powerful economically liberal forces that had hitherto governed alone. The draft of the new trade law of 1908 reveals much about the positive attitude of the coalition government towards special protection for women. Apart from the clauses on night work taken direct from the Berne Convention, the draft proposed changes in the regulations on working hours for adult women workers that, given the realities of the world of work in Hungary, could be described as quite remarkable. The main aim of the proposed sex-specific protection was quite clearly to support women in shouldering the inherited double burden of housework and paid work, and thus to stabilize this double role. Female workers who "also manage their own household or that of their parents" the plan proposed, should be released from work half an hour earlier than the normal start of the midday break, and should not have to work later than five in the afternoon on Saturdays. The working hours of all adult women over the age of 16 were to be limited to maximum eleven hours, including two hours break; a longer maximum working day of twelve hours was to be permitted only for those employed in retail who directly served customers. Women breast-feeding their own children were to receive a release of one hour until the infant reached the age of seven months. The proposed law stipulated that at their request, women were also to be provided with a heated room where the infant could be left while they were working. That no wages were to be deducted for these privileges was only explicitly stated in the case of the nursing hour; in this way it was implicitly accepted that necessary deductions would be made in the other areas. The ban on employment on machines under operation and occupation with illustrations that might threaten morality, which for males only

[52] Act 53/1908, Introduction, §§ 1–4, 7.

applied to those under 16, were to apply to women regardless of age. Women under the age of 18 were also not to be employed as waitresses.[53]

Especially the proposals for differentiation of the working hours of adult women and juvenile workers from those of men met with broad resistance from employers, chambers, and Trade Corporations. Only two groups called for divergent types of changes. The Hungarian Council of Trade Unions (*Magyarországi Szakszervezeti Tanács*) demanded a complete employment ban for girls under 16 and boys under 14 years of age thus asking for more labor protection for youngsters of both sexes though in a sex-differentiated manner. The feminist-oriented National Union of Women Employees (*Nőtisztviselők Országos Egyesülete*) called for the extension of the various proposed limitations of women's working hours to men as well, so that an equality of the sexes should be achieved. In this way the Union of Women Employees linked a class-political vision aimed at regulations favoring the employee with demands for sexual equality in the world of work. Yet unlike the Council of Trade Unions, the Union of Women Employees did not demand an extension of labor protection for the female sex compared to what the draft of the new trade law proposed. Neither organization made any comment on the proposed sex-specific limitation of the working hours of female industrial workers over the age of 16. In the case of the National Union of Women Employees this was doubtless due to the fact that they wanted to limit the demands it put forward to those regulations pertaining to their own clientele, that is woman employees alone.[54]

The end of the coalition government brought with it the end of legislative activities aimed at a general overhaul of the trade law. With the exception of the ban on women's night work this also meant the abandonment of plans for a special labor policy in support of the woman's double role.[55] The international commitment regarding women's night work made by the Habsburg Monarchy in 1906, which Hungary thus had to comply with in some form, was flexible enough to allow exceptions for key areas in which cheap female labor used to play an important role in Hungary to ensure the preservation of the liberal economic interests

[53] *Az ipartörvény módosítása* [Modification of the trade law], vol. XI, 190, 193, 198 f.

[54] *Az ipartörvény módosítása* [Modification of the trade law], vol. XIII, 373–380, 394–401.

[55] *A Magyar Királyi Kormány* [The Royal Hungarian Government] 1910, 62, already notes that a draft proposal for the implementation of the Berne Convention had been tabled.

that once again held sole power in the country.[56] According to the law of 1911 "on the ban on women's night work in industrial business"[57] the minister for commerce was able by national decree to annul the new legislation for all businesses dealing with perishable goods. In such businesses, women's hours were to be, astonishingly, "up to sixty-six hours per week," with night shifts not to exceed ten hours. A wide range of sectors of trade and commerce were indeed exempted from the new regulations from the outset. These included, for example, women employed in inns and coffeehouses, in the preparation of foodstuffs for consumption "on the premises," as well as those employed in the Hungarian state post, telegram and telephone companies. In businesses that were concerned with seasonal work and in "special circumstances"—and these might legally include factors such as adverse weather and transport considerations, as well as any form of "unusual accumulation of work"—the official night rest from work might from time to time be reduced to ten hours. In sugar beet factories and cotton spinning and carding mills as well as above-ground work in mining, the new regulations were to apply only from 1920 onwards.[58]

In justifying his proposal, the minister for commerce had made every effort to set aside any economic concerns that might be raised in opposition to a limitation on night work. In almost "every European country of any importance," the minister argued, there existed regulations limiting women's work at night, and in many other countries there were special protective regulations for women or general limitations on working hours that went beyond those of the Berne Convention and the existing Hungarian legislation. The matter of "international competition" was thus irrelevant in considering the proposal. This argument blithely ignored that,

---

[56] In the debates in the lower house there was no opposition to the draft law. *Országgyűlési Képviselőház Naplói* [Chronicle of the House of Parliamentary Representatives] 1910/1915, vol. IX, 193–208.

[57] Act 19/1911.

[58] For juvenile female workers, however, there were limitations that entered into force immediately in the latter industries. The exception clause for the cotton industry was only unanimously accepted as law (in addition to the exception clause for the sugar industry) after parliamentary debates and at the request of the Committee for Labor Affairs. The above described basic provisions of the Berne Convention entered Hungarian law unmodified. Act 19/1911, §§2–4, 14 *Országgyűlési Képviselőház Naplói* [Chronicle of the House of Parliamentary Representatives] 1910/1915, vol. IX, 208; Sámuel Dóczi, *Az iparüzemekben alkalmazott nők éjjeli munkájáról szóló 1911. évi törvénycikk* [The article of law of 1911 on the night work of women employed in industry] (Budapest 1912), 14.

internationally, intensive or cheap exploitation of the (female) labor force, independently from other factors such as productivity, constituted a competitive element some might certainly find it in their interests to preserve. The minister soldiered on, stating that the new legislation promised significant advantages of quite another type against which "arguments about production or the danger to the income of women dependent on paid labor" did not hold water. These advantages, vividly presented in the justification for the proposal, related exclusively to limiting women's night work in order to satisfy paternalistic and patriarchal interests. Besides paid work, the physically weaker woman was burdened with "the work of housekeeping and caring for children." The overburdening of women with paid work and the consequent neglect of their duties in the "home of the worker" was not only tantamount to an elimination of the "most basic requirements for the welfare of the worker" but would lead "to a coarsening of morality which … would seriously threaten the nation." The committee of the lower house of the Hungarian Parliament concerned with labor affairs supported the legislative proposal and the minister's justification. It additionally suggested that social policy should also take responsibility for the limitation of women's labor because women themselves, it implied, were incapable of doing so. Far too many women forgot, in their hard work in the "workshop of national production [their] moral obligation towards their families and also … towards their native land"; women had to shoulder the latter obligation because it was they who would ensure "the viability and magnitude of the next generation." Under these circumstances, progressive modern social policy had to avoid two extremes. It should neither prevent the dynamic development of women's labor, nor should it "sink into contemplation of misty images from the past." As the female workers themselves did not possess "the energy and organizational abilities" to improve their own situation, the law must intervene instead.[59]

It is hard, given all the above, to see Hungarian special labor protection for women as a harbinger of the extension of work protection regulations to the benefit of employees that would subsequently extend to ever newer groups of workers—although in retrospect, it was indeed to have this role. Rather, the reform was conceived and publicly presented exclusively as a step towards the creation or preservation of patriarchal family relations among the lower classes, and contribution to the good of the people and

[59] *Törvényjavaslat az iparüzemekben alkalmazott nők éjjeli munkájának eltiltásáról* [Legislative proposal for the prohibition of women's night work in industry] (no place, year given), 7 ff.

social stability as a whole. Given the concrete form of the ban on female night labor in Hungary, it was undoubtedly to be expected that some of the cheapest areas of women's night work would continue unaffected, while women lost access to other, potentially more profitable areas of night work.

IV.1.3. Labor protection for non-industrial workers

For those workers for whom the trade law did not apply—essentially workers, day laborers and bonded laborers, that is "outdoor servants" or "agricultural servants" (*külső cselédek*),[60] in the agricultural sector, and domestic servants—there were, in the sense discussed hitherto, effectively no labor protection regulations. These working relations were initially governed by the law on "the relations between employers and servants and regarding agricultural workers and day laborers" from 1876.[61] Then in 1898, after strikes by harvest workers and social unrest in 1897, there was a revision of the law with regard to agricultural and day laborers. The new law was infamously known as the "slave law," due to the fact that it made failure to fulfill the "free" work contract a punishable offence and banned strikes. There were also regulations making labor piracy a punishable offence. [62] Only in 1907 were the legal relations between farmer owners or agricultural employers and their servants also revised. This law likewise retained the spirit of a tightly binding and yet at the same time unequal relationship between employer and employee. At the same time, however, certain practices on the part of agricultural employers that had hitherto always provoked resistance, such as the press-ganging of unpaid extra labor, or payment in the form of vouchers, were forbidden or at least restricted. Apart from this, while workers gained few other rights, the state did dictate certain obligations to employers. This law too threatened punishment for those workers who failed to fulfill the duties of a contract they had entered into. Major punishment was reserved for those seditious individuals who incited or persuaded those who wished to work as agricul-

---

[60] The term "outdoor servant" (*külső cseléd)*, which will be translated as "agricultural servant" in the following, was regularly used in Hungary at the time when referring to bonded labor in the agricultural sector. The term "servant" (*cseléd)* in contrast referred to domestic servants working in and for the household in smaller and larger communities alike.

[61] Act 13/1876.

[62] Act 2/1898, §§62, 65; Heller, *Magyarország szociálpolitikája* [Social policy of Hungary], 87–93.

tural servants to refuse work, or who "in word or deed abused or threatened" those who had already accepted an obligation to work. The fact that agricultural servants who did not report for their already contracted work could be forcibly brought to their workplace by the executive authorities can be considered as an addition to these directives against the organization of workers' action.[63]

The vague and limited attempts at actual labor protection in all of these old and new laws can be swiftly listed. A minimum age of twelve for the employment of children as agricultural laborers was introduced in 1907 for the first time. The working hours of agricultural day-laborers was to last, according to the laws of 1876 and 1898, "from sunrise to sunset," and in 1899 this clause was extended to day-laborers working in infrastructure. Rest-breaks were (as in industry) to be observed. The law of 1907 contained certain regulations limiting the work of servants in the agricultural sector on Sundays. Apart from this, the employer was to ensure when allocating work that this should not exceed the "physical strength" of the servant, and to ensure that he or she had "enough time" for nightly rest "according to the general customs of management in the region and the time of year."[64] That these regulations more often than not were ignored, and the exploitation of agricultural workers continued well into the twentieth century without any constraint, was only too well known to contemporaries, from the minister to authors, to the workers concerned.[65]

Domestic servants continued after 1907 to be subject to the minimal "protection" regulations—which had been valid for all non-industrial work until 1907—set down by the law of 1876. This last was limited to the well-known formula whereby the employer was to make sure that "the workload of his employees does not exceed their physical abilities or endanger their health."[66]

---

[63] Act 45/1907, §§17, 57; Heller, *Magyarország szociálpolitikája* [Social policy of Hungary], 90–104; Gábor Gyáni, "A szociálpolitika első lépései hazánkban: Darányi törvényei" [The first socio-political steps in our homeland: Darányi's law], in *Darányi Ignác emlékkonferencia* [Ignác Darányi Memorial Conference] (Budapest 2000), 94–110.

[64] Act 13/1876, §103; Act 2/1898, §49; Act 41/1891, §2; Act 45/1907, §§3, 23, 30; Lőrincz, *Munkaviszonyok* [Labor relations], 106–110.

[65] Literary works on the subject include several short stories by Zsigmond Móricz as well as most notably the sociography "Viharsarok" [Storm region] by Géza Féja.

[66] Act 13/1876, §30; Act 45/1907, §69.

IV.2. Social Insurance and Workplace-related Social Policy (from the 1880s to 1914)

In addition to state labor protection and partly evolving out of it, in the Habsburg Monarchy from the end of the 1880s, like elsewhere in Europe, systems of state social insurance began to emerge. Following the introduction in Austria of two laws related to accident insurance and health insurance for workers that entered into force in 1888–1889, a law on health insurance was established in 1891 in Hungary too. In 1907, this was then replaced by a new law that included obligatory accident and health insurance. In Hungary labor relations in agriculture were also important for this newly emerging type of state social policy. At the heart of the relevant reforms was the law of 1900 creating an insurance for agricultural workers and [agricultural] servants[67] and ensuing laws.

The first part of this section presents the main features of the legislation and the related ordinances and reforms, as well as the interests and disputes that characterized the legislative process. The second part addresses the development of the institutional structures of the social insurance system. Particular attention is devoted to the political debates that surrounded this development, as well as the change in the role of the state it entailed. The third part then deals with the intervention of the new social insurance system into working and living conditions.[68] It focuses particularly on coverage and level of provision and, regarding specific groups and geographical areas, the mechanisms and development tendencies for inclusion or exclusion, both in law and in reality. In this way, basic concepts and political vision regarding both the preexisting and the desired reshaping of labor and social relations which inspired legislature and legal practice in the matter of social insurance will also be revealed.

---

[67] For the term "agricultural servant" (*külső cseléd*) see p. 88, fn. 60.

[68] Regulations of the social insurance system that were relevant for the policy areas addressed in sections IV.2.2. and IV.2.3 will not be discussed in the first section. The situation of mining is not dealt with. The Austria mining law of 1854 was one of those laws that remained in force in Hungary after the Compromise of 1867. The system of miners' health insurance thus for decades largely corresponded to the Austrian one. Reform efforts aimed at adapting the insurance system of the miners with that which emerged due to the development of the labor insurance system, and thus to raise the level of provision, came to nothing. Josef Sterényi, *Die Arbeiterversicherung in Ungarn. Internationaler Arbeiterversicherungskongress, 7. Tagung, Wien, 17. bis 23. September 1905* [Labor insurance in Hungary. International labor insurance congress, Vienna 17–23 September 1905] (no place, year given), 20–23; Petrák, *Szervezett munkásság* [Organized workforce], 98–101.

IV.2.1. Sectors and types of health and accident insurance: origins, development, and interests

As the preparations for the first Hungarian law on workers' insurance in general got under way in the 1880s, there was among specialists a probably rather limited debate on labor protection and labor insurance and the relationship between the two.[69] In practice, apart from various company insurance companies and miner's insurance companies, the main institution of the time was the General Worker's Sickness and Invalid's Company (*Általános munkás-betegsegélyező és rokkantpénztár*), founded in 1870 by the labor movement.[70] The Austrian trade law which came into force in Hungary in the 1850s contained initial attempts to regulate the obligations of the employer regarding accidents in the workplace or sickness of employees, as well as regulatory clauses in the area of health. Servants were in principle covered by a clause of Act 13/1876 regulating the relationship between employer and servant, according to which the employer was to pay for up to one month of sick care inside or outside the home.[71] Employees in commerce were entitled, according to the law of 1875, to continue receiving pay for up to six weeks in the case of accidents in the workplace for which they were not to blame.[72] The new trade law of 1884, however, relied for the provision of healthcare on insurance companies voluntarily created by the equally voluntarily created Trade Corporations. These insurance companies were to be managed and overseen by employees and business or workshop owners equally.[73]

---

69 Zsombor Bódy, "A 'szociális kérdés' kezelésének alternatívái a 19. század végén. Az 1891-es kötelező betegbiztosítási törvény keletkezése" [Alternatives in handling the "social question" at the end of the 19th century. The emergence of the law on compulsory health insurance of 1891]. *Korall*, no. 5–6 (2001): 72–93, here 72–76.

70 In the following, the Hungarian term (insurance) *pénztár* will be almost always translated as "company"—and qualified as public, private, or enterprise (insurance) company – so as to differentiate it from the much broader term "fund." Szterényi, *Arbeiterversicherung* [Labor insurance], 34 ff.; Petrák, *Szervezett munkásság* [Organized workforce], 18–40.

71 The law discussed in chapter II.2. on covering of costs of public healthcare of 1898 did nothing to change the fact that the employer basically had to cover the costs of hospital care for servants for up to one month. The regulations on home healthcare changed for agricultural servants from 1907 on. Act 13/1875, §32; Act 21/1898, §5; Lőrincz, *Munkaviszonyok* [Labor relations] 163 f.; Heller, *Magyarország szociálpolitikája* [Social policy of Hungary], 1–4.

72 Act 37/1875, §56.

73 Act 17/1884, §145. On the organizational structures of the Trade Corporations see p. 65, fn. 41.

From 1885 on, the preparation work for the legal foundations for workers' insurance then began to take concrete form.[74] Based on the double initiative mentioned earlier on the part of opposition representative Irányi in the lower house of the Hungarian Parliament on Sunday rest and accident insurance,[75] the house directed the government to develop a legislative proposal on accident insurance. Organized workers also demanded social protection laws, including a law on accident insurance,[76] and in 1887 a national meeting of the Trade Corporations called for the formation of compulsory public (health) insurance companies for those employed in branches of trade and industry where evidence of formal qualification was required.[77] A revised official proposal for voluntary accident insurance alone finally was presented at the end of 1888. It was based on the principle that employers could, through voluntary accident insurance, to all intents and purposes buy themselves out of otherwise carefully specified claims for compensation in the case of a work-related accident. Although important bodies intervened unambiguously in favor of the creation of compulsory insurance, the ministry held fast to its own concept. The National Industrial Union (*Országos iparegyesület*), which was later to concentrate exclusively on representing the interests of medium-sized and smaller-scale industry, and the Budapest chamber of trade and commerce argued for first introducing health insurance and then accident insurance. The various efforts at resistance, however, ultimately resulted in the plan for the creation of accident protection being temporarily shelved. Act 28/1893 on accident protection and the factory inspectorate, mentioned above, meant that for the time being in the field of social policy on work-related accidents only regulations related to labor protection and not insurance were to enter into Hungarian law. In contrast, after lengthy preparations, in August 1889 a separate bill for compulsory health insurance was presented, which eventually formed the basis of the law of 1891.[78] The debates surrounding the passing of the bill into law focused among other things on the organizational structures of the public insurance com-

[74] Bódy, "Szociális kérdés" [Social question], 77.

[75] See p. 72 f.

[76] Petrák, *Szervezett munkásság* [Organized workforce], 42.

[77] *A munkás-betegsegélyezési törvény módosítása. Hazai anyag három részben. Első rész: Joganyag. Második rész: Kivánságok és javaslatok. Harmadik rész: Statisztika* [The modification of the law on workers' sickness benefits. Domestic material in three parts. Part 1: juridical material. Part 2: wishes and suggestions. Part 3: statistics], vol. I (Budapest 1905), 30.

[78] Act 14/1891.

pany system that was to be created. While the National Industrial Union sought to introduce elements of compulsion into the planned health insurance system, the minister for justice strove to further liberalize the planned regulations for the private insurance companies, which according to the bill were allowed to continue to exist. None of these efforts, however, met with success. There was a broad consensus with regard to the extension of compulsory insurance to all businesses subject to the trade law, including smaller businesses, and with regard to the exclusion of agricultural workers from compulsory insurance. Representatives of the General Worker's Sickness and Invalid's Company were to an extent also involved in the advisory process. The law was approved in parliament not only by the liberal government but also by the major opposition party of which Dániel Irányi was a member. Criticisms and calls for amendments were kept within reasonable limits.[79]

A broader wave of reforms, in which the state intervened in social problems, began around the turn of the century. Particularly the law on the creation of the State Healthcare Fund of 1898[80] brought about the partial nationalization of finance and organization of child protection and nursing costs for various groups of indigent individuals, an area closely connected to state health insurance. The reform entailed an innovation that was remarkable even in the international context, in that state intervention was based not on the principle of compulsory contributions on the part of the affected person or the employer but rather on collecting additional taxes. In creating the State Healthcare Fund the Hungarian authorities implicitly admitted that worker's health insurance alone would not in the foreseeable future contribute in a substantial manner to reducing the continuous rush of the needy on the poor relief system. This appears to be a unique state of affairs in comparison to Austria and other European countries.

The reforms around the turn of the century also affected the agricultural workforce. Both the law on the State Healthcare Fund, and the law regulating the working conditions of agricultural workers of the same year, 1898, tried to ensure minimum of healthcare provision for the agricultural workforce as well. In accordance with Act 2/1898 and the related laws for infrastructure and forestry workers, which have already been mentioned, employers were obliged to cover up to eight days of care for sick agricultural workers who did not belong to the municipality where

[79] Bódy, "Szociális kérdés" [Social question], 78–87; Petrák, *Szervezett munkásság* [Organized workforce], 44 f., 47 f.

[80] See chapters II.2. and III.1.

they were employed, that is who did not enjoy legal residence status in this municipality.[81] The law on the State Healthcare Fund stipulated that employers had to meet the costs of hospital care for agricultural servants for up to 30 days. Connected to the reform of the legal relationship between agricultural employers and their servants of 1907, the legislators additionally required the employer to provide up to 45 days of medical treatment and medicines for sick servants. In the case of permanently employed servants, this also applied to wives and children under the age of twelve.[82] Concerning accident insurance, an important breakthrough was the creation of the National Insurance for Agricultural Workers and Servants (*Országos gazdasági munkás- és cselédpénztár*), from 1913 National Insurance Company for Agricultural Workers,[83] though the new institution was often ridiculed by contemporary sources as a "beggar's fund" that provided no more than "a pittance."[84] The new agricultural public insurance company was based on the principle of voluntary participation in various insurance categories that employees could choose. The company was financed not only by these individual contributions but also by compulsory lump sum contributions paid by the employer for each individual employed and by a state subsidy. Those insured received, in relation to their employer's contribution, compensation on a sliding scale in the case of invalidity or accident, and compensation was paid to the family in the event of their death. Those who were fully insured received a modest lump sum at the age of 65. Laborers who were not individually insured, i.e. those who were only insured by the compulsory lump sum contribution of their employers, were entitled to certain minimal compensatory payments.[85]

A reform in 1902 created possibilities for extending benefits and additionally stipulated that employers who failed to make the compulsory lump sum contribution for their employees' accident insurance should be fully liable in the event of accidents.[86] In 1907 the lower house explicitly called on the minister for agriculture in relation to the debate on the new workers' insurance law to lay before the house "as soon as possible" a

---

[81] Act 2/1898, §33; Act 41/1899, §20; Act 28/1900, §18.

[82] Act 21/1898, §5; Act 45/1907, §28

[83] Act 16/1900.

[84] *Országgyűlési Képviselőház Naplói* [Chronicle of the House of Parliamentary Representatives] 1910/1915, vol. XIV, 204.

[85] Act 16/1900, esp. §§2, 7–10, 19, 23.

[86] Act 14/1902, esp. §§24–26; Heller, *Magyarország szociálpolitikája* [Social policy of Hungary], 112–115.

(yet to be drafted) legislative proposal for accident and health insurance that was to include agricultural servants and workers.[87] Yet in 1910 the board of directors of the National Insurance for Agricultural Workers and Servants publicly stated that where the agricultural labor force was located, namely on the "periphery," it was first necessary to create an adequate healthcare system before the introduction of health insurance could be even considered.[88]

The nationally centralized structure of the National Insurance for Agricultural Workers and Servants created in 1900 can be seen as a model for the major reforms of social insurance of workers in Hungary that were soon to follow. The actual passing into law in this second case in fact dragged on until 1907. However, as early as 1899, the minister responsible had officially announced that the preparatory work for a reform of the law on health insurance had been completed. He had "come to the conclusion in the course of the year of 1899" that "the obstacles that stand in the way of the prosperity and development of the health insurance companies lie partly in the law."[89] In the following years, the agenda for the reform of health insurance and the introduction of accident insurance were handled separately, though there was lengthy and detailed discussion about a possible unification of these two branches of social insurance. The process of entry into law then got under way, starting with the presentation of a separate bill on accident insurance in 1903. From 1905 the authorities aimed at creating a new law on both branches of insurance. The authorities made clear at this point that the reform should address a number of problems[90] that had emerged from the health insurance law of 1891 and related legal practice. In the matter of accident insurance in particular (large-scale) employers pushed for the creation of compulsory insurance. This was because of a trend in Hungarian legal practice based on clauses of the trade law of 1884 and the 1893 law on accident prevention that proved to be of considerable concern from the point of view of the employer. Specifically, legal practice partly interpreted the matter of responsibility for accidents in the workplace in such a way as to apportion exten-

---

[87] *Országgyűlési Képviselőház Naplói* [Chronicle of the House of Parliamentary Representatives] 1906/1910, vol.VI, 410.

[88] *Munkásügyi Szemle* 1 (1910): 272.

[89] *A Magyar Királyi Kormány* [The Royal Hungarian Government] 1899, 56.

[90] One concern was the diversity and lack of centralization of the diverse health insurance companies operating under the 1891 law. On this and other problems regarding the organization of the system of health insurance companies under this law, to which the reform of 1907 was addressed, see chapter IV.2.2.

sive civil liability to the employer, leading to the award of damages for victims of accidents. While this was a thorn in the side of the employers, the same legal practice still did not ensure for the other party, the victim of the accident—according to the justification for the bill—"appropriate care."[91]

When the economically liberal forces that had hitherto held power were replaced by the coalition government (1906–1910) that was committed to national rhetoric, the new law rapidly became reality under the professional leadership of József Szterényi. The 1907 law covered both areas of social insurance in one framework, although based on quite different principles.[92] From 1910 the ministry pushed for an amendment to the 1907 law already, but this did not happen before 1914.[93] From 1911, preparations for the creation of legal provisions for old age insurance for private and commercial employees got under way.[94]

IV.2.2. Institution and policy

The development of social insurance in Hungary was marked by a whole range of persistent institutional and political conflicts. The historical analysis of the relevant debates provides an insight not only into the insti-

---

[91] Act 19/1907, Justification of the Legislative Bill, *Magyar Törvénytár* [Hungarian corpus juris] 1907, 184; Zsombor Bódy, "A 'társadalom kora'. Munkásbiztosítás és munkaügy Magyarországon a 19. és a 20. század fordulóján" [The "age of society." Labor insurance and labor affairs in Hungary at the turn of the 19th to 20th Century]. *Aetas* 19, no. 1 (2004): 5–29, here 16–20; Szterényi, Arbeiterversicherung [Labor insurance], 67; *A munkások baleset ellen való biztositása. I. rész. Hazai és külföldi anyag-gyűjtemény* [The insurance of workers against accidents. Part I. Domestic and international collection of materials] (Budapest 1903), 75 f.; *A munkás-betegsegélyezési törvény módosítása* [Modification of the law on workers' sickness benefits], 22; *Az ipartörvény módosítása* [Modification of the trade law], vol. II, 180–183; *A Magyar Királyi Kormány* [The Royal Hungarian Government] 1903, 9; 1905, 52.

[92] In the free city of Fiume and the corresponding insurance district the new law—with certain additional clauses regarding the use of the Italian language—first entered into force in 1911. In and for Croatia–Slavonia, a National Insurance Company practically identical with the Hungarian one (see p. 105) was to be created with its headquarters in Zagreb, which held its first general meeting in early 1910. The founding of the Zagreb institution of the revised labor insurance system did not go smoothly, however. Act 19/1907, §§99, 208; *A Magyar Királyi Kormány* [The Royal Hungarian Government] 1911, 64; *Munkásbiztositási Közlöny* 5 (1911): 235 ff; *Munkásbiztosítás* 2 (1909): 13–14, 3 f.; *Munkásügyi Szemle* 1 (1910): 242.

[93] *A Magyar Királyi Kormány* [The Royal Hungarian Government] 1910, 62; 1911, 64.

[94] *A Magyar Királyi Kormány* [The Royal Hungarian Government] 1911, 64.

tutional history of the workers' insurance itself, but also makes clear how the development of the insurance system influenced the relationships between a wide range of institutional and political actors, and was in turn shaped by these relations on both national and local levels. It will also become clear how and to what extent the organization and politics of compulsory insurance can be seen as a new sphere of activity and a new partially state-formed institution of the social democratic labor movement.

The process of organization of the health insurance system, based on the law of 1891, began to take concrete form in 1893. The minister for commerce had first established by decree the districts and the registered office for each of the 98 District Health Insurance Companies (*Kerületi betegsegélyző pénztárak*) that were now created, a process in which political interests regarding the location of the district offices in those places where the labor movement was strongest were taken into account.[95] At the same time, in parallel with the newly created District Health Insurance Companies, the law permitted the continued functioning and creation of health insurance companies operated by enterprises, the Trade Corporations, and civil actors (as well as the separate and highly particular system of health funds in the mining sector, which is not discussed here). At the general assembly of the District Companies, employers were to make up a third of the members—a proportion corresponding to their share in the contributions to the insurance companies—and at least one third of the management and the board of trustees. The District Companies had the right, without obligation, to create a national "insurance union." If created, the general assembly of the union was to decide on matters such as the appointment of doctors and the conclusion of contracts with pharmacies. If the membership of a District Health Insurance Company remained constantly below 100 members or if it was definitively financially unviable, the trade authorities were entitled in agreement with the minister to close it down or to amalgamate it with another. Of key importance in foreshadowing the contested role of the workers' movement and its General Worker's Sickness and Invalid's Company in the future system—which will be discussed below—were the regulations about compulsory membership in the different types of insurance companies and compulsory

[95] *Pallas Nagylexikon* [Pallas encyclopedia], 18 vols. (Budapest 1893–1900), vol. III, 216; Ordinance no. 2343/1892, Minister for the interior; Petrák, *Szervezett munkásság* [Organized workforce], 57; Dorottya Szikra, "Az 1891. évi betegbiztosítási törvény végrehajtása" [The enforcement of the health insurance law of 1891]. *Aetas* 19, no. 1 (2004): 31–48, here 41.

change of membership. Those employed by a company that had its own insurance company were required to join this fund unless they were, at time of entry into the relevant company or at the time of granting of the statute of the company insurance fund, already insured with the District Health Insurance Company or with another fund. In relation to company funds and other types of supplementary insurance companies in general, it was stipulated that employees of companies who ensured their workers in either of these types were obliged to join the system provided by their company only if they could not provide evidence of membership of the District Health Insurance Company or another fund. Transferring from District Insurance Companies and those of the Trade Corporations to private insurance companies—and thus also to the General Worker's Sickness and Invalid's Company—was forbidden.[96]

The creation and development of the District Health Insurance Companies went very slowly in many places, as did the progress of many other insurance companies. This was partly due to the competition between the different companies and the fragmentation of the system as a whole, the latter being the object of the probably most prominent public criticism at the time.[97] In 1898 there were, within the insurance system based in the labor insurance law of 1891, a total of 617,000 insured in 453 different insurance companies, of which 142, that is nearly one third, had less than 300 members each. Only ten funds achieved a membership of between 5,000 and 10,000 individuals, another ten had more than 10,000 members. The last category included the Budapest District Health Insurance Company and the fund of the Hungarian State Railways.[98]

There were, however, a number of other reasons for the agonies of the health insurance system that operated on the basis of the law of 1891. The most important of these were related to the legal and factual organization and management of the new insurance system.

---

[96] Act 14/1891.

[97] Gyula Sárdi, *A Kaposvári kerületi betegsegélyező pénztár története 1894–1916* [History of the Kaposvár District Health Insurance Company 1894–1916] (1996, no place given), 24, 29–32; Szikra, "Az 1891. évi betegbiztosítási törvény végrehajtása" [The enforcement of the health insurance law of 1891], 42; Petrák, *Szervezett munkásság* [Organized workforce], 63; *A munkás-betegsegélyezési törvény módosítása* [Modification of the law on workers' sickness benefits], 259–267; Act 19/1907, Justification, *Magyar Törvénytár* [Hungarian corpus juris], 183.

[98] Heller, *Magyarország szociálpolitikája* [Social policy of Hungary], 45; *A munkás-betegsegélyezési törvény módosítása* [Modification of the law on workers' sickness benefits], 499.

One feature that, thanks to repeated media reports of (supposed) scandals, constantly attracted public attention were irregularities of the insurance companies themselves, including excessive or unusually high administrative costs, misuse of funds, insufficient transparency of management, and other forms of mismanagement or corruption.[99] It also became clear that those in important positions, particularly in the management of funds, frequently lacked any training of how such insurance funds should be managed, or indeed any understanding of the very meaning of insurance autonomy, or the commitment to substantially engage with these matters.[100]

A range of more serious, and publicly less prominently discussed, problems emerged, however, from the cooperation with those local actors and institutions that the lawmakers had expected compulsory labor insurance to integrate with smoothly. The law on health insurance created a wide range of new obligations and duties for those local officials and authorities who functioned as trade authorities—this meant the District Administrator (*szolgabíró*) in small municipalities; in larger ones, depending on the status of the municipality, the chief of police or the city council, and in the capital, the district councils. The trade authorities not only played an important role in the founding of District Health Insurance Companies and the formulation of their statutes. They also were to have supervisory responsibility for all local insurance companies, who were required, for example, annually to submit their balance of accounts to these authorities. In addition, the trade authorities had to decide on exemptions from compulsory insurance, and at regular intervals to determine, separately for men, women and apprentices, the "average general daily wage" that served as the basis for the calculation of insurance contributions. They were required, on the basis of evidence of employment in their possession, to verify disclosures by the insurance companies regarding possible arrears in contributions, to adjudge the opening or closing of companies located in the given administrative district, to share in the resolution of disputes, and to intervene in the case of petty offenses.[101]

The complaints over the unwillingness or inability of the local authorities to fulfill these duties, or conversely the complaints of the authorities

[99] Petrák, *Szervezett munkásság* [Organized workforce], 60; Sárdi, *A Kaposvári kerületi betegsegélyező pénztár* [Kaposvár District Health Insurance Company], 30, 52; Heller, *Magyarország szociálpolitikája* [Social policy of Hungary], 44; Act 19/1907, Justification, *Magyar Törvénytár* [Hungarian corpus juris], 184.

[100] Sárdi, *A Kaposvári kerületi betegsegélyező pénztár* [Kaposvár District Health Insurance Company], 37.

[101] Act 17/1884, §166; Act 14/1891, §§6, 16, 24, 26, 35, 47, 53, 55, 57, 58, 61, 75–81, 84.

themselves that they were unable, due to overload or to administrative difficulties, to address these tasks in a suitable manner, did not decrease as time went by. Particularly when it came to finding confidants, that is agents willing to take responsibility for handling the collection of contributions and registering and deregistering the insured, there was a lack of qualified individuals willing to do the job.[102] The District Health Insurance Company of Kaposvár, for example, struggled with the consequences of the fact that it was the local notaries who were supposed to take this role. Although the confidants were even entitled to a percentage of the insurance premiums collected, many local notaries still refused to take on the job. In many municipalities belonging to the district of the Kaposvár Health Insurance Company, a person responsible for the handling of the relevant duties was not even named. An additional problem was the fact that neither the agents nor the staff of the health insurance companies had the legal right to examine the company documents *in situ* so as to assess whether employers had failed to register any of their employees for health insurance. In 1899 the County Head Official [*alispán*] of Somogy County—the seat of which was Kaposvár—finally enacted two decrees obliging the local notaries to take on the role of confidant and the trade authorities to collect outstanding payments without fail.[103]

A further key area of problems with regard to the position of insurance companies in relation to local institutional power struggles was the matter of cooperation with the medical community, the arrangement of which the law left to be regulated by the statutes of the District Insurance Companies. Many doctors in private practice refused to treat patients whose treatment cost was to be covered by a health insurance company at all, charged patients with compulsory health insurance particularly high fees, or showed a strong tendency simply to refer patients to hospitals. Local physicians who were not under contract with the District Health Insurance Company also demanded a guaranteed fixed annual income to be paid by the District Company before they agreed to cooperate. From the point of view of the insurance companies this was simply not affordable.[104] Added

[102] *A munkás-betegsegélyezési törvény módosítása* [Modification of the law on workers' sickness benefits], 279, 299–303; Sárdi, *A Kaposvári kerületi betegsegélyező pénztár* [Kaposvár District Health Insurance Company], 24, 52.

[103] Sárdi, *A Kaposvári kerületi betegsegélyező pénztár* [Kaposvár District Health Insurance Company], 32, 35–38, 40, 44.

[104] After the turn of the century, the tendency in the district funds was towards abolishing the system of free choice of doctors. Sárdi, *A Kaposvári kerületi betegsegélyező pénztár* [Kaposvár District Health Insurance Company], 45–51; *A munkás-betegsegélyezési*

to this was the frequently discussed fact that, particularly in rural areas, there were simply not enough doctors, and often not even the position of district medical officer, who the authorities were in principle obliged to appoint, was filled.[105] As a consequence of all these problems, there were health insurance companies that in practice were completely unable to offer any kind of comprehensive medical coverage within their district.[106]

Another problem area was the financial situation of the insurance companies, which in many cases was permanently insecure to disastrous.[107] The reasons for this, apart from the general structure of the system of health insurance companies described above, were first of all the sheer and simple failure to meet insurance obligations—the fact that large numbers of workers who in principle were subject to compulsory insurance in actual reality were not registered with any health insurance company—and the consequent decline in the number of those insured.[108] Second, the fact that many insurance companies had to deal constantly with enormous arrears in the payment of insurance contributions had dire consequences for the management of their finances. "[T]he employer registers his workers and then doesn't pay a *filler* into the fund; the employee falls ill, he [is sent] to hospital, which demands that the insurance company meet the costs of medical treatment; and when it finally comes to the collection of arrears [by the insurance company], the notary submits proof of lack of funds" or a "negative bailiff's return is submitted."[109] In the year 1900, by the end of the year, the health insurance companies were able to register 90 percent of premiums as being paid, while arrears made up the remaining 10 percent. When calculated only for District Health Insurance Companies, the percentage of arrears rose to 18, and if the district of Budapest is excluded, the figure reached 21 percent. There were a consider-

törvény módosítása [Modification of the Law on Workers' Sickness Benefits], 283–292; Petrák, *Szervezett munkásság* [Organized Workforce], 64; Szikra, "Az 1891. évi betegbiztosítási törvény végrehajtása" [The enforcement of the health insurance law of 1891], 44; *Közigazgatási elvi határozatok. Új-folyam* [Principle administrative decisions. New series], vol. I, 503.

105 Szikra, "Az 1891. évi betegbiztosítási törvény végrehajtása" [The enforcement of the health insurance law of 1891], 44.

106 Heller, *Magyarország szociálpolitikája* [Social policy of Hungary], 44.

107 *A munkás-betegsegélyezési törvény módosítása* [Modification of the law on workers' sickness benefits], 533 f.

108 See also chapter IV.2.3 on this point.

109 According to the annual report of the Kaposvár District Company of 1897, cited in Sárdi, *A Kaposvári kerületi betegsegélyező pénztár* [Kaposvár District Health Insurance Company], 35, 40 f.

able number of individual insurance companies where the rate of arrears was even higher.[110]

The position of the workforce regarding labor insurance changed in two ways as a consequence of the introduction of compulsory insurance in 1891. First, the state thus created for the first time an extensive institutional framework of social policy within which representatives of the working population had a place of their own. Second, the introduction of the law on health insurance led to a change in the status of the General Worker's Sickness and Invalid's Company, which had been founded and served for two decades as an important institution of the organized labor movement. The General Company, as it was commonly referred to by the contemporaries, continued to exist within the new system as one of the private health insurance companies, but at the same time its autonomy and the possibilities to make decisions for itself decreased. The General Company lost the freedom that it had hitherto enjoyed due to its status as a duly constituted civil association, and like all other insurance companies was teamed up with the local trade authorities and was obliged to conform its statutes regulations contained in the law of 1891 and pertaining to all insurance companies. In addition, the General Company had to be strictly separated from the Social Democratic Party in terms of organizational structure. These restrictions notwithstanding, the changes after 1891 did mean a first step towards the incorporation of the workers' movement into institutional structures of and political projects pursued by the Hungarian state, in this case the development of a social insurance system. Workers' representatives were assigned a significant position within the newly created insurance system, and in the 1890s the membership of the General Company, which itself now formed a part of this system, after a brief dip immediately following the introduction of compulsory insurance, remained stable at just under 50,000.[111]

The incorporation of organized labor and the General Company into the new institutional structure of workers' health insurance was not without problems. As regards the General Company, it had in the process of creation of the law argued strongly but unsuccessfully against any form of organization of the insurance system that would give too much leeway to

[110] *A munkás-betegsegélyezési törvény módosítása* [Modification of the law on workers' sickness benefits], 504–511.

[111] Petrák, *Szervezett munkásság* [Organized workforce], 22–40, 51f.; István Lackó, *A magyar munkás- és társadalombiztosítás története* [The history of Hungarian labor and social insurance] (Budapest 1968), 60 ff.

insurance companies operated by companies and thus to initiatives by employers. In practice, however, the government lent massive support to the creation of company insurance within the new system. The General Company, in contrast, was forbidden, even before the entry into force of the law, to set up new branches outside the capital, after it had tried to get around the above described legal restrictions to be imposed by Act 14/1891 with a preemptive geographical expansion before the law came into effect. Further ordinances in 1892 and 1893 denied private companies the right to create national or regional unions, and explicitly forbade the maintenance of multiple branches as such. The same ordinances also abolished the right of any individual health insurance company to expand its area of activity beyond the territory officially established by the state for the District Health Insurance Company on whose territory it had its seat. By 1898 in the whole of Hungary there were 111 District Health Insurance Companies, 182 insurance companies operated by companies, 101 companies of Trade Corporations and 58 private health insurance companies (each limited to a single district) within the system created by the law of 1891. The efforts to repress and limit the General Company evident not only in the actions described here were a regular feature of the political landscape of the 1890s.[112]

As regards the relationship between the workers' movement and the District Health Insurance Companies, one can assume that the former at best only partly recognized the political possibilities that lay in the organized participation in the system of District Companies, at least in the 1890s. The competition between the District Companies and the General Company and the policy of defending the latter within the new state labor insurance system was in fact hardly conducive to the development of a systematic social democratic labor insurance policy. In addition, there was infighting within the workers' movement as well as the very real experience that the non-socialist forces involved in state workers' insurance were not prepared to cooperate with the workers' movement and sought to marginalize it. Finally, one further factor was that the workers' movement was not so well established among the workforce across the country as to have a sufficiently well-organized political foundation that would permit a

[112] The law came into force on 1st April 1892. Act 14/1891, §86; Petrák, *Szervezett munkásság* [Organized Workforce], 51–56; Sárdi, *A Kaposvári kerületi betegsegélyező pénztár* [Kaposvár District Health Insurance Company], 35 f., 55; Heller, *Magyarország szociálpolitikája* [Social Policy of Hungary], 45; Szikra, "Az 1891. évi betegbiztosítási törvény végrehajtása" [The enforcement of the health insurance law of 1891], 45 f.

systematic workers' insurance policy. In the case of the Kaposvár District Health Insurance Company, for example, many company owners felt safe to send their own workers as representatives of the management to the general assembly of the District Company. As a result, in one general assembly held in the 1890s, 20 out of 35 management representatives were in fact members of the workforce.[113]

After the turn of the century, the Social Democratic Party and the trade unions pushed hard for a broadening and nationalization of workers' insurance. Nationalization should be carried out in such a way as to ensure the self-government of the insured within the insurance system and appropriate representation of the workforce on management committees. As the preparations for the legal reform of the workers' insurance got under way with the new century, and it became clear that a more centralized structure of insurance companies would indeed be created, it looked likely that the Budapest district company would be amalgamated with the General Company of the workers' movement. And after a hard fought process for a compromise that was also tolerable for the General Company—with pressure from the ministry, which wanted to have done with the legal reform that was to bring about the abolition of the private insurance companies—this did indeed take place as of 1 July 1906.[114] The new law on health and accident insurance of 1907, however, brought a bitter backlash for the efforts of the labor movement. On the grounds that employers and employees were henceforth to pay equal shares of insurance contributions, the principle of parity in the representation of both sides in the insurance funds was introduced.[115]

The 1907 law of health and accident insurance constituted a dramatic intervention in the organization of Hungarian social insurance in other regards as well, and led to far-reaching changes in how the social insurance system was positioned within the institutional and political structures of the

[113] Petrák, *Szervezett munkásság* [Organized workforce], 57–61, 66 f.; Sárdi, *A Kaposvári kerületi betegsegélyező pénztár* [Kaposvár District Health Insurance Company], 29–33.

[114] *A Munkás-betegsegélyezési törvény módosítása* [Modification of the Law on Workers' Sickness Benefits], 251, 253; *A Budapesti kerületi betegsegélyző pénztár XIII. évi jelentése, zárószámadása és kimutatásai az 1905. évről* [13th annual report, account settling and statement of the Budapest District Health Insurance Company for the year 1905] (Budapest 1906), 7–32; *A Budapesti kerületi általános munkás-betegsegélyző pénztár évi jelentése, zárószámadása és kimutatásai az 1906. évről* [Annual report, account settling and statement of the General Budapest District Workers' Insurance Company for the year 1906] (Budapest 1907), 12; Petrák, *Szervezett munkásság* [Organized workforce], 61 f., 67–72.

[115] Act 19/1907, §§41, 104, 106, and justification.

Hungarian state. First of all, the new law brought an end to the companies of the Trade Corporations and also, with a small number of specific exceptions, to private health insurance companies. The mining insurance companies managed to preserve their special status and independence. The remaining health insurance companies, operated on the district level or by companies—the latter being henceforth required by law to have at least 200 members—were incorporated into the National Workers' Health and Accident Insurance Company (*Országos betegsegélyző és balesetbiztosító pénztár*) as its local organs. The principle of parity applied for the general assembly, the management, and the board of directors. In the course of the parliamentary negotiations over the new law, however, without casting into question the basic principle of health insurance centralization, but contrary to the original legislative proposal, the District Insurance Companies were granted a right of disposal over part of any financial surpluses they might have. Secondly, the State Bureau for Workers' Insurance (*Állami munkásbiztosítási hivatal*) was created, a body that was to have a very powerful role in the new system. For example, the top positions in the newly created National Workers' Health and Accident Insurance Company could only be assigned with the endorsement of the Bureau; the Bureau was responsible for the closure or reorganization of workers' insurance companies, and it had extensive powers of inspection and review in any of their decisions. Within the State Bureau for Workers' Insurance the key positions were filled by state officials, and the roles of representatives of employers and employees were marginal. Thirdly, the new law created a large number of new decision-makers with regard to resolving various different disputes between employers and employees, employers and the National Insurance Company, and between the Company and those insured, and the Bureau for Workers' Insurance was one of these.[116]

While the new organizational structure brought with it new problems, it contributed little to solving some of the old ones. One new problem was the "constant … friction" that quickly was to become the distinguishing feature of the relationship between the new National Insurance Company as the main self-governing institution of workers' insurance and the State Bureau, which was appointed to supervise the Company.[117] This "friction"

---

[116] Act 19/1907; *A Magyar Királyi Kormány* [The Royal Hungarian Government] 1907, 68 f.; 1908, 70 f.; Heller, *Magyarország szociálpolitikája* [Social policy of Hungary], 47 f.

[117] There were also disagreements at the outset in the relationship between the Zagreb Workers' Insurance Bureau and the Zagreb National Company. *Munkásügyi Szemle* 1 (1910): 242. For conditions in the Hungarian Kingdom, *A magyar társadalombiztosítás*

began as early as the preparation and decision-making regarding the statutes of the newly established National Company and the convocation of its first general meeting,[118] and continued with constant disagreements over such matters as the level of contributions and many other questions.[119] Given that the lawmakers had settled on a complex diversity of channels and decision-makers in labor insurance, the constant need for clarification and the "friction" between the National Company and the Bureau for Workers' Insurance was unavoidable.[120] All this was well known both to those involved and to the general public. In the opinion of opponents of the National Company, it was the representatives of this body itself who broadcast the constant "dissonance" in the relationship between the Bureau and the National Company "to the public at every single opportunity." As a result of this publicity, those who took an interest were well aware that workers' insurance was an area of many unresolved and contentious legal and political problems, and that this situation offered ample opportunity to pursue particular interests at all times. This made "the situation of the [National] Company in dealing with doctors and the authorities even more difficult."[121]

Opponents of workers' insurance or of self-government within the insurance system seized on the creation of the State Bureau for Workers' Insurance in addition to the National Company as an excuse to get up in arms about the rapidly increasing costs that they saw as a consequence. In reality, however, the Bureau was an administrative instrument that, as a newly created separate body, was concerned with social insurance agendas that had hitherto been dealt with within the ministry. As a consequence of this hate campaign against the new organizational structure of the Hungarian workers' insurance system, the National Company felt the need to defend this structure against wide-ranging accusations in its first annual report. It pointed out that the State Bureau, contrary to accusations, was not financed from insurance contributions but by the state. In turn, the National Company, as an institution of labor insurance must continue to exist, and to exist

ötven éve 1892-1942 [Fifty years of Hungarian social insurance 1892–1942] (Budapest, no year given), 21.

[118] E.g. *Munkásbiztositási Közlöny* 1 (1907): 211–224.

[119] E.g. *Munkásbiztositási Közlöny* 4 (1910): 468 f., 482–490; 5 (1911): 37–44, 137 f., 172 f.

[120] Heller, *Magyarország szociálpolitikája* [Social policy of Hungary], 52 f., and e.g. *Munkásbiztositasi Közlöny* 1 (1907): 109, 115 f., 203 f.; 2 (1908): 37 f., 189, 275 f., 317 f., 1321, 1314 f., 1442; 3 (1909): 109, 134 f.

[121] *Szociálpolitikai Szemle* 3 (1913): 215; *A magyar társadalombiztosítás ötven éve* [Fifty years of Hungarian social insurance], 21.

on the basis of self-government.[122] In the final years before the war, the attacks on the existing structure of labor insurance continued to grow. The high point was the inaugural address of the new prime minister, Kálmán Tisza, to Parliament in 1913, in which he attacked workers' insurance head on as a system that already "in its inception had set off in the wrong direction." Criticisms against the labor insurance system in the Hungarian press now reached fever pitch. There were calls for the management of the insurance system to be partly or completely taken over by the state, effectively amounting to the abolition of the National Company or at least of its self-government. The State Bureau for Workers' Insurance also became once again the target of the opponents of the health and accident insurance companies. The "discrete silence" of the Bureau over the years, it was said, hid nothing more than weakness and hesitancy, and the Bureau had failed to curb the rowdy, politically red misdeeds of the Fund.[123]

The institutional integration of labor in the system of the National Company in fact played a significant role in the development of "dissonance" between the Company on the one hand, and the Bureau and the opponents of self-governance on the other. The National Company developed to a large extent into an institution of the organized labor movement. This was partly due to the fact that the labor movement—otherwise scarcely perceived as an acceptable or respectable policymaker on the Hungarian political scene—now recognized and sought to make use of the new social and socio-political possibilities provided by labor insurance as a state-organized institution integrated into the network of public infrastructure and authorities. In its party conference of 1907, the Social Democratic Party reached a decision—in the light of the upcoming elections to the self-government of the National Company—that made it clear that the Party would make every effort to secure as many positions as possible in the management of the National Company. And indeed thereafter many top members of the party were elevated to leading positions in the Company, and for a small host of comrades from the second and third ranks, employment with the Company became the mainstay of their personal existence. The Party also pushed for such training, attainment of academic

[122] *Az Országos munkásbetegsegélyző és balesetbiztosító pénztár első évi jelentése (1907–1908)* [First annual report of the National Company for Workers' Health and Accident Insurance (1907–1908)] (Budapest 1909), 31 ff.

[123] *Országgyűlési Képviselőház Naplói* [Chronicle of the House of Parliamentary Representatives] 1910/1915, vol. XIX, 76; *Szociálpolitikai Szemle* 3 (1913): 186 f., 204, 215–220; 4 (1914): 192, 257; *Munkásbiztositási Közlöny* 7 (1913): 34 ff; 8 (1914): 409 f.

rank and so on as were necessary to make its representatives eligible for higher-ranking positions within the National Company.[124] At the same time, like in other countries, the almost proverbial lack of interest on the part of employers in using the potential of joint decision-making that was their right, based on the parity principle for representation in the National Company, soon became evident. As a result, the organized labor force was able to take disproportionate advantage of its influence within the Company. Accordingly, the quasi-state Bureau for Workers' Insurance was conceived by the workers' movement as its key political opponent within the labor insurance system. In turn, those political forces who struggled against the influence of the organized labor movement within the national labor insurance system sought to maximize their influence over the Bureau. There were also efforts to limit the influence of the workers' movement in the National Company through amendments to the law. For example, there were attempts to change the method of voting within the management of the Company so that regardless of the number of those present from either side, the number of votes would be equally balanced, or to transfer the right to appoint personnel of the health and accident insurance companies to the state.[125]

In another problem area of the workers' insurance system, the relationship with the medical profession, the reform of 1907 initially exacerbated the conflict. During the preparations for the new law, the policy of the medical profession was geared towards, on the one hand, reducing the upper income limit for obligatory insurance so as to gain a larger number of private patients. On the other hand, there were efforts to improve the remuneration of doctors who treated insured patients. Before and after the enactment of the law, the doctors persistently demanded a fee of six crowns per individual member of an insurance company or nine crowns per member with a family.[126] Another point of contention was the ques-

[124] There was also criticism within the Social Democratic Party of the insurance policy pursued by the party being one of seeking material benefit and employment opportunities, and opportunistic currying of favor with the government. Petrák, *Szervezett munkásság* [Organized workforce], 78–83.

[125] *Magyar Ipar* 31 (1910): 33; *Munkásbiztositás* 1, no. 2 (1908): 4 f.

[126] The National Company estimated that at such a payment rate it would have had to pay out 60 to 70 percent of its annual income for the payment of doctors. In reality in 1908 on average for every health service doctor there were 329 insured members and an average annual contribution per member per year of 3.51 crowns. *Az Országos pénztár jelentése 1907–1908* [Annual report of the National Company 1907–1908], 56 ff, 60–64; *Munkásbiztositási Szemle* 3, no. 1 (1910): 3.

tion whether there should be a system of free choice of doctor, as the doctors themselves demanded, or a "fixed system." From the point of view of the National Company, the advantage of the fixed system was greater control over the quality of the doctors, that their selected doctors were at least in principle interested in cooperation with the Fund, and that the Company gained a certain supervisory role regarding the treatment of the insured by its selected doctors.[127] Yet negotiations between the Company and the medical profession over the creation of a nationwide system failed. Because according to §133 of Act 19/1907, the District Insurance companies were still able to make their own agreements with doctors, the conflict was shifted increasingly back to the local level, where the District Companies met with an increasingly well-organized medical profession. The vast majority of District Companies outside the Budapest district rapidly decided, after the 1907 reforms, in favor of a "system of permanent appointment" of doctors. The management of the National Company too soon spoke out in favor of such a system.[128] The powerful Budapest District Company—since 1906 amalgamated with the former General Company of the workers' movement—had initially worked with a system of free choice of doctors in the 1890s. After the resistance of the workers' representatives, who feared the freedom of the insured to choose their own doctor, had delayed the reform for years, in 1899 a system of salaried doctors was finally introduced, with the doctors under the supervision of the District Company. As a compromise towards the interests of the patients, the insured could still choose between a considerable number of doctors—excluding only practices in further away districts. In addition, an outpatients' clinic for insured patients was created.[129] In 1906 the already

127 *Az Országos pénztár jelentése 1907–1908* [Annual report of the National Company 1907–1908], 58 f.

128 *Az Országos pénztár jelentése 1907–1908* [Annual report of the National Company 1907–1908], 56 ff, 60–64, 70; *Az Országos munkásbetegsegélyző és balesetbiztosító pénztar második évi jelentése (1909)* [Second annual report of the National Company for Workers' Health and Accident Insurance (1909)] (Budapest 1910), 201.

129 *A Budapesti kerületi betegsegélyző pénztár I. évi jelentése, zárószámadása és kimutatásai 1892 decz. 15-től 1893 decz. 31-ig* [First annual report, account settling and statement of the Budapest District Health Insurance Company from 15 December 1892 to 31 December 1893] (Budapest 1894), 11; *A Budapesti kerületi betegsegélyző pénztár IV. évi jelentése, zárószámadása és kimutatásai az 1896. évről* [4th annual report, account settling and statement of the Budapest District Health Insurance Company for the year 1896] (Budapest, 1897), 8; *A Budapesti kerületi betegsegélyző pénztár VII. évi jelentése, zárószámadása és kimutatásai az 1899. évről* [7th annual report, account settling and statement of the Budapest District Health Insurance Company for the year

amalgamated District Company in and around Budapest—the Budapest district was larger than the capital city itself—employed 229 doctors. In its capacity as the district "organ" of the new National Company, the Budapest District Company then concluded a new agreement on medical provision, and also placed great emphasis on the further development of the system of outpatients' clinics and the creation of new doctor's positions. By the end of 1908, the Budapest District Company already employed 370 doctors within and outside the city of Budapest, of which 136 were working in the Company's own outpatient's clinics.[130]

As a whole, in the years following the 1907 reform of labor insurance, increasing numbers of the supporters of the system of workers' insurance took the position that it would be sensible to make concessions to doctors with regard to remuneration. In this way conflicts might be reduced, an increasing level of medical care ensured, and as these political forces put it, the interests of the insurance companies and the doctors could be merged. In addition, it was argued, such a policy would help to fill the district medical officer positions that in some places were still unoccupied. If the position of a health insurance physician was added to the position of district medical officer, moving to a remote district would become financially more attractive for doctors. The additional costs incurred by the insurance companies, if the higher salaries or benefits for doctors were accepted, would ultimately have to be met by increasing the insurance contributions deducted from employers and employees.[131] The minister officially put paid to this plan to combine the role of official district doctor and health insurance physician, however, clearly taking sides for the interests of the anti-workers' insurance doctors' lobby. This was not the only topic to remain contested.[132] A significant part of the organized medical profession continued over the years to

1899] (Budapest 1900), 31–38; *A Budapesti kerületi betegsegélyző pénztár IX. évi jelentése, zárószámadása és kimutatásai az 1901. évről* [9th annual report, account settling and statement of the Budapest District Health Insurance Company for the year 1901] (Budapest 1902), 29 ff.

130 *A Budapesti kerületi általános munkás-betegsegélyző pénztár 1906* [The General Budapest District Workers' Health Insurance Company 1906] (Budapest 1907), 19; *A Budapesti kerületi munkásbiztositó pénztár évi jelentése, zárószámadása és kimutatásai az 1908. évről* [Annual report, account settling and statement of the Budapest District Workers' Insurance Company for the year 1908] (Budapest 1909), 5, 18.

131 *Munkásügyi Szemle* 1 (1910): 62 f.; *Munkásbiztositási Közlöny* 5 (1911): 511 ff., 659.

132 *Munkásbiztositási Közlöny* 2 (1908): 455; *Munkásügyi Szemle* 2 (1911): 704; *Szociálpolitikai Szemle* 3 (1913): 289 f.

openly pursue a professional policy that was directed against the interests of labor insurance.[133]

There was also systemic conflict, however, between the different institutions within the system of labor insurance. Particularly, the relationship between the National Company and the district funds was far from straightforward. A large share of the problems in this relationship basically stemmed from the construction of financial relations between the two sides on the legal level. Specifically, the District Companies were required to pay two thirds of their annual surpluses to the National Company, while the National Company was obliged to take responsibility for the possible financial shortfall of any subordinated company. Moreover, the district funds had a certain independent decision-making power with regard to their expenditures, although the National Company and the State Bureau for Workers' Insurance took their rights of supervision and intervention very seriously in this regard.[134] The fact that financial relations were constructed this way within the workers' insurance system facilitated the propensity for some District Companies to allocate benefits generously, and generally to adopt a laid-back attitude to the collection of arrears and other budgetary questions.[135] Added to this was the introduction of obligatory benefits for family members and dependants according to the law of 1907, which turned out to be a very expensive innovation.[136] Farkas Heller, a balanced and experienced expert of the subject matter pointedly summarized the consequences of the legal construction of the relationship between the National Company and workers' insurance on the local level. "[T]he surpluses" of the district funds, Heller wrote, "were counted against the arrears" of these funds so that the National Company received its share of the surplus only theoretically, "while [the National Company] itself had to pay the shortfalls of the district funds in cash."[137]

The inherited problem of outstanding contributions plagued Hungarian labor insurance up to World War I, accompanied by constant complaints about the situation and fruitless efforts to create the conditions for change. There was no real solution to the aversion of employers to insurance and

---

[133] *Munkásügyi Szemle* 3 (1912): 101; *Szociálpolitikai Szemle* 3 (1913): 289 f.

[134] Act 19/1907, §§102, 105, 118, 122, 124, 133; *Munkásbiztositási Közlöny* 3 (1909): 223 f.; 7 (1913): 746 f.

[135] *Munkásbiztositási Közlöny* 2 (1908): 1331 f.; 8 (1914): 189 ff., 293.

[136] The minimal scope of services for non-earning family members living in the same household as the insured was 20 weeks of medical care and midwifery. Act 19/1907, §50; Heller, *Magyarország szociálpolitikája* [Social policy of Hungary], 59.

[137] Heller, *Magyarország szociálpolitikája* [Social policy of Hungary], 47 f., 54 ff.

to the—in fact fraudulent—practice of deducting the 50 percent employee's contribution from his or her wages without registering the employee or paying the contributions. Even the state itself left much to be desired in its capacity as an employer in this regard. According to the law of 1907, civil servants were required to be registered in the insurance system, yet in reality as a rule employees in the relevant institutions were often not registered, while at the same time the Budapest District Company initially still had to pay for their treatment. Eventually, the problem was resolved: the National Company received a lump sum payment of arrears for the years from 1907 to 1910, and at the same time a regulation was passed freeing civil servants from obligatory registration in the workers' insurance system. From the point of view of the National Company, this was not a sustainable solution however, because the coverage of labor insurance, that is the percentage of the labor force that was subject to compulsory workers' insurance, was reduced as a result. Similar longstanding problems with other public, i.e. local and regional authorities as employers also remained unaddressed. As regards other employers, the various health and accident insurance companies demonstrated again and again that without a change to the legal system on which the collection of contributions was based, there would be no change in their reluctance to pay and its consequences. The National Company tried repeatedly to anticipate such a reform on its own initiative. For example, in 1912 it instructed its district subsidiaries to use whatever means possible to get the overburdened local authorities to employ an executor, paid by the insurance company, to collect outstanding contributions. In 1913 it was once again legally established[138] that employers who collected the employee's contribution without paying it into the fund were guilty of the crime of embezzlement. The minister for the interior for his part instructed local authorities in 1909, and again in 1914, to make greater efforts in the collection of insurance arrears. Yet there was no real improvement in this regard before the outbreak of the war. In the final years before the war, the Budapest District Company revealed even higher outstanding debts than in the previous years, amounting to 30–40 percent of the actually required contributions. A comparison of the outstanding accounts of the Austrian and Hungarian social insurance companies makes clear that the problem

[138] There had already been a ruling of this sort by a higher court in 1895, however, the insurance funds could gain little benefit from it because in order to prove embezzlement it was first necessary to prove that employee's share of the contributions had actually been deducted. *Magyar Ipar* 19, no. 22 (1898), supplement: 1.

of contribution arrears really did occupy a central place in Hungarian labor insurance. While in 1909 the outstandings of the Austrian fund amounted to 6.7 million crowns or 8.3 percent of a total income of 80.8 crowns, in Hungary in 1911, outstandings amounted to 8.1 million crowns or 27.1 percent of the total income of 29.9 million crowns.[139]

The permanently difficult to hopeless financial situation of Hungarian labor insurance with regard to income was not only due to the issue of arrears, however. There was in addition the serious problem that the resistance of various groups of employers as well as the attitude of the legislative body and other higher ranking public authorities than labor insurance prevented an appropriate configuration of the system of contributions. Disagreements in this regard focused on two main issues. One constant bone of contention was the fact that the law of 1907 prohibited the health and accident insurance companies for a period of five years from levying more than two percent of the daily wage as a health insurance contribution in the case of small businesses, specifically businesses which did not regularly employ more than five people.[140] The new National Company kicked up a fuss from the outset about this reduced scale which amounted to an attack on "the finances of the Company in its very foundations." When the five-year period ran out in 1912, the National Company ordered an immediate switch to the three-percent scale that applied for all other enterprises.[141] The second area of disagreement was the question whether the calculation of contributions should be based on seven or six days' wage per week. From August 1908 to the end of 1910—"to the great surprise and disappointment of the Company"—a variation of the six-day scale was applied, according to which contributions were to be calculated on the basis of days actually worked. From the point of view of the National Company, who held on fast to its divergent interpretation of the legal regulations, this had considerable negative consequences with regard to loss of revenue. Only in 1911, after years of resistance, did the State Bu-

139 *Munkásbiztositási Közlöny* 3 (1909): 157 f., 301; 4 (1910): 301, 449; 6 (1912): 169, 918; 7 (1913): 113, 128 f., 132 f., 935 f., 949 ff.; 8 (1914): 409, 919 f.; *Az Országos pénztár jelentése 1907–1908* [Annual report of the National Company 1907–1908], 30; *A Budapesti kerületi munkásbiztositó pénztár évi jelentése, zárószámadása és kimutatásai az 1913. évről* [Annual report, account settling and statement of the Budapest District Workers' Insurance Company for the year 1913] (Budapest 1914), 7, 14 ff., 21.

140 According to the law, the contribution scale was allowed to vary between two and four percent. Act 19/1907, §25.

141 *Az Országos pénztár jelentése 1907–1908* [Annual report of the National Company 1907–1908], 29; *Munkásbiztositási Közlöny* 6 (1912): 903.

reau for Workers' Insurance decide that at least for those businesses with more than five regular employees, a seven-day scale should be used.[142]

With regard to expenditures too, apart from the easy budget morals of local insurance companies and the new and expensive obligatory health care for family members mentioned above, there were numerous problems. Just one of these was the fact that when members of one of the health and accident insurance companies existing in one district had exhausted the 20 weeks of health care benefits they were entitled to, they switched to a different district in order to claim new health care from another fund. There were attempts to circumvent this last problem since 1909 through regular publication of an ever increasing list of names of company members who had exhausted their 20-week entitlement.[143] Another common concern evolved around the question of decision-making power in cases when it was to be determined whether or not an insured individual should be hospitalized. The insurance companies argued that they were liable to recourse of the costs of hospitalization only in those cases when the responsible insurance company itself had recommended the hospitalization. Conversely, there were regular complaints and criticisms from the regulatory authorities that the insurance companies did not reimburse the expenses of hospitals punctually or regularly (and this was indeed the case), that the funds delayed referral for inpatient treatment even after this was recommended by health insurance physicians, and so on.[144] A problem of significantly greater consequence occurred due to particular policies of financing the hospital care of the poor as part of the official state care financed by the State Healthcare Fund. In the grey area between this state welfare obligation and the—albeit clearly limited—responsibility of the workers' insurance for the hospital care of its insured and their dependents without income, diverse authorities and decision-making bodies made sure that the insurance companies had to shoulder ever increasing responsibilities and financial burdens.[145]

All in all, it can be seen that Hungarian labor insurance suffered not only from organizational and administrative problems, and from obstructive behavior on the part of employers and to an extent also the medical

[142] *Munkásügyi Szemle* 2 (1911): 61 f.; *Munkásbiztosítás* 2, no. 16 (1909): 4 ff.; *A Budapesti kerületi pénztár 1913* [The Budapest District Company 1913], 6 f.

[143] E.g. *Munkásbiztositási Közlöny* 3 (1909): 11 f., 76.

[144] Added to this there was also often an extreme shortage of beds. *Az Országos pénztár jelentése 1907–1908* [Annual Report of the National Company 1907–1908], 72 ff.; *Munkásbiztositasi Közlöny* 2 (1908): 1343; 3 (1909): 45, 170; 4 (1910): 449.

[145] See the section on "Social insurance and welfare" in chapter IV.2.3.

profession, but also from the fact that in determining rates for contributions, constantly conflicting interests had to be taken into account. Added to this were the two great structural problems of low coverage and the limits to the capacities of social-political action from which social insurance suffered. The low numbers and quotas of insured—a fact underlined for example in comparison to Austria[146]—had serious negative administrative and budgetary consequences. The causes of limited coverage were not only the structural-administrative problems within the workers' insurance as an institution within a particular political and social context (described above), and a number of additional developments to be described in the next chapter, but also the low level of industrialization of the country. As far as the capacities of social-political action were concerned, it was a key problem that the workers' insurance system was, and could be, only partly successful in separating social insurance from the responsibility for the far-reaching problems of poverty and social marginality. This was not only because the insurance companies themselves and other important authorities had not made sufficient efforts. Rather, labor insurance was constantly under pressure in various ways from a social "environment" in which other basic elements necessary for making a living and of social welfare were absent or highly inadequate. This was a common problem across several individual areas of social policy—such as the child protection system described in chapter III.1—in which the state saw itself obliged to turn its back on the classical liberal philosophy of minimalism in welfare-policy.

In spite of all these problems, however, Hungarian labor insurance did become an important component of a clearly visible expansion of social governance and the welfare-political role of the state. Organized labor also played a role in this development, as against all odds and despite ongoing political struggle it acquired a position within the system of social insurance. The status of the workers' movement within social insurance, a new element in the local and national network of institutions and public authorities in Hungary of the time, was unique as compared to the overall status of the workers' movement in the country. This fact at least partly explains why the Hungarian social insurance met with such vigorous resistance from so many sides.

[146] For the data and the comparison to Austria, see the section "Coverage: overview and comparison of long-term trends" of chapter IV.2.3.

IV.2.3. Coverage, boundaries, dissociations and relations: social insurance and the formation and differentiation of working and living conditions

The extent to which the overall population and the workforce were covered by the various types of health and accident insurance changed over time and varied greatly between different regions, groups and types of employment or labor relations. The remainder of this chapter explores the long-term development of overall coverage and variation and its underlying causes, as well as the boundary lines that were drawn by and within the system of social insurance between workers to be insured and those excluded from compulsory social insurance. It also describes how in various areas these boundaries were constantly contested. This process was closely related to particular visions of social and labor relations, at times controversial political interests, and the problem of material need experienced by large parts of the population. The politics of including various employment sectors, labor relations, and groups of the population into social insurance while excluding others from the same system had a considerable impact on the formation and differentiation of working and living conditions of the working population and their family members.

Coverage: overview and comparison of long-term trends

Although the socio-political relevance of social insurance for a growing share of the working population—and beyond the insured individual to their dependents—was uncontested, coverage as a whole remained limited. This was true for social insurance for both agricultural workers and employees in trade and industry.

The share of the population (workforce and dependents) in agriculture and forestry in the Kingdom of Hungary in 1910 was still 63 percent—more than a fifth higher than in Cisleithania, where it was 48 percent.[147] For this reason, but also due to the outstanding importance of agricultural (export) production in the Hungarian economy as a whole and sectors of industry directly dependent on and related to it, the special form of agri-

[147] Birgit Bolognese-Leuchtenmüller, *Bevölkerungsentwicklung und Berufsstruktur, Gesundheits- und Fürsorgewesen in Österreich 1750–1918* [Population development and occupational structure, the healthy and welfare system in Austria 1750–1918] (Vienna 1978), 179–208, Table 60; *1910. évi népszámlálás* [Census results 1910], vols. XLVI, XLVIII; own calculations.

cultural accident and invalid insurance in the Kingdom of Hungary was of particular importance in the political process and in public debate. The figures in Table 3, however, show that the coverage of voluntary agricultural insurance remained marginal, while agricultural compulsory accident insurance, albeit providing very limited benefits, nonetheless included one employee in every ten in primary production.

Table 3: Numbers and Share of Insured in National Insurance for Agricultural Workers and Servants

Year	Voluntary insurance		Compulsory accident insurance			
	Number of insured	Share of insured as percentage of the workforce in primary production	Number of insured	Share of the insured as percentage of the workforce in primary production	Agricultural machine operators (among the compulsory insured)	
					Number of insured	Percentage among compulsory insured
1902	14,602	-	420,807	-	-	-
1904	30,399	-	487,867	-	-	-
1906	34,167	-	491,093	-	-	-
1908	37,784	-	525,447	-	-	-
1910	40,119	0,86%	543,399	11,7%	128,130 [(a)]	23,6%

(a) This figure is based on an estimate by the National Insurance for Agricultural Workers and Servants that calculated 10 machine operators per "machine operator policy."

Sources: *Az Országos gazdasági munkás- és cselédsegélypénztár első tíz évi működése (1901–1910) és X. évi jelentése a pénztár 1910 évi működéséről* [The first ten years activity of the National Insurance for Agricultural Workers and Servants (1901–1910) and 10th annual report on the activity of the insurance in 1910] (Budapest 1911); *1910. évi népszámlálás* [Census results 1910], vol. XLVIII; own calculations.

The figures for workers' insurance also show that its coverage related to the population as a whole, the labor force and for the labor force excluding primary production remained limited. It has to be taken into account, however, that even before 1907, and after the 1907 reform in much larger numbers, dependents, who are not included in Table 4, also benefited from the insurance.

Table 4: Insurance Figures and Share in Health Insurance (HI) and Accident Insurance (AI) in Hungary and Selected Insurance Districts[(a)] 1900 and 1910

Year, Insurance branch, Insurance district	Number of insured (annual average)	Share of the population (%)	Share of the labor force (%)	Share of the labor force without primary production (%)
1900 – HI				
Kingdom of Hungary	593,588 [(b)]	3.5	7.9	22.7
Budapest [(c)]	250,351 [(b) (d)]	27.5	55.0	60.9
1910 [(e)] – HI				
Kingdom of Hungary	1,007,586	5.5	13.4	32.6
Budapest [(c)]	368,654 [(d) (f)]	31.1	60.2	65.6
	282,903 [(f) (g)]	23.9	46.2	50.4
Pozsony	25,216 [(h)]	11.1	24.0	40.3
Nagyvárad	25,165 [(h)]	4.3	9.6	32.7
Temesvár	20,773 [(h)]	8.3	18.9	73.0
1910 [(e)] – AI				
Kingdom of Hungary	850,677	4.0	9.4	23.7
Budapest [(c)]	368,654	26.0	50.3	54.8
Pozsony	19,655	8.6	18.7	31.4
Nagyvárad	18,557	3.1	7.1	24.1
Temesvár	15,972	6.3	14.5	56.3

(a) The selected districts are those where the largest number of employees in trade and industry were counted at the beginning of the 1890s. In 1910 these districts still belonged to those with the highest numbers of insured.

(b) Number of insured at the end of the year.

(c) The Budapest District Insurance company also covered a considerable part of the outer conurbation area of the city. The figures for population and labor force occasionally might apply to a marginally different area.

(d) Including those insured by insurance funds operated by companies who were resident in the insurance district of Budapest; these data in some cases included insured who were in fact employed in branches of the relevant companies outside the Budapest district.

(e) The figures for the number of insured are for 1911; those for the population and labor force are from the census of 31 December 1910.

(f) A small number of individuals exceptionally insured by still existing private funds are not included.

(g) Not including those insured by the company insurance fund of the Hungarian State Railways, the largest company fund in the country with around 85,000 members; all Hungarian State Railways workers were registered under those insured in the Budapest insurance district.

(h) Amongst the company funds only those based in Pozsony, Nagyvárad or Temesvár are included. The area for which the figures for population and labor force apply might differ slightly from the area covered by the district insurance companies.

Sources: *Az Országos munkásbetegsegélyező és balesetbiztosító pénztár negyedik évi jelentése (1911)* [Fourth annual report (1911) of the National Workers' Health and Accident Insurance Company] (Budapest 1912); *1900. évi népszámlálás* [Census results 1900], vol. II; *1910. évi népszámlálás* [Census results 1910], vols. XLVIII, LVI; *A Budapesti kerületi munkásbiztosító pénztár évi jelentése, zárószámadása és kimutatásai az 1913. évről* [Annual report, account settling and statement of the Budapest District Workers' Insurance Company for the year 1913] (Budapest 1914); own calculations.

As regards workers' insurance, the share of those insured and the development of this share over time was basically influenced by four factors. First there was the fact that a considerable number of individuals were not insured in spite of an existing obligation. After a tour of Somogy County in 1899, for example, the representative of the relevant trade inspectorate reported to the minister responsible that here "only some 30–40 percent of commercial workers" were insured. When the secretary of the District Insurance Company himself examined the situation in the county in 1900, he discovered that in the district of Marcali, in which not one insured individual was registered, several trade companies with employees were operating. [148] The second factor was the changes in work relations in the area of commercial work, or work outside the agricultural sector, such as the decline of small-scale industry or the diminishing number of domestic servants, that is the transformation of bonded labor not covered by the workers' insurance, into free labor. The third important factor was the fact that agricultural production was losing ground in the economy in comparison to industry and commerce, and the share of the workforce employed in this area, or in primary production as a whole, was decreasing, as mentioned above. And finally, reforms in the regulations on labor insurance also played an important role—whether at the legal level or by government decree—as did changes in legal practice. The sudden spurt in those insured as a share of the labor force as a whole in Hungary in the first decade of the new century, as can be seen from the figures in Table 4, was in no small part due to the reform of the legal framework in 1907. This increase also represents a process of catching-up in terms of insurance coverage with Cisleithania, where the relevant share of insured grew from

[148] Sárdi, *A Kaposvári kerületi betegsegélyező pénztár* [Kaposvár District Health Insurance Company], 44, 52, including original quotations.

18.2 to 23.3 percent between 1900 and 1910.[149] The catching-up process, however, started from a comparatively very low level.

There was marked regional diversity in terms of the share of insured as part of the labor force in both health and accident insurance. This was true when those selected insurance districts are compared that were centers of trade and commerce[150] and are highlighted in Table 4. If these selected districts are compared to the national average, the differences are very marked. With the exception of the Nagyvárad district, the share of insured in all of the insurance districts selected here was far higher than the national average, though at the same time the Pozsony and Temesvár districts lagged far behind the district which included the Hungarian capital. This outstanding status of Budapest and its outer conurbation in the matter of health insurance coverage is very much comparable with the ratio in Cisleithania, where the share of insured among the labor force in the imperial capital, Vienna, reached 64.8 percent in 1910.[151] The figures in Table 4 also show that the backwardness of the districts of Pozsony, Temesvár and Nagyvárad was to a large—though in each case different—extent due to the comparatively higher share of the workforce employed in primary production. The high level of coverage of labor insurance in the districts of Budapest and Temesvár was doubtless related to what contemporary writers liked to call the progressive and even industrial character of labor relations in trade and commerce in these areas in comparison to other regions.

All in all then, labor insurance increased the distance between rural and urban social relations, and between "progressive" and "less progressive" labor relations. The politics of workers' insurance in effect privileged urban areas as well as "progressive" labor relations. Thus it created new distinctions between the working and living conditions of those who enjoyed work-related social security and those who did not. As shown in

[149] The figures for Cisleithania are taken from Susan Zimmermann, "Geschützte und ungeschützte Arbeitsverhältnisse von der Hochindustrialisierung bis zur Weltwirtschaftskrise. Österreich und Ungarn im Vergleich" [Protected and unprotected labor relations from the peak of industrialization to the Great Depression], in: Andrea Komlosy, Christof Parnreiter, Irene Stacher, Susan Zimmermann, eds. *Ungeregelt and unterbezahlt. Der informelle Sektor in der Weltwirtschaft* [Unregulated and underpaid. The informal sector in the world economy] (Frankfurt/M. – Vienna 1997), 87–115, here 91, Table 1.

[150] See note (a) in Table 4.

[151] The municipal area of Vienna had been enlarged in 1904/1905 so as to include larger parts of the conurbation. Zimmermann, "Geschützte und ungeschützte Arbeitsverhältnisse" [Protected and unprotected labor relations], 91, Table 1.

Table 5, beyond the distinctions already discussed, the politics of workers' insurance also involved a gendered dimension.

Table 5: Paid Employment and Health and Accident Insurance (HI and AI) of Women in Hungary 1910(a)

<table>
<tr><th rowspan="3">Area</th><th colspan="2" rowspan="2">Women insured (annual average):</th><th colspan="3">Percentage of women:</th></tr>
<tr><th rowspan="2">in the labor force</th><th colspan="2">among the insured</th></tr>
<tr><th>in HI</th><th>in AI</th><th>in HI</th><th>in AI</th></tr>
<tr><td>Kingdom of Hungary</td><td>145,289</td><td>106,331</td><td>23.6%</td><td>13.0%</td><td>12.2%</td></tr>
<tr><td>Budapest (b)</td><td>48,552 (c)
46,742 (d)</td><td>36,816</td><td>34.9%</td><td>13.2% (c)</td><td>12.0%
16.5% (d)</td></tr>
</table>

(a) The figures for the numbers insured are for 1911, those for the (working) population from the census of 31 December 1910.
(b) The figures for the labor force are for the administrative area of Budapest, those for the insured for the insurance district of Budapest, which also included a significant part of the surrounding area of the capital.
(c) Including the Company Fund of the Hungarian State Railways; see also note (g) in Table 4.
(d) Excluding the Company Fund of the Hungarian State Railways; see also note (g) in Table 4.

Sources: *Az Országos munkásbetegsegélyző és balesetbiztositó negyedik évi jelentése (1911)* [Fourth annual report of the National Workers' Health and Accident Insurance Company (1911)] (Budapest 1912); *1910. évi népszámlálás* [Census results 1910], vols. XLVIII, LVI; *A Budapesti kerületi munkásbisztositó Pénztár statisztikai kimutatásai az 1918. évről* [Statistical disclosure of the Budapest District Workers' Insurance Company for the year 1918] (Budapest, no year given); own calculations.

The percentage of women amongst the insured in both health and accident insurance remained markedly lower than the percentage of women in the labor force as a whole. In Budapest, the difference between the share of women in the workforce (which was considerably higher than the national average) and the share of women amongst the insured was more pronounced than in the country as a whole. Comparison with the imperial capital, Vienna, makes clear just how glaring this difference between the percentage of women among the insured and within the workforce in Budapest was. The share of women in the working population in Vienna, at 36.6 percent, was negligibly higher than that in Budapest, while the share of women amongst the insured in Vienna, at 29.9 percent, was more than double that in the insurance district of Budapest.[152]

For Hungary, the comparison of the overall national figures with those of Budapest is a particularly clear indication that the underrepresentation of women in labor insurance was closely related to the criteria for inclusion or exclusion from labor insurance in trade and commercial employment as established by the workers' insurance. The new social insurance created distinctions between the insured and the uninsured in a gender-politically highly relevant way, which in effect resulted in gendered discrimination against working women.[153] Those areas of employment and sectors of the labor market where women dominated—most notably the large sector of domestic service—were characterized in a more pronounced manner than other areas of employment and sectors of the labor market, some of them dominated by men, by labor relations which were not covered by social insurance. For this reason, and for other reasons that will be discussed below,[154] the development of a separate area of socially insured employment relations contributed—besides the special labor protection for women discussed earlier—to increasing the distance between women's and men's working and living conditions.

Compulsory insurance of workers and differentiation of commercial labor relations

The previous section has shown that the character and changes to employment relations and conditions in trade and commerce—referred to here as commercial employment relations—were some of the key factors that had a major influence on coverage and the percentage of those (among the population and the labor force) with labor insurance. This section explores how this state of affairs came about through the drawing of various boundary lines between those who had compulsory insurance and those sectors of the workforce and groups of individuals who contin-

---

[152] The figures for Vienna are taken from Susan Zimmermann, "Frauenarbeit, soziale Politiken and die Umgestaltung von Geschlechterverhältnissen im Wien der Habsburgermonarchie" [Women's labor, social policies and the transformation of relations between the sexes in Vienna under the Habsburg Monarchy], in: Lisa Fischer, Emil Brix, eds. *Die Frauen der Wiener Moderne* [Women in modern Vienna] (Vienna–Munich 1997), 34–52, here 45, Table 1.

[153] The relevant mechanisms for Vienna are discussed in detail in Zimmermann, "Frauenarbeit" [Women's labor], 45–48.

[154] See the section on "Compulsory insurance of male and female workers" in this chapter.

ued to lack compulsory insurance (though they could have taken out such insurance voluntarily).

Regulations regarding which types of company and employment relations were to be included in compulsory insurance and which excluded were one important factor responsible for the drawing of these lines. Insofar as particular groups of the workforce, such as for example workers in rural areas or women, were disproportionately represented in those types of companies and employment relations that did not involve compulsory insurance, they were consequently disproportionately excluded. Secondly, practices aimed at bypassing compulsory insurance, such as illegal employment, failure to register employees and so on, as well as disputed interpretation of the existing regulations, played an important role in the shaping of these dividing lines.

There were three particularly problematic areas in defining who was to be insured. These were the treatment of small businesses, home workers and the problems connected to insecure employment, i.e. employment that was irregular, not formalized, or paid on a daily basis. The handling of these three problem areas of the world of work within the historically new policy framework of labor insurance was contentious not only in Hungary and Austria, but also in other countries. The at times bitter altercations on the related elements of the definition of who was and who was not to be insured played their part in shaping perceptions of what was proper work, as well as in some ways normatively establishing hierarchical distinctions between different types of labor relations.

The Hungarian health insurance law of 1891 contained distinctions between workers who were obliged to be insured and "other" workers that were in several regards ambiguous. In consequence, legal practice was repeatedly concerned with the exact definition of the boundaries and with establishing the exact meaning of the existing legal prescriptions. Agricultural employees and domestic servants were unambiguously excluded from labor insurance. However, certain grey areas between agricultural and commercial labor became a constant bone of contention between the responsible institutions and authorities, and in some sub-areas these conflicts were exacerbated by the competition between compulsory workers' insurance and (compulsory) agricultural insurance.[155] With regard to domestic servants[156] too, there were frequent areas of legal and administra-

[155] See the section on "Compulsory insurance of workers in agriculture" in this chapter.

[156] On the gender-specific meaning of the exclusion of domestic servants, see the section on "Compulsory insurance of male and female workers."

tive conflict. Notably, the very fact that this form of employment was clearly excluded—thus tempting insurance-shy employers to present their employees as servants instead of as commercial workers liable for compulsory insurance—was the cause of disputes over the boundaries of compulsory insurance. At least in the final years before the war, however, the relevant authorities insisted on compulsory insurance in those cases where these so-called "servants" were clearly carrying out commercial work. Thus the State Bureau for Workers' Insurance decreed on the basis of a specific case that cooks, chambermaids, porters, maids-of-all-work, and coachmen employed in the hotel and catering business were subject to compulsory insurance, regardless of whether they were contracted as workers or as servants. In another case, the authorities made clear that a chambermaid employed in an inn was under no circumstances to be classified as a servant because in the case of an inn or hostel she was not concerned with the employer's own housekeeping but with that of a commercial business.[157]

Compulsory insurance applied, according to Act 14/1891, to all those employed in businesses that came under the regulations of the trade law of 1884, as well as a few additional areas. The ambit of the trade law, however, was not always explicitly and unambiguously defined. In principle it was intended—with the exception of agriculture and forestry, "home work (*házi ipar*)," "ordinary day-labor" (*közönséges napszámosmunka*) and a few other areas—to encompass the whole area of commercial work.[158] Over the decades, areas of business such as photography or particular printing techniques were included into the trades coved by the 1884 law on the grounds that technological developments had subsequently changed the nature of these trades. As a result, workers employed in these areas were included in the ambit of compulsory health insurance.[159] In addition, the health insurance law explicitly included mining, larger construction sites and companies connected to transportation as areas of employment requiring compulsory insurance. All those workers who earned not more than eight crowns per day were to be insured, as well as all apprentices

[157] *Közigazgatási döntvénytár. Szerkeszti Dr. Marschalkó János. Kiadja a Jogtudományi Közlöny szerkesztősége* [Collection of decisions in public administration. Edited by Dr. János Marschalkó. Published by the editorial office of the *Jogtudományi Közlöny*], 11 vols. (Budapest 1908–1922), vol. VI, 312 f.; *Munkásbiztositási Közlöny* 5 (1911): 1329 f.

[158] *Az ipartörvény módosítása* [Modification of the trade law], vol. I, 22; Act 17/1884, §183.

[159] *A Magyar Királyi Kormány* [The Royal Hungarian Government] 1902, 66.

and trainees. Insurance was not required for those workers for whom at the time of their employment "the employer … had clearly specified that the employment was for a period of less than eight days."[160]

As far as small business was concerned, by the time of the birth of Hungarian labor insurance in 1891, the conditions were clear from a legal point of view. Dependent employees in this sector were to be insured. With regard to home work and insecure work, the situation was less clear. On the one hand, the rationale of the bill that formed the basis of Act 14/1891 established that compulsory insurance included "those employed in a commercial capacity, or so-called auxiliary personnel" and "regardless whether those concerned are employed on an annual, monthly, weekly or daily basis and whether they can leave their position only with notice or without notice." "Accordingly, those employed on a daily basis in the enterprises cited in the bill are also obliged to be insured."[161] On the other hand, however, for the "ordinary" day laborer, the trade law did not apply. As a result, as was to be seen, the situation with regard to certain areas of day labor remained unclear. In addition, the clause regarding employment contracts that lasted for less than eight days definitely excluded widespread forms of irregular work from compulsory insurance and opened the doors to numerous attempts at manipulation with regard to day labor. As for home work, the health insurance law of 1891 contained a clause according to which persons, "occupied in home work," could voluntarily join an insurance fund.[162] Thus the law emphasized the intention, already present in the trade law, to exclude this group of employees from the circle of those classified as commercial workforce, and thus from compulsory health insurance under the workers' insurance act.

As was to be expected, these boundaries, which were intended to exclude particular forms of uncertain employment and home work, were constantly disputed. As far as home work was concerned, the decision-makers in health insurance played a limited role. They were, according to a decision by the minister for commerce in 1894, simply to adhere to the clause according to which individuals who were active in "home work" were not to be insured under the compulsory health insurance scheme.[163]

160 Act 14/1891, §§2, 3.

161 *Képviselőház Irományai* [Documents of the House of Representatives] 1887/1891, vol. XXIII, 167 f.

162 Act 14/1891, §4.

163 *A betegsegélyezési törvény módosítása* [Modification of the law on sickness benefits], 40.

The disputes over a possible compulsory insurance for home workers thus played themselves out on a different legislative territory. These focused around the question of what forms of production outside commercial companies and factories could be classified as commercial, rather than "home work," and thus recognized as falling under the trade law and therefore requiring compulsory insurance. At the time of the enactment of the health insurance law of 1891, there existed no general provisions that would have afforded even partial clarity in answering this question. Decisions regarding the application of the trade law were to be made on a case-to-case basis, taking into account local circumstances, by the trade authorities of the first instance.[164] The principal guideline in such cases was to be whether a "commercial activity" was being practiced "regularly and for profit." Obviously more important than the use of "external workers" in this context was the question of whether external raw materials were being processed in the course of production and the products commercially sold to third parties. There was a conspicuous tendency to assign effectively commercially practiced activities outside commercial companies and factories to the trade law, and thus require compulsory insurance. For example, in corresponding decisions, weaving, brick-making, pottery and distilling of spirits were named as activities that in certain circumstances could clearly be considered and falling within the ambit of the trade law. In contrast, the production of peasant clothing or the direct sale of home-baked bread, for example, were to be classified as "domestic business," even if in some circumstances the "women baking the bread" did not produce the flour themselves. The same applied to the activities of "Gypsy smiths" as long as they did not employ any external labor.[165]

In contrast to home work, the definition of boundaries in the area of insecure work proved to be a more serious bone of contention. A circular letter from the Budapest Trade Corporation of master builders, bricklayers, masons and carpenters to its members triggered a long series of attempts to exclude workers employed on insecure terms from access to compulsory health insurance. The letter advised members that for day laborers there was no requirement of registration for health insurance so long as these were informed "every week" that their services were "only required until Saturday or possibly for a shorter period." The Budapest District Health Insur-

[164] For the specification of these diverse bodies see p. 99 f.

[165] *Az ipartörvény módosítása* [Modification of the trade law], vol. I, 102–106; *Közigazgatási elvi határozatok, Új-folyam* [Principle administrative decisions. New series], vol. II, 429.

ance Company did not hesitate to alert the minister. In his decision on the case in 1893, the minister expressed his dismay at such obstructiveness and circumvention of the "humanitarian goals" of the health insurance law, and made it plain that day laborers in the building industry were subject to compulsory insurance.[166] Yet a whole decade later the minister for commerce found himself obliged to repeat the same statement in a subsequent decision.[167] In 1897 he had conversely established that "general day laborers" who as already mentioned were exempt from the regulations of the trade law, were not subject to compulsory insurance.[168]

It can thus be assumed that an appreciable share of those employees statistically classified as "commercial employees" were excluded from compulsory insurance on the grounds of the insecure nature of their employment, whether *de facto* or *de iure*. The authorities of Temesvár, for example, at the beginning of the twentieth century, gave a characteristic description of the employment conditions of "at least 6,000–8,000" individuals out of a total of 24,108 local workers and day laborers, together classified as "commercial employees." Some "6,000–8,000," that is a quarter to a third of these "commercial employees," were "simple unskilled day laborers performing the coarsest physical work" such as "woodcutters, water carriers, sack haulers and all sorts of other working persons who possess no regular weekly or monthly income" and earned "scarcely more than 30–40 crowns" a month.[169]

The changes made to the treatment of insecure employment by the new law on accident and health insurance of 1907 can be seen as a reaction to the various problems and debates in this area. The earlier eight-day clause allowing exemption from compulsory health insurance had already disappeared from the draft law. The justification of the draft included an explanation that the earlier eight-day clause had been justified by practical ad-

---

166 The quotations related to the circular letter are taken from the indirect reproduction of the letter's content as contained in the decision by the minister for commerce. *Közigazgatási elvi határozatok* [Principle administrative decisions], vol. II, 635 f.

167 *A betegsegélyezési törvény módosítása* [Modification of the law on sickness benefits], 32.

168 *A betegsegélyezési törvény módosítása* [Modification of the law on sickness benefits], 34. In the debates on compulsory insurance for day laborers, it was repeatedly made clear which groups should not be considered as "ordinary day laborers," while in the available sources it remains rather unclear which groups actually did fall into this category. It may be that the hitherto untraceable ordinance, 58541/1897, Minister for commerce, might provide clarification of this.

169 Geml, *Temesvár lakáspolitikája* [The housing policy of Temesvár], 105 f., 117.

ministrative procedures with the health insurance companies, but that the new law was designed differently.[170] It also mentioned that it would now finally be possible to include in labor insurance the "mobile element of the workforce whose employment is not permanent and extends only over a short period of time."[171] This statement can be read as a belated confession of the fact that this "element of the workforce" was indeed important for the Hungarian economy and constituted a problem in terms of its inclusion into the workers' insurance system—both within and beyond the strategies described above for avoiding health insurance for *de facto* continuously employed day laborers.

The new law of 1907 and the legal practice based on it clearly sought to include in compulsory health insurance all employees in those areas of work subject to the trade law or working in additional areas listed in the new law. Henceforth, this meant not just those regularly employed in businesses where health or accident insurance was compulsory, but all those members of the workforce of these same businesses who were "permanently or occasionally, temporarily or transitorily" employed. Admittedly, as far as health insurance was concerned, the "ordinary day laborer" was once again listed amongst those groups who could only be voluntarily insured.[172] This group thus continued to be excluded from compulsory healthcare insurance.

The legal practice that developed in the following years with regard to these new regulations was rather unequivocal. It was very quickly established that employees of enterprises subject to compulsory insurance were to be registered with the responsible insurance company even if they were employed for fewer than eight days. It was also clarified that only those day laborers could be classified as "ordinary day laborers" who were "not employed in commercial enterprises and generally not in such employment, work or business" to which "compulsory insurance extends" according to the terms of the new law on health and accident insurance. It would not avail an employer to claim, for example, that the employee in question only worked for him "for the odd day or two, sometimes only half days." The relevant rulings were repeated over and over, and the higher authorities

---

170 In the new law, the eight-day clause only played a role in the regulations regarding the time-frame during which the employer had to register a new employee with the insurance company. Act 19/1907, §12.

171 *Képviselőház Irományai* [Documents of the House of Representatives] 1906/1910, vol. IX, no. 186, 160 f.

172 Act 19/1907, §§1, 3, 7.

often overturned the rulings of lower courts in favor of insurance-shy employers.[173] Both the contradictory rulings and the need to repeat the rulings endlessly show that employers continued to make extensive and diverse efforts to exclude insecure work from access to labor insurance, in spite of the now much more explicit regulations. Insofar as the legislature and legal practice succeeded in enforcing the new regulations, however, labor insurance no longer contributed to increasing the distance between the realm of normalized, increasingly protected work on the one hand and insecure employment and the living conditions of the affected groups on the other.

The new labor insurance law of 1907 brought an important change with regard to the matter of home work. Unlike in 1891, when the health insurance law had relied on the woolly and diversely construable regulation of the trade law on (not compulsorily insurable) "home work," dependent home work was now clearly and explicitly subject to compulsory insurance. The obligation for insurance applied, according to the law, to those home workers, male or female, who "worked in their own workshops or homes at the behest of other contractors and on their account ... including when they procure the raw and auxiliary materials themselves and as a sideline also work on their own account." Every employer who employed home workers of this sort was obliged to register them for health insurance.[174]

Clear words were followed by decisive deeds in the controversies about the interpretation of these words that rapidly ensued. In principle, the vague maxim inherited from the legal practice connected to the trade law was adhered to, by which the District Insurance Companies, "in keeping with local circumstances" were responsible for the implementation of the new legal regulations, given the "diverse types and character" of home work.[175] Nevertheless there were often policy decisions which were unmistakably concerned with making home work that was connected in a dependent rela-

[173] *A munkásbiztositási törvény* (1907: XIX. t.-c.) *és választott bírósági eljárás kiegészítve a vonatkozó jogesetekkel és rendeletekkel* [The labor insurance law (Act 19/1907) and arbitration proceedings, supplemented with the relevant legal cases and acts] (Budapest 1912), 8 f., 35; Aladár Halász, *A munkásbetegsegélyezés és balesetbiztositás kézikönyve. Az 1907. évi XIX. t.-c. magyarázata a vonatkozó rendeletek, határozatok, ítéletek és utasításokból álló teljes joganyag feldolgozásával* [Handbook of workers' accident and health insurance, commentary on act 19/1907 taking into account all legal materials comprising the relevant regulations, decisions, judgments and directives] (Budapest 1909), 32; *Munkásbiztositási Közlöny* 1 (1907): 166–169; 2 (1908): 260, 528 f., 1135 f.; 4 (1910): 283 f., 328 f., 361 f.

[174] Act 19/1907, § 2.

[175] *Munkásbiztositási Közlöny* 1 (1907): 153 f.

tionship to industry and commerce compulsorily insurable. Home workers who processed materials distributed from a factory at home, and especially if the factory then marketed the products as its own, were to be insured. This rule also applied despite all kinds of qualifying circumstances, such as when the home workers in question were only engaged by the factory for a part of the year, namely in the so-called dead season in agriculture, if no written contract existed and if piecework rates were paid. The argument presented by one defaulting employer that the registration of such workers was associated with "insuperable difficulties" was dismissed out of hand by the minister for commerce: "Incidentally, the difficulties mentioned are not in fact insuperable." Another important area in which legal practice attempted to enforce obligatory insurance was that of home workers who also worked on their own account and thus themselves employed auxiliary staff. Such home workers were themselves to be classified as employers in relation to their staff, and thus obliged to ensure them. There were, however, certainly hesitations and ambivalence as to how the practical procedures for combining the insurance obligations of factory owners, intermediary employers working from home and their employees should look. In contrast, those individuals who produced commercial products "independently" and not for manufacturers, or only for their own family or "at most for a certain more or less restricted circle of consumers" or for trade were classified as not requiring compulsory insurance.[176]

Yet the new law of 1907 also introduced a fundamental differentiation in matters of home work between the two branches of insurance that henceforth operated in parallel, that is between the revised health insurance on the one hand and the newly introduced accident insurance on the other. The new obligation to accident insurance did not apply to home work, though it was included in the revised compulsory health insurance. The lawgivers thus chose a quite different path in treating home work as compared to insecure employment in both classes of insurance. Insecure employment was treated largely equally in both branches of insurance in that the law used the same wording when describing which groups of employees working in those businesses declared subject to compulsory insurance were to be insured. Home work, in contrast, was not mentioned at all in the regulations on compulsory accident insurance, and legal practice explicitly made it

---

[176] Halász, *A munkásbetegsegélyezés és balesetbiztosítás kézikönyve* [Handbook of workers' accident and health insurance], 15 f.; *A Munkásbiztositási törvény* [The workers' insurance law], 14; *Munkásbiztositási Közlöny* 1 (1907): 155 f.; 2 (1908): 276 f.; 4 (1910): 1672–1675.

clear that this—particularly in view of the fact that health insurance regulations did refer specifically to home work– was to be interpreted to the effect that home workers should be excluded from accident insurance. Home workers were also not to be included even when establishing the size of a business, a criterion which helped determine whether the relevant production facility was to be included in compulsory accident insurance or exempted on the grounds of it being a small business.[177]

With the appearance of size of an enterprise as a factor in deciding on whether or not accident insurance was to be compulsory, a new element in the definition of the ambit of insurance was introduced into Hungarian social security for the first time, namely the distinction between factories and other large-scale businesses on the one hand and small business enterprises on the other. Austrian accident insurance, which was introduced almost two decades earlier, operated with exactly this distinction from the outset.[178] In the Hungarian process of entry into law, the question of whether to except small businesses from compulsory insurance was fought over to the last. Even the final bill that was eventually discussed in parliament had anticipated establishing the sphere of insurance for accident insurance so as to correspond to that of health insurance. Yet in the course of the parliamentary proceedings, those forces that sought to see small scale business and trade—except in those areas of work where there was an increased risk of accidents, and these were individually listed in the law—exempted from compulsory insurance prevailed.[179] Insurance

---

177 *A Munkásbiztositási törvény* [The workers' insurance law], 17, 20; *Közigazgatási döntvénytár* [Collection of decisions in public administration], vol. II, 72 ff.

178 Peter Lachnit, Staatliche Sozialpolitik für and gegen die Arbeiterschaft. Arbeiterbewegung and Sozialversicherung in Österreich von den Anfängen bis 1918 [State social policy in favor and against the workforce. The workers' movement and social insurance in Austria from the beginnings to 1918], Phil. Diss. Vienna 1989, 93 f.

179 *Képviselőház Irományai* [Documents of the House of Representatives] 1906/1910, vol. XI, no. 360, 264–266. There was thus a return to the perceptions that were also prevalent in the years before 1906. Just as in an earlier bill from 1890, the bill issued by the ministry of commerce in 1903 listed the types of business that were subject to compulsory insurance individually (and the list of these was more tightly limited than in the law of 1907). The bill of 1903 also provided that motorized small businesses were only to be included in those cases where the business concerned had at least five permanent employees. *A munkások baleset ellen való biztositása. I. rész* [The insurance of workers against accidents. Part I], 37; *A munkások baleset ellen való biztositása. II. rész. Törvényjavaslat és indoklás* [The insurance of workers against accidents. Part II. Legislative Proposal and Justification] (Budapest 1903), 334, 430–433; Halász, *A munkásbetegsegélyezés és balesetbiztositás kézikönyve* [Handbook of workers' accident and health insurance], 21.

was only generally compulsory for factories and "commercial business premises" for a company size of twenty or more employees, and for all companies with steam generators which were subject to authorization, or with machinery driven by wind or water power.[180]

For compulsory accident insurance, first introduced in 1907, the group of those insured was thus markedly narrower than for health insurance. In addition, the boundaries once established in this case were restrictively interpreted in policy decisions related to a number of key questions. These decisions were relevant for all types of business not explicitly listed in the law because they were not considered particularly accident prone. Thus amongst "commercial workshops" employing 20 or more workers, only those in which material was processed with the use of tools were subject to compulsory insurance. In counting the workforce, office workers were only to be included if their activities supplemented the actual shop floor work. In addition it was made clear that small, motorized businesses were only subject to compulsory accident insurance when the machines were used on "commercial business premises."[181] For those areas of the world of work, however, that were considered particularly accident-prone, and for which the exemption of small businesses from compulsory insurance therefore did not apply, highly inclusive regulations were established. This went so far, for example, as to include day laborers in "domestically conducted" building construction in compulsory accident insurance, although the same group remained excluded from compulsory health insurance. The only exemptions from compulsory accident insurance in the construction sector were simple, "domestically conducted" building projects at ground level.[182]

Naturally, disputes over the limits of compulsory insurance were not limited to the problem zones of home work, small businesses, and insecure employment. The relevant authorities were also particularly concerned with the problem of compulsory insurance of employees who were active in the marginal areas of work defined as dependent employment in trade and commerce. These included, for example, office clerks in lawyer's offices, nuns employed as nurses, journalists employed in editorial offices, prostitutes employed in brothels, or orchestral musicians. All these groups were exempt from compulsory insurance. Those required to

180 Act 19/1907, §3.

181 *A Munkásbiztositási törvény* [The workers' insurance law], 17, 20 f.

182 In "commercial" building construction day laborers were also subject to health insurance. *A Munkásbiztositási törvény* [The workers' insurance law], 18; Act 19/1907 §3, section 4.

be insured, in contrast, included those employed in the workshops of state basket weaving schools, those employed in boring wells, raft workers, and feather pluckers employed by feather and down dealers as well as commercial agents even then when they were working for several employers.[183] Compulsory insurance for employees of certain public institutions and bodies was officially and legally confirmed many times, however, in 1910 the authorities were still forced to admit that the insurance of these groups was "carried out only sporadically throughout the country."[184]

Compulsory insurance of male and female workers

In the comments on Table 5 above, it has already been pointed out that the introduction of social insurance served, in effect, to increase the distance between men's and women's work. It is hard to guess just how far each of the differentiations of commercial work discussed in the previous section—and no doubt several other factors not considered here that influenced the drawing of boundaries between the sectors subject to compulsory insurance and those that were not—contributed to increasing this distance. One key, statistically measurable area of nonagricultural women's work that was not subject to compulsory insurance is domestic service. The new labor insurance law of 1907 once again excluded domestic servants from compulsory health insurance on the grounds that with regard to the "notifying [the authorities] about" this category of workers and "keeping them registered" there were "no legal regulations yet" and thus compulsory insurance could not be enforced.[185] As late as 1910, national census results showed 40.0 percent of the female nonagricultural workforce as belonging to the category of domestic servants, and in the capital, Budapest, this figure was negligibly lower at 39.6 percent.[186] The strong representation of domestic servants among the female labor force no doubt contributed greatly to the low representation of women amongst those included in compulsory health insurance. As mentioned above, however, in cases of dispute, and perhaps in other cases, not all employees

---

[183] *A Munkásbiztositási törvény* [The workers' insurance law], 4–12.

[184] *Munkásbiztositási Közlöny* 4 (1910): 872 f.

[185] With reference to the costs incurred by employers regarding their obligation to contribute to the hospital costs of their employees in accordance with Act 21/1898 on the State Healthcare Fund, the new law granted the possibility of voluntary participation in labor insurance. Act 19/1907, §7b; *Képviselőház Irományai* [Documents of the House of Representatives] 1906/1910, vol. IX, 164.

[186] *1910. évi népszámlálás* [Census results 1910], vol. LVI.

who possessed a servant's papers rather than work papers were automatically excluded from health insurance.

Social insurance policy also contributed to the engendered formation of labor relations proper through the design of protective measures specific to women in the workplace as part of social insurance—mainly via the granting of continued pay for female workers in the period after the birth of a child, as discussed in chapter IV.1.2.

These dimensions of the gender-relevant configuration of working conditions not only influenced the gendered construction of the world of work itself, but also impacted on the living conditions of men and women, and social relations between the sexes in the wider sense. For example, the greater social-welfare security protection of the paid employment of a husband or partner and family man, or the childbed benefit for a wife or female partner and mother was certainly not without consequences for family relations. The gendered impact of social insurance policy beyond the world of paid work, however, reached far beyond such immediate consequences of the differentiation of men and women's status in the world of work. Social insurance policy was also of relevance for the living conditions of and relations between men and women, particularly due to regulations on co-insurance of family members and indeed through the references to family contained in, and the implicit and explicit relevance for the (re)construction of family relations of many regulations and procedures. This dimension of social insurance policy was based in large part on a particular image of existing relations and the existing social division of labor between the sexes, and in turn many procedures and decisions in this sphere were arranged to normatively support and promote particular types of family relations and relations between the sexes, at the same time discriminating socio-politically against others.

The regulations on coinsurance of family members—while legally extended by the new workers' insurance law of 1907—were repeatedly construed in a restrictive way. This created particular disadvantages for women and their children for two reasons. First of all, women, as can be deduced from the figures in Table 5 above, relied more than men on coinsurance rather than labor insurance. Second, women were more likely than men to be in the situation of living with children but without the second parent. The newly created State Bureau for Workers' Insurance decided as early as 1908 that "a woman living in a common home outside the legal bonds of wedlock... no matter how much assistance she might be due in individual cases, has no entitlement to benefits stipulated for family members." This position, at least according to the press, stood in diametric opposition to the practice pursued by the local insurance companies hitherto, and indeed the National Company soon officially appealed against the decision of the Bureau, referring to its own alternative interpretation of the terms of the labor insurance law. It sought to provide or maintain access to the maternity benefit available for coinsured dependent family members and medical treatment for common-law wives as well. Yet the Bureau remained unmoved, and its position was finally endorsed by a verdict of the Higher Administrative Court in 1913. In contrast, the costs for inpatient treatment of the mother of an insured individual who lived in a common household with this head of the family, were indeed to be borne by the Company. The reason given, unlike in the case of a female cohabitant, was the fact that the relevant paragraph of Act 19/1907 "generally" referred to family members in the same household.[187] A few years earlier, the Court had also ruled that step-children—in contrast to legitimate, illegitimate, and adoptive children—did not count as family members "of the stepfather," and that the Fund should therefore not pay the costs of their medical care as part of benefits for dependents.[188] This meant in practice that a child from an earlier relationship, when its mother lived with a new partner and was not herself insured, was not covered by the insurance of the step-father. A further ruling established that women who gave up employment with compulsory health insurance, married and concerned themselves with household work lost the right to continued independent voluntary insurance, which previously compulsorily insured persons who were no longer employed were normally entitled to. The explanation was that "now her husband will take care of her upkeep." The access of such women to health insurance thus depended entirely on the status of this husband. The wife, regardless of her previous status, and like the other members of the insured's household, only had the right to be voluntarily[189] insured if her husband's employment belonged to the category of those subject to compulsory insurance. Wives who did not pursue any gainful employment of their own were thus entirely dependent on their husbands in matters of health insurance. The justification for the relevant decision of the board of the National Company referred exclusively to wives, thus not even taking the unlikely case of a househus-

[187] *Munkásbiztositási Közlöny* 2 (1908): 1443 f.; 7 (1913): 1227 f., 1517; 8 (1914): 207 f.; *Munkásbiztositás* 2, no. 1 (1909): 5 f.; 2, no. 11 (1909): 3 f.

[188] Act 19/1907, §§50.5, 72; *Munkásbiztositási Közlöny* 5 (1911): 1457 f.

[189] The provisions on voluntary insurance, however, made this option basically dependent on the state of health of the person concerned, and the National Company moreover limited participation to individuals under the age of 40. Co-insurance as a family member, in contrast, was not subject to any age limit.

band into consideration. However, there was at least one case documented in which the Administrative Court eventually forced the Company to cover the hospital costs of a husband who was not separately insured (for whom the provision on coinsurance as a family member applied). Better treatment was reserved for "individuals," for example single mothers, who after terminating compulsorily insured employment "cared for their children and were provided for by a member of their family" who was not subject to compulsory health insurance. These individuals were able to continue to insure themselves voluntarily.[190] Children or families where the mother was insured but the father was not, were also disadvantaged. In such cases the father, with reference to the primary duty of care of the male parent, based on family law, unless he was unable to pay, was obliged to pay for all costs of inpatient medical care of the child himself.[191] In general, the level of contributions of voluntarily insured family member was set at half of the contribution of the insured, however, according to the 1907 Act only "his wife" was entitled to sickness benefits on this basis, that is in the capacity of a voluntarily insured family member.[192] A husband who chose to insure himself in this way—a case obviously not even hypothetically considered by the lawgiver—would thus have been considerably worse off in comparison to a voluntarily insured wife.

The regulations and rulings discussed above make it quite clear that the Hungarian workers' insurance system particularly supported the traditional form of marriage. This had negative consequences for women, and thus for common-law partnerships that did not conform to these norms. Children born outside marriage, however, were not so consistently discriminated against. The system of regulations and rulings discussed above marginalized them only in cases where a female partner (or in principle also a male partner) who was not subject to compulsory insurance brought children with her into a (new) marriage or relationship. As long as illegitimate children lived in the same household with the insured parent, they were explicitly placed on an equal footing with the legitimate children of the same parent as regards their entitlement to health insurance. [193] Last but not least the system supported the inclusion of single, previously compulsorily insured mothers into the extended family of origin.

---

[190] Act 19/1907, §§7f, 60; *Munkásbiztositási Közlöny* 1(1907): 205; 5 (1911): 1177–1181; 8 (1914): 751.

[191] *Munkásbiztositási Közlöny* 7 (1913): 1293 f., 1703 f.

[192] Act 19/1907, §26.

[193] *A Munkásbiztositási törvény* [The workers' insurance law], 69.

The support and privileging of traditional forms of marriage in labor insurance did, however, have positive consequences for women whose relationships did not depart from this tradition. This was the case, for example, regarding surviving female as compared to male survivors in the case of accident insurance. While a widow as a rule was entitled lifelong—or until remarriage—to 20 percent of the annual income of her husband as a widow's pension, the same was true for a widower only if his insured wife had "maintained him due to partial or complete inability to work."[194] This amounted to the recognition of housework and childcare as the basis for legal entitlement to insurance only for married women.

Compulsory insurance of workers in agriculture

For many of the workforce who were not classified as employed in trade and commerce or as domestic servants, the regulations for agrarian social welfare and insurance, or the regulations pertaining to either of these sectors of agrarian social policy applied. In this area of social policy, as mentioned earlier, a minimal compulsory accident insurance on the part of the employer for his laborers was introduced in 1900. From 1902 a similar provision also existed for an important group of agricultural machine workers. Owners of threshing machines and chaff cutters were henceforth required to insure those employed in the use of these machines against accidents under the agricultural social insurance system.[195] The introduction of this provision was partly thanks to the fact that operators of these types of machine were particularly vulnerable to accidents. Apart from this, the legislators were keen to increase the numbers insured by the new National Insurance for Agricultural Workers and Servants, given that this institution had not met original expectations, especially in terms of numbers of insured.[196] As a result, there existed even before the introduction of compulsory workers' accident insurance in 1907—and indeed perhaps

[194] Parents and grandparents who had been "predominantly" maintained by the insured deceased had a similar right to benefits "for as long as they require such assistance"; here again the level of benefits was maximum 20 percent, but might not exceed the amount of such assistance as had earlier been provided (by the deceased) for the person concerned. Act 19/1907 §§72, 73; *Munkásbiztositási Közlöny* 5 (1911): 444 f.; 6 (1912): 755 f.

[195] Act 14/1902, §26.

[196] Gyula Fáy, *Az Országos gazdasági munkás- és cselédsegélypénztár* [The National Insurance for Agricultural Workers and Servants] (Budapest 1904), 22 f.; Heller, *Magyarország szociálpolitikája* [Social policy of Hungary], 111, 115.

because the preparations for the introduction of this branch of insurance within the framework of the workers' insurance were delayed year after year—a form of obligatory accident insurance for agricultural (so-called "outdoor") servants and for certain agricultural workers. In comparison to later workers' accident insurance the obligatory insurance in agriculture can however only be described as minimalistic.

In the debates over the distinction between labor relations that were subject to compulsory workers' insurance and agricultural labor relations, the interrelation of these factors characterizing the *status quo* and development in the field of accident insurance played an important role. First of all, it was clear that workers and "outdoor" servants in agriculture and forestry, as well as in viticulture, were essentially not subject to compulsory health insurance. The same was true for work of commercial or industrial nature, as long as it was carried out within individual farms or estates and by their employees. This category also included independent ("hired") craftsmen who were attached to such farms, as long as they did not carry out further commercial work for other farms or estates or private individuals. Those workers whose area of activity was not strictly agricultural but was clearly not commercial in nature, such as for example those who were employed by municipalities or other authorities as swineherds or "mountain guards" and the like, were classified as agricultural servants and thus not subject to compulsory health insurance. At the same time, the institutions and authorities responsible for the system of workers' insurance (as opposed to agrarian insurance) identified several groups of workers at the margins of agricultural and primary production who from their point of view were subject to compulsory workers' health insurance. These included those employed in manufacturing facilities of an industrial nature that were not owned by farmers, estates, and companies engaged in primary production, and those employed in facilities which over time had grown beyond primary production (for example by taking on new types of production). Examples of this group of the workforce included employees of "agrarian" breweries and distilleries, those employed in commercial wineries (even if these used grapes from their own production), in sawmills, and in subsidiary commercial businesses attached to estates. Those employed in logging and wood processing businesses that processed wood from forests that were not the property of the owner of the relevant company, or were only purchased by him for direct commercial processing, were also subject to compulsory insurance. With accident insurance, the question of the danger involved in the relevant activity was also taken into account. The workers' insurance law of 1907 clearly stated that even those factories that were concerned with processing agricultural materials that were largely from their own production—even if this was a type of business that did not fall under the 1884 trade law—were subject to accident insurance within the workers' insurance system. Legal practice after 1907 also confirmed for example the necessity of this type of insurance for "commercial wood production." An exception was made only for the employees of a forest owner engaged for the purposes of cutting firewood in the employer's own forest, without the use of power machinery. Attempts to avoid insurance by registering employees for voluntary insurance with the National Insurance for Agricultural Workers and Servants were, in those cases where compulsory insurance applied, (initially) not legally tolerated in either of the two insurance systems.[197]

In sum, in the first years after the introduction of the new labor insurance law of 1907 there were frequent conflicts over obligatory insurance for workers who were employed in borderline grey areas; however, legal practice as a whole was unequivocal in interpreting extensively and inclusively the existing regulations on obligatory insurance. In a number of special areas—notably those of operators of threshing and chaff cutting machines, who as mentioned above, had occupied a special position since 1902—substantial conflicts developed. These conflicts became increasingly acrimonious over the years and were finally to end in victory for the interests of manorial farming and agribusiness.

Initially, these agrarian and agro-industrial interests ensured, via the appropriate formulation of the regulations on compulsory accident insurance in the new workers' insurance law of 1907, that all agricultural machine workers should be excluded from the newly introduced workers' accident insurance. The new law modified the legal regulations in this regard on agrarian accident insurance so that henceforth not only operators of threshing and chaff cutting machines but all agricultural machine operators were required to be insured by the owner of the machine with the National Insurance for Agricultural Workers and Servants.[198] The existence of significantly cheaper agricultural social insurance was thus used to keep an important sector of the workforce out of labor insurance. This

---

[197] Act 19/1907, §3; *A Munkásbiztositási törvény* [The workers' insurance law], 4–12, 17–22; Béla Perneczky, *A gazdasági cselédek szolgálati viszonyai* [Conditions of service of agricultural servants] (Budapest 1928), 11; *Közigazgatási döntvénytár* [Collection of decisions in public administration], vol. V, 213 f.; *Munkásbiztositási Közlöny* 4 (1910): 225, 1161 ff.

[198] Act 19/1907, §3.

group of workers was of strategic importance for employers' interests, which were increasingly linked to the progressive industrialization of agriculture. The legal definition of these workers as henceforth belonging to the world of agriculture really stood symbolically in opposition to the idea that one day the armory of a modern social policy—spearheaded by the integration of agro-industrial machine workers into labor insurance designed for commercial workers—might conquer the world of commercial agriculture.

Not surprisingly, representatives of the National Workers' Health and Accident Insurance Company and the district insurance companies fought back. It was clear to them that large-scale farming and agribusiness were gaining in strategic importance in the world of work in Hungary, and that as a consequence the policy on agricultural machine workers was of great significance for the future of labor insurance. At first the minister for commerce and the minister for agriculture, supported by the State Bureau for Workers' Insurance, the supervisory body of the National Workers' Health and Accident Insurance Company that strongly represented the interests of the state, strove to reach a compromise solution that would broadly take into account agrarian and agro-industrial interests. A by-law of 1908 decreed that at least those workers employed by owners of agricultural machinery who used their machinery "mainly" to process the products of others, in other words who operated "commercially," would be subject to workers' insurance. Those cases were excluded, however, where such workers were agricultural servants or contracted workers of the farmer or estate-owner for whom the owner of the machinery was carrying out the work. The ordinance aimed at clarifying the boundaries of another sector of commercial work related to or on the periphery of large-scale agriculture. The so-called "hired" craftsmen who were engaged by agricultural enterprises, the ordinance clarified, fell strictly outside the sphere of influence of workers' insurance. An exception was to be made only in cases where "large manors" maintained their own workshop in which at least ten workers, including young workers and apprentices, or otherwise at least twenty workers, pursued the same trade. In such cases both workers' health and accident insurance were to be compulsory.[199]

Once representatives of workers' insurance had made clear that they would not be satisfied with such a compromise on the matter of agricultural machine workers as was unmistakably in the interests of agribusiness, the Bureau for Workers' Insurance tried again to impose checks on

[199] *Munkásbiztositási Közlöny* 2 (1908): 1100 f.

the workers' insurance companies. It ordered the latter sharply to adhere to the act of 1908 and made clear that insurance with the National Insurance for Agricultural Workers and Servants was to take place even when only some of the machine operators were employed by the farmer or landowner for whom the work was done.[200]

When in 1911–1912 a reform of the law on the National Insurance for Agricultural Workers and Servants was under discussion which initially appeared unconnected with these conflicts, large-scale agricultural interests felt that the time for a decisive offensive had come. With the help of an additional proposal that was not even presented to deputies in printed form, they succeeded in slipping a new regulation on the matter of agricultural machine workers into the law. With the exception of certified machine operators, henceforth all agricultural machine workers, whether the work took place within the business of the owner of the machine or elsewhere, were to be insured against accidents with the National Insurance for Agricultural Workers and Servants. In his defense of the planned reform in parliament, the minister for agriculture begged the deputies to finally acknowledge "that this country cannot be measured by foreign yardsticks; here agricultural and industrial workers must, due to ethnographic and various other circumstances, enjoy different treatment." There was some resistance in parliament to this ambush-style approach and the "significant detriment" to the interests of the workers involved, as well as the socio-political step backwards that this proposal entailed, but without success. There was a similar initiative with regard to workers in water regulation and state earthworks, however it was finally agreed to resolve this question later through an additional by-law. [201]

The reform of 1912 was, however, by no means the end of the altercations on this matter. On the contrary, there was soon much more at stake, namely the obligatory health insurance of agricultural machine operators and thus their assignment to a branch of workers' insurance that did not exist in agricultural social insurance. The minister for commerce now decreed—surprisingly, in the light of legal practice hitherto—that these workers were under no circumstances subject to workers' health insurance, even when the owner of the machinery was conducting the work commercially and outside his own farm or estate. In reaction to this on-

[200] *Munkásbiztositási Közlöny* 3 (1909): 707 f.

[201] *Képviselőház Irományai* [Documents of the House of Representatives] 1910/1915, vol. XI, no. 286, 376; *Országgyűlési Képviselőház Naplói* [Chronicle of the House of Parliamentary Representatives] 1910/1915, vol. X, 63; vol. XIV, 201–209; Act 8/1912, §5.

slaught, the National Company for Workers Health and Accident Insurance chose a course of open confrontation. In the decision-making procedure on questions of compulsory insurance, it argued, different entities were empowered to make decisions in different subareas, and not always the minister for commerce. The legal opinion of the National Company on the matter of compulsory health insurance of agricultural machine workers was diametrically opposed to the new opinion of the minister, and thus the Company intended to continue to pursue with every effort its demands with regard to the relevant employers.[202] However, against the agricultural and agro-industrial lobby and its allies, the National Company stood no chance. A sweeping legal reorganization in 1913 put an end to the conflict with a few brief clauses. From now on, with the exception of certified machine operators, all agricultural machine workers were excluded from workers' health insurance and subject to agricultural accident insurance. And while they were at it, several other birds were killed with the same stone. One of these was the matter of agricultural servants. The disagreement between those political forces representing the agro-lobby and the representatives of workers' insurance in this area had never been as acute as in the case of agricultural machine workers. This was because those forces that sought to extend the scope of compulsory workers' insurance could be only concerned in this field of action with bringing workers from the comparatively limited grey areas on the fringe of the mass of agricultural servants under their umbrella. Conversely, agricultural employers knew that as far as the vast majority of their "outdoor" servants were concerned, the creation of an alternative to compulsory agricultural accident insurance was just not on the cards. Act 20/1913 now in any case made this explicitly clear. Firstly, all agricultural servants were to be excluded from worker's health insurance. This also applied to servants who "carried out commercial work for the relevant estate" and for "so-called hired craftsmen employed by estates, insofar as these are not carrying out gainful commercial work for others too." Secondly, the law now established that in the future other possible problems that might arise in the grey area between agricultural and commercial work were to be resolved from above, that is through collaborative ordinances to be jointly issued by the minister for commerce and the minister for agriculture.[203] The argument of the National Company for Workers Health and Accident Insurance trying to exploit the ambiguity of administrative channels between agri-

[202] *Munkásbiztositási Közlöny* 6 (1912): 882, 1264–1271.

[203] Act 20/1913, §§2, 3.

cultural and workers' insurance was thus from a legal point of view swept from the table.

Restrictive interpretations of the new regulations, which clearly went hand in hand with limitations on compulsory insurance according to the provisions on labor insurance of 1907, followed hard behind. Already in 1914 the minister for commerce established that the employees of an "agricultural distillery," so long as they were the servants of the owner of the factory, were not subject to the regulations on workers' insurance.[204] Now it made sense, as it had not in the first years after the passing of the labor insurance law of 1907, for labor-insurance-shy agricultural employers to register their workers as agricultural servants. In 1916 the minister for agriculture made the numerous seasonal agricultural workers, known as piece-workers (*summások*), into agricultural servants so long as—and such was generally the case—during the period of employment they had contracted to work for an employer, they only worked for him.[205]

Social insurance and welfare

In addressing the last important dividing line erected by the national system of social insurance that emerged from the early 1890s, the chapter now returns to the issue this study started with, namely poor relief and welfare provision. The borderline between social insurance and welfare was a constant problem in legal practice and in every day decision-making within social insurance. This was true not only in Hungary but in Austria and other countries as well. In Hungary, the particularly minimalist nature of poverty policy, the comparatively limited scope of both agricultural and labor insurance, and the modest state of development of other aspects of welfare, social reform and social policy exacerbated the tensions in this regard. For like the state-communal child protection system or the relief action for unemployment in the capital city, labor insurance was constantly confronted with the problem of delimiting its scope in relation to the "misery of every kind" that came knocking at its door in the absence of any other system of support.[206] Contemporary experts were well aware

[204] *Munkásbiztositási Közlöny* 8 (1914): 825 f.

[205] Perneczky, *A gazdasági cselédek szolgálati viszonyai* [Conditions of service of agricultural servants], 10.

[206] For the related analysis and the context of the quotation, which is taken from Ferenczi, "A főváros első munkanélküliségi akciója" [The first action of the Capital against unemployment], see p. 68.

of this difficult situation. Farkas Heller, for example, in his (for its time) authoritative study on the history of Hungarian social policy, referred to the enormous importance "in our native circumstances" of the introduction of compulsory coinsurance of dependent family members under worker's health insurance in the law of 1907. At the same time, he perceptively pointed out that the "extension of the blessing of insurance to the families of the members" of the insurance companies constituted a step that contributed to skyrocketing costs in service provision for Hungarian health insurance to an extent that he could "hardly emphasize in adequate terms."[207]

Another problem area closely related to the peculiarities and limitations of the Hungarian social and welfare system stemmed from the question of how to distinguish between traditional hospital care of the poor and the services provided by labor insurance in the area of hospital care. Responsibility for covering the costs of hospital care for indigent members of the population were shared between labor insurance and the State Healthcare Fund, and in the grey area that thus developed the "misery of every kind" which social reformers especially in the capital city of Budapest also had to address became strikingly apparent. In this context, the divided responsibility led, not unexpectedly, to major conflicts, which ultimately had equally major financial consequences for the health insurance companies. Because the State Healthcare Fund was financed from taxes, it was entirely in the interests of all authorities and institutions except the workers' insurance itself to pass on as large a part of the costs of hospital care as possible to the health insurance companies. As early as 1908, the Bureau for Workers' Insurance, which represented state interest within the system of labor insurance, instructed hospitals to immediately check with all[208] admitted patients whether they were subject to compulsory insurance under the workers' insurance law of 1907. If patients could thus be proved to be subject to workers' health or accident insurance, the insurance companies were "categorically" obliged to bear the costs of hospital care of those concerned, according to the provisions of the labor insurance law regarding hospital care. At the same time admittance to the

[207] Heller, *Magyarország szociálpolitikája* [Social policy of Hungary], 49 f., 59.

[208] An exception was mental illness and venereal disease as well as trachomatous illness, the hospital treatment of which, according to the law of 1898, was to be paid by the State Healthcare Fund, even in cases where the individual involved was insured. However the insurance company was required to provide certain services for these patients if they were insured. *Munkásbiztositási Közlöny* 3 (1909): 306, 643; 5 (1911): 421 f.

hospital was not to be made dependent on a previously issued permission from the insurance company. Of course many of those who were classified in this way as insured had—as described above—in reality not been registered for compulsory insurance by their employers. The Administrative Court finally ruled that the insurance companies were liable to recourse by the hospitals in all cases, regardless of whether they were able to collect insurance contributions (retrospectively) from employers.[209] In the same year, the court also ruled that in cases of accident-related hospitalization, the insurance funds were obliged to cover the costs of hospital care not just for 28 days, but until the patient was fully recovered.[210] Soon there were complaints from higher authorities to the Bureau for Workers' Insurance about the "overflowing" tide of complaints submitted to them as the insurance companies attempted—regardless of the now legally clarified situation—to cope with the additional burden. As a result, the companies were rapidly forced to abandon their desperate resistance.[211] Further decisions burdening the financial situation of the funds, clearly designed to relieve the State Healthcare Fund, were to follow. In 1911, for example, the Higher Administrative Court rendered a policy decision according to which the insurance company had to bear (up to a specified maximum amount) half the hospital costs of the indigent daughter of an insured person, who had been admitted to hospital by the authorities because of a highly infectious illness. The State Healthcare Fund was only required to pay the remaining half of the costs. Conflicts were only rarely settled in favor of the Fund in individual cases and in peripheral areas.[212]

[209] *Munkásbiztositási Közlöny* 2 (1908): 59–62; 4 (1910): 1103 f., 1284 f.
[210] *Munkásbiztositási Közlöny* 4 (1910): 1592 f.
[211] *Munkásbiztositási Közlöny* 4 (1910): 1771 f.; 5 (1911): 385, 1514 f.
[212] *Munkásbiztositási Közlöny* 3 (1909): 563 ff.; 5 (1911): 1075 f.; 6 (1912): 1545.

V. Conclusion

Confronted with the "critical economic circumstances" and the ensuing unemployment debacle of 1913, the capital city, Budapest, tried to take action as did other authorities outside the capital. It established a system of municipal unemployment benefits which foreshadowed a branch of social insurance entirely missing from Hungarian social policy as it was in other countries. Faced with the doubling of daily admission figures of children to the state childcare system, the minister for the interior called upon the local authorities to proceed with "utmost care" when deciding about admission or rejection of those in need.[1] Only a few months later he had to admit in parliament that there was indeed a fundamental problem. "Hungary in the field of child protection at that time misjudged its strength and has, as demonstrated by the consequences, taken regulatory action which overtaxed its capacity; nevertheless, these regulations are, measured against our poverty, truly beautiful, human, and might serve as a model for richer countries." One idea to solve the crisis was that state children from the age of seven should contribute to their maintenance by "their own work."[2]

The need-related policies unfolding in Hungary in the second half of the 19th and the early 20th centuries were indeed characterized both by limited room for maneuver given the existing socio-political balance of forces in the Hungarian market economy, and by imaginative innovation and reform. Socio-political innovation took place on national and local levels and in the context of transnational transfer of strategies in welfare and social policy.

As regards the limited room of maneuver, this study has shown that in Hungary developments towards a more socially integrative poverty policy, like reforms aimed at social inclusion and a more far-reaching state social policy, bore only limited fruit. This has to be read bearing in mind that in the course of Hungarian economic development the situation of

---

[1] BFL-C IV 1407b 1056/1908-IX, which includes Ordinance 160.633/1913-XII, Minister for the interior, and other material. The doubling of the daily admission figures was experienced in Budapest.

[2] As quoted in *A gyermekvédelem lapja* 10 (1914): 127 f.

large sectors of the population by and large remained socio-economically unstable or marginal.

In poverty policy there certainly was no overall trend toward retracting repressive measures such as the criminalization of certain social consequences of poverty. Just how deeply or systematically the repressive side of poverty policy—which like in other countries in particular areas even expanded—actually affected the living conditions of the lower classes is difficult to assess, especially as comparative data are rare.[3] However, local authorities, the police, and the Hungarian state undoubtedly made every effort to ensure that they possessed far-reaching legal rights to intervene against life-styles deemed inappropriate and not respectable. This affected the Roma population in particular. The normative expectations about what counted as an appropriate life-style differed markedly between the sexes, in that the moral judgment of women was sexualized whereas this was not the case for men. The expectation that the able-bodied should work and were therefore not entitled to relief, while put forward in gender-neutral terms, clearly discriminated against many women. In these repressive sectors of poverty policy in Hungary integrative reform did not take place. This was different in Austria. Here the regulations on legal residence status (*Heimatrecht*) enacted in 1863, which drastically exacerbated the politics of legal exclusion from access to poor relief for those who didn't live in their place of origin, were changed in 1896 so as to alleviate the circumstances of those who had left their place of origin in search of a better life.[4]

As for provision, the other side of poverty policy, public assistance was extremely scant. The level of benefits remained low and the portion of the population who actually received benefits remained small. This is true not only if the capital city of Hungary, Budapest, is compared with the capital city of the empire as a whole, Vienna,[5] but also on the national and local level when Hungary is compared with other countries. In England and Wales under the poor laws after 1834, for example, the ratio of recorded paupers on relief in 1910 – the lowest ratio in the period from 1840, and

3 For an international overview—though also lacking quantitative data—of the in-part intensified emphasis on strategies of exclusion, especially in the context of urbanization and social change in later decades, see Daniel T. Rodgers, *Atlantic Crossings. Social Politics in a Progressive Age* (Cambridge–London 1998), 213–216.

4 Sabine Veits-Falk, "Öffentliche Armenfürsorge in Österreich im 19. Jahrhundert" [Public poor relief in Austria in the 19th century], in: Alexander Prenninger, ed. *"Mercy or Right." Development of Social Security Systems*, (Vienna 2005), 31–44, 37 ff.

5 A more detailed comparison than provided in this study is contained in chapter 4 of Zimmermann, *Prächtige Armut* [Splendid poverty].

taking into consideration a ratio that did not represent all those on relief at different times of the given year—was 26 per thousand of the population. For Hungary this ratio was—for the municipalities and the secondary cities (without Budapest) alone, that is without taking into consideration the smaller communities, and using a potentially more inclusive figure—2.3 per thousand of the population.[6] The level of provision was lower in the rural areas of Hungary as compared to the municipalities and secondary cities and also when comparing for example one rural district in Somogy County to rural communities in Germany.[7] Even if private and denominational charity seems to have paid a significant complementary role—as was the case in many other European countries[8]—this does not change the overall finding of this study that poverty policy in Hungary provided very limited relief. Developments in Ireland which took "account of the greater extent of poverty and destitution" as compared to England support the finding that under certain circumstances minimalist poor relief was likely to occur in tandem with widespread social marginalization. The Irish poor law of 1838 "contained no provision for outdoor relief." In the early 1870s the proportion of those receiving relief was a quarter of that in England, with only 24 percent of those on relief receiving outdoor relief.[9]

---

[6] Many more dimensions of difference pointing in the same direction become visible when comparing other data and information contained in part II and III of Lynn Hollen Lees, *The Solidarities of Strangers. The English Poor Laws and the People, 1700–1948* (Cambridge–New York–Melbourne 1998), with data and information contained in chapters II.3.1. and II.3.2. of this study.

[7] In a number of small communities in two different regions of Germany, these figures ranged from two to three (at the low end) up to 16 or respectively 15 individuals per 1,000 receiving aid in the 1880s. In all communities taken together of the district of Igal in Somogy County in Hungary, 1.3 individuals per 1000 were registered as receiving aid in 1900, and they received the most minimalistic type of support. Thomas Küster, "Der Einfluss von Industrialisierung und sozialer Gesetzgebung auf die ländliche Armenfürsorge in Westfalen (1850–1920)" [The impact of industrialization and social legislation on rural poor relief in Westfalia (1850–1920)], in: Brandes, Marx-Jasulski, *Poor Relief and Charity*, 47–72, here 63; Katrin Marx-Jaskulski, *Armut und Fürsorge auf dem Land. Vom Ende des 19. Jahrhunderts bis 1933* [Poverty and poor relief in the country-side. From the end of the 19th century to 1933] (Göttingen 2008), 115.

[8] A number of recent case studies published in Brandes, Marx-Jasulski, *Poor Relief and Charity*, and elsewhere certainly confirm this fact.

[9] In later decades there were more expansive tendencies in Irish poor relief. Virginia Crossman, "The Humanization of the Irish Poor Laws. Reassessing Developments in Social Welfare in Post-Famine Ireland," in: Andreas Gestrich, Steven King, Lutz Raphael, eds. *Being Poor in Modern Europe. Historical Perspectives 1800–1940* (Frankfurt/M.–Berlin–Berne–Bruxelles–New York–Oxford–Vienna 2006), 229–249, here 230–236.

As for social policy, the rise of workers' insurance introduced from the early 1890s certainly eased significantly the burden of social risk related to illness, and later occupational accident, for a considerable part of workforce in trade, services, and industry. The access of family members improved over time. Yet the proportion of the overall workforce employed in these sectors remained comparatively low, and the workforce covered by workers' insurance was distributed extremely unevenly throughout the country. In addition, workers' insurance definitely privileged certain types of labor relations within trade and commerce. Specifically, men gained more from workers' insurance as compared to women, and those sectors of the workforce whose labor relations were particularly insecure and whose income tended to be unstable had less access to workers' insurance than others. These trends were much less pronounced in neighboring Austria. In contrast, in the Western half of the empire "home industry" or home work was a much more significant bone of contention compared to Hungary, and the tendency to exclude this group of workers was more pronounced. Overall coverage, however, was significantly higher in Cisleithania.[10] In Germany, the birth place of Bismarkian social insurance, agricultural workers were included in health and accident insurance in 1886, and additional groups other than the 'classical' workers in trade and commerce followed. While overall coverage in Hungary in workers' health insurance (there was no compulsory health insurance in agriculture) after the 1907 reform was less than six percent of the population, in Germany health insurance in 1900 covered 18 percent of the population. Accident insurance in Hungary covered—including those insured in workers' and agrarian insurance—less than 8 percent of the population in 1910, as compared to 31 percent in Germany in 1900.[11] While this was certainly partly due to the higher level of economic 'development' in Germany, these and comparable data still underline the fact that social insurance in Hungary contributed

[10] See Zimmermann, "Geschützte und ungeschützte Arbeitsverhältnisse" [Protected and unprotected labor relations]; Eckardt Reidegeld, *Staatliche Sozialpolitik in Deutschland. Historische Entwicklung und theoretische Analyse von den Ursprüngen bis 1918* [State social policy in Germany. Historical development and theoretical analysis from the beginnings to 1918] (Opladen 1996), 235.

[11] Reidegeld, *Staatliche Sozialpolitik in Deutschland* [State social policy in Germany], 210–273; Herbert Pruns, "Soziale Sicherung im Bereich der Landwirtschaft. Versuch eines internationalen Vergleichs" [Social policy in the area of agriculture. An attempt at international comparison]. *Vierteljahresschrift für Sozial- und Wirtschaftsgeschichte* (1991), supplement no. 95: 295–357, here 299, 309–312.

far less than in other countries to protecting the population against material lack and social risk within the overall framework of need-related policy.

Workers' protection at the workplace in Hungary was also weak. The weight of employers' interest in Hungarian politics at both national and local levels was amply demonstrated, for example, by the hesitant implementation and supervision of existing provisions and the equally halting progress of special protection of women. While in Austria patriarchal interest in "family protection" largely contributed to a decisive enlargement of special labor protection for women in the 1880s,[12] in Hungary comparable perspectives, though represented in the parliament, had no chance to assert themselves against employers' interest.

Despite the limited room for maneuver and the low level of provision in Hungarian need-related policy in the areas discussed above, there was also imaginative innovation and reform on both national and local levels. For sure, many characteristic legal and institutional features of Hungarian need-related policy resembled the legislation and institutions of other countries. Important elements of workers' insurance were largely built on the Bismarckian model. Key elements of poverty policy, such as the "home town" or legal residence status principle, had been directly imported in the early days from Austria. Special labor protection for women and the—by European standards—early introduction of social insurance,[13] as well as the emergence of certain features of social reform such as the establishment of a national system of labor exchanges, were clearly influenced by international developments. More examples could be added. And yet, divergent social and economic circumstances and political interest constellations triggered change and innovation too. This is true for a whole number of more specific features of individual areas of need-related policies, such as the particularly restrictive approach taken by the Budapest poor relief authorities in relation to single moth-

[12] Ingrid Mairhuber, *Die Regulierung des Geschlechterverhältnisses im Sozialstaat Österreich* [The regulation of gender relations in the Austrian welfare state], Frankfurt/M.–Berlin–Berne–Bruxelles–New York–Vienna: Peter Lang, 2000, section II.2.

[13] Without reference to Hungary but to many other smaller and bigger, more or less "developed" European states, Gerhard A. Ritter, *Der Sozialstaat. Entstehung und Entwicklung im internationalen Vergleich* [The welfare state. Emergence and development in international comparison] (Munich 1991), 87–95; Stein Kuhnle, Anne Sander, "The Emergence of the Western Welfare State," in: Francis G. Castles, Stephan Leibfried, Jane Lewis, Herbert Obinger, Christopher Pierson, eds. *The Oxford Handbook of the Welfare State* (Oxford 2010), 61–80, here 64–71.

ers.[14] In some contexts institutional features transferred basically unaltered from abroad brought unexpected innovation to the landscape of Hungarian politics. This was the case with the integration of the workers' movement into the institutions of public social insurance, even if the new institution was constructed in such a way in Hungary as to ensure stricter control of the labor movement than in Austria or Germany.[15]

Yet Hungarian need-related policy produced more far-reaching adaptations and highly distinctive innovations too, in both rural and urban contexts, and at both national and local levels. Two issues were of particular importance here. First, the significant role of large-scale agrarian and agro-industrial interest in the economy and in Hungarian politics, together with the dependency of the economy on the agricultural workforce, gave rise to specific developments in housing policy in the countryside, as well as agrarian social insurance and labor policies. From a comparative perspective, Hungary made itself into one of the pioneers in agrarian social policy. By including agricultural workers in labor insurance as early as 1886, Germany for decades remained an exception in Europe. Hungary followed with compulsory accident insurance in agriculture, Belgium and Luxemburg with partial inclusion of the agricultural labor force in social insurance in 1909. Many other countries lagged far behind.[16] In Austria, as regards legal stipulations and in terms of actual coverage as related to working period, a significantly lower proportion of the agricultural workforce was included in workers' health insurance than was the case for agrarian health insurance in Hungary.[17] Employers' interest played a major role in Hungarian agrarian

[14] Lees, *The Solidarities of Strangers*, 196–210; Susan Zimmermann, "Das Geschlecht der Fürsorge. Wohlfahrtspolitik in Budapest und Wien 1873–1914" [The gender of poor relief. Welfare policy in Budapest and Vienna 1873–1914]. *L'Homme* 5, no. 2 (1994): 19–40.

[15] In both Austria and Germany, representatives of the labor force were stronger represented in the institutional bodies governing social insurance, while there was also constant tension over the influence of the labor movement on and within the insurance companies. For Austria, see Robert Grandl, "Die Geschichte der Selbstverwaltung in der österreichischen Sozialversicherung. Von den Anfängen bis 1918" [The history of self-government in Austrian social insurance. From the beginnings to 1918], in: Prenninger, *Mercy or Right*, 81–102, here 93–98; for Germany, inclusive retrograde tendencies in the years before 1914 see Reidegeld, *Staatliche Sozialpolitik in Deutschland* [State social policy in Germany], 228–241, 256.

[16] Pruns, "Soziale Sicherung im Bereich der Landwirtschaft" [Social policy in the area of agriculture], 312–318.

[17] For Austria see Ernst Bruckmüller, Roman Sandgruber, Hannes Stekl, *Soziale Sicherheit im Nachziehverfahren. Die Einbeziehung der Bauern, Landarbeiter, Gewerbetreibenden*

social policy. Social insurance and labor policies in this field combined innovative adaptations of basic principles of labor insurance for the field of agricultural labor with the legal strengthening and expansion of restrictions on bonded and even "free" labor in this economic sector. There were distinct limits to benefits from agricultural accident and even more so health insurance. Yet the very invention of agrarian social insurance and the ensuing struggle over the inclusion of industry-type work in the agricultural sector into either workers' or agricultural insurance were indicative of the strategic importance of the agro-business for developments in and beyond Hungarian social policy.

Second, given widespread social marginalization and unstable living conditions, the limited scope of provision based in poor relief or social insurance, and considerable social tension and unrest, Hungarian authorities eventually resorted to innovative types of social reform. It was a decisive feature of the emerging social reform that it targeted clearly circumscribed "hubs" of what was now perceived more explicitly than earlier as the "social question." These included the extreme housing shortage and the tenants' movement in Budapest, children's misery and later "neglect," and the unemployment crises around the turn of the century and in 1913. As these problems played out or were perceived to play out in the most dramatic form in the capital city, the municipality of Budapest played a key role in these reforms. To an extent, municipal social policy and reform seemed to replace national policy. The municipal authorities fought hard to make the capital city into a "laboratory of socio-political reform" which should and could attract attention and generate recognition well beyond the borders of Hungary.[18] Budapest indeed took the lead in the field of municipal housing for the working classes on the European continent.[19] The state, however, also took its share. Triggered by alarming fi-

und Hausgehilfen in das System der österreichischen Sozialversicherung [Belated social security. The inclusion of peasants, agricultural workers, craftsmen and servants into the Austrian social insurance system] (Salzburg 1978), 60–66.

[18] Ferenczi, "A főváros szociálpolitikai programmja" [The socio-political program of the Capital City], 7.

[19] While there is no exhaustive comparison of municipal housing in the large cities of the European continent, the available information strongly suggests this conclusion. See a number of contributions in Juan Rodríguez-Lores, Gerhard Fehl, eds. *Die Kleinwohnungsfrage. Zu den Ursprüngen des sozialen Wohnbaus in Europa* [The question of small scale apartments. On the origins of social housing in Europe] (Hamburg 1988); M.J. Daunton, ed. *Housing the Workers. A Comparative History*, 1850–1914 (Leicester 1990).

nancial imbalances in the area of health care for the poor and the equally burning question of stabilizing poor families, the state created a childcare system that was characterized by a number of extraordinary features (though certainly it did not serve as a "model for richer countries"). What was genuinely lacking from the Hungarian state childcare system was the principle of socio-political "productivity" or efficiency, according to which the social system should generate not only costs but also income. Internationally the issue of "efficiency" of public intervention was a key feature in triggering and shaping modernist social reform that departed from old traditions of poor relief.[20] In Hungary it was the Budapest municipality rather than the state that adopted these new perspectives, building many elements of municipal social reform on the productivity principle. Yet it was not the lack of socio-political "productivity" alone that made the state childcare system into what contemporaries soon perceived as a bottomless pit, and the minister for the interior as something that definitely overstrained Hungary's resources. Rather, as a result of the limited social-integrative capacities of need-related policies in the other areas discussed in this study, the isolated reforms targeted at specific nodal points of the social question invited "misery of every kind" to come knocking at its door.

There were similarly intense struggles over the boundaries regulating access to provision in many other fields of Hungarian poverty policy, social policy and social reform. These were indicative of the continuing mismatch on the one hand between the magnitude of social need, and on the other the willingness and—within the given pattern of economic development and the related constellation of political interest—the ability of the authorities to provide for the needy and to mitigate social risk in Hungarian society.

[20] Rodgers, *Atlantic Crossings*, 213.

Bibliography

Archival material

BFL-C = Budapest Főváros Levéltára [Budapest Capital Archive]
Budapest Székesfőváros Tanácsának iratai [Documents of the Administrative Council of the Capital and Royal Seat Budapest] IV 1407b

SML = Somogy Megyei Levéltár [Somogy County Archive]
Igali Járás [District of Igal]
Kaposvár rtv. Képviselő testület [Secondary City of Kaposvár. Municipal Council]

Printed sources and secondary literature

A gyermekvédelem lapja, 9 (1913), 10 (1914).

A Budapesti kerületi általános munkás-betegsegélyező pénztár évi jelentése, zárószámadása és kimutatásai az 1906. évről [Annual report, account settling and statement of the general Budapest District Workers' Insurance Company for the year 1906], Budapest: Budapesti kerületi általános munkás-betegsegélyző pénztár, 1907.

A Budapesti kerületi betegsegélyző pénztár .... évi jelentése, zárószámadása és kimutatásai ... [First annual report, account settling and statement of the Budapest District Health Insurance Company ...]. 15 Dec. 1892–31 Dec. 1893, Budapest: Budapesti kerületi betegsegélyző pénztár, 1894; 1896: 1897; 1901: 1902; 1905: 1906.

A Budapesti kerületi munkásbiztositó pénztár évi jelentése, zárószámadása és kimutatásai az .... évről [Annual report, account settling and statement of the Budapest District Workers' Insurance Company for the year ...]. 1908: Budapest: Budapesti kerületi munkásbiztosító pénztár, 1909; 1913: 1914.

A Budapesti kerületi munkásbiztositó pénztár statisztikai kimutatásai az 1918. évről [Statistical disclosure of the Budapest District Workers' Insurance Company for the year 1918], Budapest: Országos munkásbiztosító pénztár, no year given.

A Magyar Királyi Kormány ... évi működéséről és az ország közállapotairól szóló jelentés és statisztikai évkönyv [Report and statistical yearbook on the activities of the Hungarian Royal Government and the Public Conditions in the Country in ...]. 1899: Budapest: Athenaeum, 1900; 1901: 1902; 1902: 1904; 1903: 1904; 1905: 1906; 1906: 1907; 1907: 1909; 1908: 1909; 1909: 1910; 1910: 1911; 1911: 1912; 1912: 1913; 1913: 1915; 1914: 1916.

A Magyar Korona Országainak az 1891. év elején végrehajtott népszámlálás eredményei. I. rész. Általános népleírás [Census of the lands of the Hungarian Crown conducted at the beginning of the year 1891. Part I. General description of the population]. Magyar Statisztikai Közlemények. Új Folyam [Hungarian statistical publications. New sequence], Budapest: Pesti Könyvnyomda Rt., 1893, vol. I.

A Magyar Szent Korona Országainak 1900. évi népszámlálása. Második rész. A népesség foglalkozása községenként [Census of the lands of the Holy Hungarian Crown for the year 1900. Employment of the population by municipality]. Magyar Statisztikai Közlemények. Új Sorozat [Hungarian statistical publications. New series], Budapest: Pesti Könyvnyomda Rt., 1904, vol. II.

A Magyar Szent Korona Országainak 1910. évi népszámlálása. Második rész. A népesség foglalkozása [Census of the lands of the Holy Hungarian Crown, 1910. Part two. The occupation of the population]. Magyar Statisztikai Közlemények. Új Sorozat [Hungarian statistical publications. New series], Budapest: Athenaeum, 1913, vol. XLVIII.

A Magyar Szent Korona Országainak 1910. évi népszámlálása. Negyedik rész. A népesség foglalkozása a főbb demográfiai adatokkal egybevetve s a népesség ház- és földbirtokviszonyai [Census of the lands of the Holy Hungarian Crown in 1910. The occupations of the population compared with the most important demographic figures and conditions of property and land ownership of the population]. Magyar Statisztikai Közlemények. Új Sorozat [Hungarian statistical publications. New series], Budapest: Athenaeum, 1915, vol. LVI.

A magyar társadalombiztosítás ötven éve 1892–1942 [Fifty years of Hungarian social insurance 1892–1942], Budapest: Országos társadalombiztbiztosító intézet, no year given.

A magyarországi szocziálisztikus munkásmozgalmak az 1906. évben [The socialist workers' movements of Hungary in the year 1906], Budapest: Országos Központi Községi Nyomda, 1907.

A munkásbiztositási törvény (1907: XIX. t.-c.) és választott bírósági eljárás kiegészítve a vonatkozó jogesetekkel és rendeletekkel. Jegyzetekkel, utalásokkal és magyarázatokkal ellátta Dr. Lévai Tibor budapesti ügyvéd [The labor insurance law (Act 19/1907) and arbitration proceedings, supplemented with the relevant legal cases and acts. With comments, suggestions and clarifications by Dr. Tibor Lévai, lawyer in Budapest], Budapest: Ráth, 1912.

A munkások baleset ellen való biztositása. I. rész. Hazai és külföldi anyag-gyűjtemény. II. rész. Törvényjavaslat és indoklás. Kiadja a kereskedelmügyi m. kir. miniszter [The insurance of workers against accidents. Part I. Domestic and international collection of materials. Part II. Legislative proposal and justification. Published by the Hungarian Royal Minister of Commerce], 2 vols, Budapest: Athenaeum, 1903.

A munkás-betegsegélyezési törvény módosítása. Hazai anyag három részben. Első rész: Joganyag. Második rész: Kivánságok és javaslatok. Harmadik rész: Statisztika [The modification of the law on workers' sickness benefits. Domestic material in three parts. Part 1: juridical material. Part 2: wishes and suggestions. Part 3: statistics], vol. I, Budapest: Athenaeum, 1905.

Allgemeines Reichs-Gesetz- und Regierungsblatt für das Kaiserthum Österreich, Kaiserliches Patent vom 27. Mai 1852 [General Imperial legislative and governmental gazette of the Austrian Empire, Imperial patent of 27 May 1852].

Angyal, Pál, Gyula Isaák. *A Kihágási Büntető Törvénykönyv. Jegyzetekkel, utalásokkal, magyarázatokkal és bírói gyakorlattal* [Criminal code for minor offences. With comments, indications, explanations and judicial practice], 2 vols, Budapest: Grill, third edition, 1937.

Beliznay, Kinga, et al. *Magyar jogtörténet* [Hungarian Legal History], Budapest: Osiris, 1996.

Az ipartörvény módosítása. Hazai anyag két részben. Első rész: Joganyag (Az iparra vonatkozó törvények, rendeletek és határozatok gyüjteménye). Második rész: Kívánságok és javaslatok (Az ipartörvény módosítására nezve felmerült kivánságok és javalatok, valamint törvény- és szabályrendelet-tervezetek gyüjteménye) [Modification of the trade law. Domestic material in two parts. Part one: Juridical material (Collection of laws, regulations and decisions on trade). Part two: Wishes and suggestions (Collection of wishes and suggestions on the amendment to the trade law as well as drafts of the law and statutes)] (part one in two partial vols., vols. I and II, part two as vol. III), Budapest: Athenaeum, 1904.

Az ipartörvény módosítása. Negyedik rész. Törvényjavaslat az ipar gyakorlásáról, valamint az ipari és kereskedelmi alkalmazottak védelméről. Előadói tervezet [Modification of the trade law. Part four. Legislative proposal for the practice of trade and the protection of employees in commerce and trade. Preliminary draft], vol. XI, Budapest: Athenaeum, 1908.

Az ipartörvény módosítása. Vélemények az ipar gyakorlásáról, valamint az ipari és kereskedelmi alkalmazottak védelméről szóló törvényjavaslat előadói tervezetére [Modification of the trade law. Responses to the preliminary draft of the legislative proposal for the practice of trade and the protection of employees in commerce and trade.], vols. XII-XIV, Budapest: Athenaeum, 1909.

Az Országos gazdasági munkás- és cselédsegélypénztár első tíz évi működése (1901–1910) és X. évi jelentése a pénztár 1910. évi működéséről [The first ten years activity of the National Insurance for Agricultural Workers and Servants (1901–1910) and 10th annual report on the activity of the insurance in 1910], Budapest: Franklin, 1911.

Az Országos munkásbetegsegélyző és balesetbiztosító pénztár első évi jelentése ... [... annual report ... of the National Workers' Health and Accident Insurance Company]. 1907–1908: Budapest: Pesti Könyvnyomda Rt., 1909; 1909: 1910; 1911: 1912.

Bolognese-Leuchtenmüller, Birgit. *Bevölkerungsentwicklung und Berufsstruktur, Gesundheits- und Fürsorgewesen in Österreich 1750–1918* [Population development and occupational structure, the healthy and welfare system in Austria 1750–1918]. Wirtschafts- und Sozialstatistik Österreich-Ungarns [Economic and social statistics of Austria-Hungary], vol. I, Vienna: Verlag für Geschichte und Politik, 1978.

Bódy, Zsombor. "A 'szociális kérdés' kezelésének alternatívái a 19. század végén. Az 1891-es kötelező betegbiztosítási törvény keletkezése" [Alternatives in handling the "social question" at the end of the 19th century. The emergence of the law on compulsory health insurance of 1891]. *Korall. Társadalomtörténeti folyóirat*, no. 5–6 (2001): 72–93.

———. "A 'társadalom kora'. Munkásbiztosítás és munkaügy Magyarországon a 19. és a 20. század fordulóján" [The "age of society." Labor insurance and labor affairs in Hungary at the turn of the 19th to 20th century]. *Aetas. Történettudmányi folyóirat* 19, no. 1 (2004): 5–29.

Bősze, Sándor. "*Az egyesületi élet a polgári szabadság...*" *Somogy megye egyesületei a dualizmus korában* ["The activity of associations is civic freedom..." The societies of Somogy County under the Dual Monarchy], Kaposvár: Somogy Megyei Levéltár, 1997.

Brandes, Inga, Katrin Marx-Jasulski. "Armut und ländliche Gesellschaften im europäischen Vergleich." Eine Einführung [Poverty and rural societies in European comparison. An introduction], in: Inga Brandes, Katrin Marx-Jasulski, eds. *Armenfürsorge und Wohltätigkeit. Ländliche Gesellschaften in Europa, 1850–1930 / Poor Relief and Charity. Rural Societies in Europe, 1850–1930.* (English-German). Inklusion/Exklusion. Studien zu Fremdheit und Armut von der Antike bis zur Gegenwart [Inclusion/exclusion. Studies on foreignness and poverty from antiquity to present], vol. XI, Frankfurt/M.–Berlin–Berne–Bruxelles–New York–Oxford–Vienna: Peter Lang, 2008, 9–45.

Bruckmüller, Ernst, Roman Sandgruber, Hannes Stekl. *Soziale Sicherheit im Nachziehverfahren. Die Einbeziehung der Bauern, Landarbeiter, Gewerbetreibenden und Hausgehilfen in das System der österreichischen Sozialversicherung* [Belated social security. The inclusion of peasants, agricultural workers, craftsmen and servants into the Austrian social insurance system]. Geschichte und Sozialkunde [History and social studies], vol. III, Salzburg: Neugebauer, 1978.

Budapest fő- és székváros közigazgatási bizottságának jelentése a közigazgatás összes ágainak állapotáról az 1891. év II-ik felében [Report of the administrative committee of the Capital City and Royal Seat of Budapest on the state of all branches of the administration in the second half of the year 1891], Budapest: Budapest Főváros Közigazgatási Bizottsága, 1892.

Budapest Fő- és Székesvárosi Állami Rendőrség .... évi működése [The activities of the State Police in the Capital City and Royal Seat of Budapest in ...]. 1895: Budapest: A Pesti Lloyd-Társulat Könyvnyomdája, 1896; 1897: Budapest, Rózsa Kálmán és Neje Könyvnyomdája, 1898; 1899: *Jelentés a Budapest Fő- és Székesvárosi Állami Rendőrség 1899. évi működéséről,* Budapest: Rózsa Kálmán és Neje Könyvnyomdája, 1900; 1908: *Jelentés a Budapesti Állami Rendőrség 1908. évi működéséről,* Budapest: Radó Izor Nyomdai Műintézete, 1909.

Buday, László. *Magyarország községeinek háztartása az 1908. évben. Különlenyomat a Magyar statisztikai közlemények új sorozatának 39. kötetéből* [The budget of the smaller communities in Hungary in 1908. Special edition of volume 39 of the new series of Hungarian statistical publications], Budapest: Pesti Könyvnyomda Rt., 1913.

Crossman, Virginia. "The Humanization of the Irish Poor Laws. Reassessing Developments in Social Welfare in Post-Famine Ireland," in: Andreas Gestrich, Steven King,

Lutz Raphael, eds. *Being Poor in Modern Europe. Historical Perspectives 1800–1940,* Frankfurt/M.–Berlin–Berne–Bruxelles–New York–Oxford–Vienna: Peter Lang, 2006, 229–249.

Csizmadia, Andor. *A magyar közigazgatás fejlődése a XVIII. századtól a tanácsrendszer létrejöttéig* [The development of Hungarian administration from the 18th century to the emergence of the (1919) Soviet system], Budapest: Akadémiai Kiadó, 1976.

———. *A szociális gondoskodás változásai Magyarországon* [Changes in social welfare in Hungary], Budapest: MTA Állam- és Jogtudományi Intézet, 1977.

Csorna, Kálmán. "Az állami gyermekvédelem és a főváros" [State child protection and the Capital]. *Városi Szemle. Közlemények a városi közigazgatás és statisztika köréből* 12 (1926): 78–90.

Czettler, Jenő. *Magyar mezőgazdasági szociálpolitika* [Hungarian agricultural social policy], Budapest: Pátria, 1914.

Daunton, M. J., ed. *Housing the Workers. A Comparative History, 1850–1914*, Leicester: Leicester University Press, 1990.

Dóczi, Sámuel. *Az iparüzemekben alkalmazott nők éjjeli munkájáról szóló 1911. évi törvénycikk* [The article of law of 1911 on the night work of women employed in industry], Budapest: Országos Iparegyesület kiadványai, 1912.

Dudeková, Gabriela. "Das soziale Wohnmodell für Arbeiter in Preßburg am Ende des 19. Jahrhunderts" [The social housing model for workers in Bratislava at the end of the 19th century], in: Viliam Čičaj, Othmar Pickl, eds. *Städtisches Alltagsleben vom Mittelalter bis zum Ende 19. Jahrhunderts. Die Referate des Internationalen Symposions in Častá-Píla vom 11. bis 14. September 1995* [Urban every-day life from the medieval age to the end of the 19th century. The presentations given at the international symposium in Častá-Píla, 11 to 14 September 1995], Bratislava: AEP, 1998, 339–346.

Fáy, Gyula. *Az Országos Gazdasági Munkás- és Cselédsegélypénztár* [The National Insurance for Agricultural Workers and Servants], Budapest: Országos Központi Községi Nyomda, 1904.

Fényes, Elek. *A magyar birodalom statisticai, geographiai és történeti tekintetben. Részletes és kimerítő leírása Magyar és Erdélyországnak* [The Hungarian empire in statistical, geographical and historical perspective. Detailed and extensive account of Hungary and Transylvania], Pest: Beimel, 1848.

———. *Magyarország ismertetése statisztikai, földirati s történeti szempontból* [Description of Hungary from the statistical, geographic and historical point of view], vols. I-1 and I-2, Pest: Pollák Nyomda, 1865, 1866.

Ferenczi, Emerich. *Die kommunale Wohnungspolitik in Ungarn, namentlich in Budapest 1910. Sonderdruck anlässlich des IX. Internationalen Wohnungskongresses in Wien* [Municipal housing policy in Hungary, specifically in Budapest 1910. Special print on the occasion of the IX International Housing Congress in Vienna], no place, publisher, year given.

———. *Die behördliche Organisation des Arbeitsmarktes in Ungarn. Sonderdruck aus der Zeitschrift für Volkswirtschaft, Sozialpolitik und Verwaltung* [The Official organization of the labor market in Hungary. Separate print from *Zeitschrift für Volkswirtschaft, Sozialpolitik und Verwaltung*], Vienna, 1917.

Ferenczi, Imre. "A magyar lakásügy haladása az utolsó öt évben" [The progress of Hungarian housing affairs in the last five years]. *Városi Szemle* 3 (1910): 351–364.

———. "A főváros szociálpolitikai programmja" [The socio-political program of the Capital]. *Munkásügyi Szemle* 2 (1911): 3–7.

———. "A főváros első munkanélküliségi akciója" [The first action of the capital against unemployment]. *Városi Szemle* 6 (1913): 503–538.

———. *A lakásügy állása és haladása Magyarországon az utolsó három évben* [The situation and progress of housing in Hungary in the last three years]. Special print of an article originally published in *Városi Szemle*, Budapest, 1913.

Finkey, Ferencz. A csavargás és koldulás szabályozása kriminálpolitikai szempontból [The regulation of vagabondage and mendicancy from the point of view of criminal policy]. Special print from *Jogállam,* Budapest, 1909.

———. "A csavargás, koldulás és iszákosság törvényhozási szabályozáshoz" [On the legal regulation of vagabondage, begging and drunkenness]. Büntetőjogi értekezések, vol. IIX, Budapest: Révai és Salamon Nyomda, 1910.

Forbáth, Tivadar. *A magyar szegényügy rendezése* [The regulation of the poor relief system in Hungary], Budapest: Márkus S. Nyomda, 1910.

Források Budapest történetéhez [Sources on the history of Budapest], 4 vols., Budapest: Budapest főváros levéltára, 1971–1973.

Fővárosi Közlöny. Budapest székesfőváros hivatalos lapja 12 (1901), 17 (1906).

Gaál, Ibolya. A szegényügy- és felnőttvédelmi szociálpolitika története Szabolcs-Szatmár megyében 1867–1989 [History of poverty policy and the social policy of the protection of adults in Szabolcs–Szatmár County]. A Szabolcs-Szatmár-Bereg Megyei Önkormányzat Levéltárának Kiadványai III. Tanulmányok [Szabolcs-Szatmár-Bereg County Self-Government Archives Publications III. Studies], vol. V, 2 partial vols., Nyíregyháza: Szabolcs-Szatmár-Bereg Megyei Önkormányzat Levéltára, 1997.

Geml, József. *Temesvár lakáspolitikája. Tanulmány a munkáslakások kérdéséhez* [The housing policy of Temesvár. A study on the question of workers' housing], Temesvár: Uhrmann, 1906.

———, ed. *Temesvár szabad királyi város közállapotai az 1910. évben* [The public conditions in the Royal Free City of Temesvár in 1910], Temesvár: Uhrmann, 1910.

Geyr, Géza von. "Die Wekerlesiedlung in Budapest. Staatliche Arbeitersiedlung und Gartenstadt" [The Wekerle settlement in Budapest. State workers' housing and garden city], in: *Ungarn Jahrbuch. Zeitschrift für die Kunde Ungarns und verwandter Gebiete*, vol. XVII, 1989, 71–94.

Grandl, Robert. "Die Geschichte der Selbstverwaltung in der österreichischen Sozialversicherung. Von den Anfängen bis 1918" [The history of self-government in Austrian social insurance. From the beginnings to 1918], in: Alexander Prenninger, *"Mercy or Right". Development of Social Security Systems*. ITH-Tagungsberichte [ITH Conference proceedings], vol. XXXIX, Vienna: Akademische Verlagsanstalt, 2005, 81–102.

Gyáni, Gábor. A szociálpolitika múltja Magyarországon [The Past of Social Policy in Hungary]. História Kvt. Monográfiák. Előadások a történettudomány műhelyeiből, vol. IV, Budapest: MTA Történettudományi Intézet, 1994.

———. "A szociálpolitika első lépései hazánkban: Darányi törvényei" [The first socio-political steps in our homeland: Darányi's law], in: *Darányi Ignác emlékkonferencia* [Ignác Darányi memorial conference], Budapest: Magyar Mezőgazdasági Múzeum, 2000, 94–110.

Halász, Aladár. *A munkásbetegsegélyezés és balesetbiztosítás kézikönyve. Az 1907. évi XIX. t.-c. magyarázata a vonatkozó rendeletek, határozatok, itéletek és utasításokból álló teljes joganyag feldolgozásával* [Handbook of workers' accident and health insurance, commentary on Act 19/1907 taking into account all legal materials comprising the relevant regulations, decisions, judgments and directives], Budapest: Lampel, 1909.

Halász, Sándor, Gyula Mandello, eds. *Közgazdasági Lexikon* [Economic encyclopedia], 3 vols., Budapest: Pallas, 1898–1901.

Hanák, Péter. "Das Zeitalter des Dualismus, 1867–1919" [The Dualist period, 1867–1919], in: Barta, István et. al., eds. *Die Geschichte Ungarns* [The history of Hungary], Budapest: Corvina, 1971, 379–495.

Heller, Farkas. *Magyarország szociálpolitikája* [Social policy of Hungary], Budapest: Németh, 1923.

Hlavács, Kornél. "Az iparfelügyelők tevékenysége az 1909. évben" [The activity of the trade inspectors in the year 1909] (third sequence). *Munkásügyi Szemle* 1 (1910): 718–721.

Illustrierter Führer durch Pozsony (Pressburg) und Umgebung [Illustrated guide to Pozsony (Pressburg) and its surroundings], Pressburg: Sigmund Steiner's Buchhandlung, no year given.

Internationales Übereinkommen vom 26. September 1906 betreffend das Verbot der Verwendung von weissem (gelbem) Phosphor in der Zündholzindustrie [International convention as of 26 September 1906 on the abolition of the use of white (yellow) phosphorus in the matchstick industry], available at http://www.admin.ch/ch/i/rs/c0_822_15.html and http://www.swissembassy.org.uk/eda/de/home/topics/intla/intrea/dbstv/data22/e_19060022.html, 24/01/2011.

Jelentés az állami gyermekmenhelyek 1907–1910. évi munkásságáról [Report on the work of the state children's asylums from 1907–1910], Budapest: Schmidl Nyomda, 1913.

John, Michael. Hausherrenmacht und Mieterelend 1890–1923 [Landlord power, tenants' misery 1890–1923]. Österreichische Texte zur Gesellschaftskritik, vol. XIV, Vienna: Verlag für Gesellschaftskritik, 1982.

Kácser, Romulus. *Temesvár emberbaráti intézményei* [The philanthropic institutions of Temesvár], Temesvár: Uhrmann, 1906.

Képviselőház Irományai [Documents of the House of Representatives]

Killyen, Hansgeorg von. "Zur Geschichte des siebenbürgisch-sächsischen Fürsorgewesens" [On the history of Transylvanian-Saxon welfare]. *Zeitschrift für Siebenbürgische Landeskunde* 8 (1985): 163–172.

———. "Zur Geschichte der siebenbürgisch-sächsischen Kinderschutzbewegung und der Säuglingspflegerinnen-Schule in Hermannstadt" [On the history of the Transylvanian-Saxon child protection movement and the infant nurse's school in Hermannstadt]. *Zeitschrift für Siebenbürgische Landeskunde* 21 (1998): 26–37.

Kőrösy, Josef von. *Die Armenpflege der Haupt- und Residenzstadt Budapest in den Jahren 1900–1902* [Poor relief in the Capital City and Royal Seat of Budapest in the years 1900–1902]. Publikationen des Statistischen Amtes der Haupt- und Residenzstadt Budapest, vol. XXXVII, Berlin: Puttkammer und Mühlbrecht, 1905.

Közigazgatási döntvénytár. Szerkeszti Dr. Marschalkó János. Kiadja a Jogtudományi Közlöny szerkesztősége [Collection of decisions in public administration. Edited by Dr. János Marschalkó. Published by the editorial office of the *Jogtudományi Közlöny*], 11 vols., Budapest: Franklin, 1908–1922.

Közigazgatási elvi határozatok egyetemes gyüjteménye. Összeállította és kiadja a Magyar közigazgatás szerkesztősége [Universal collection of principle administrative decisions. Assembled and published and by the editorial office of *Magyar közigazgatás*], 3 vols., Budapest: Pallas, 1895.

Közigazgatási elvi határozatok egyetemes gyüjteménye. Összeállította és kiadja a Magyar közigazgatás szerkesztősége. Új-folyam [Universal collection of principle administrative decisions. Assembled and published by the editorial office of *Magyar közigazgatás*. New series], 3 vols., Budapest: Pallas, 1900, 1906, 1910.

Kuhnle, Stein, Anne Sander. "The Emergence of the Western Welfare State," in: Francis G. Castles, Stephan Leibfried, Jane Lewis, Herbert Obinger, Christopher Pierson, eds. *The Oxford Handbook of the Welfare State,* Oxford: Oxford University Press, 2010, 61–80.

Küster, Thomas. "Der Einfluss von Industrialisierung und sozialer Gesetzgebung auf die ländliche Armenfürsorge in Westfalen (1850–1920)" [The impact of industrialization and social legislation on rural poor relief in Westfalia (1850–1920)], in: Brandes, Marx-Jasulski, *Poor Relief and Charity* 2008, 47–72.

Lachnit, Peter. Staatliche Sozialpolitik für und gegen die Arbeiterschaft. Arbeiterbewegung and Sozialversicherung in Österreich von den Anfängen bis 1918 [State social policy in favor and against the workforce. The workers' movement and social insurance in Austria from the beginnings to 1918], Phil. Diss. Vienna, 1989.

Lackó, István. *A magyar munkás- és társadalombiztosítás története* [The history of Hungarian labor and social insurance]. Budapest: Táncsics Kiadó, 1968.

Lees, Lynn Hollen. *The Solidarities of Strangers. The English Poor Laws and the People, 1700–1948,* Cambridge – New York – Melbourne: Cambridge University Press, 1998.

Lichtblau, Albert. "Boykott, Krawall, Gewalt, Demonstration. Die Budapester Mieterbewegung 1906 bis 1912 und exkursive Vergleiche zu ähnlichen Vorgängen in Wien" [Boycott, riot, violence, demonstration. The Budapest tenants' movement 1906 to 1912 and some elements of comparison to similar events in Vienna], in: *Archiv. Jahrbuch des Vereins für Geschichte der Arbeiterbewegung*, vol. IIX, 1992, 65–82.

———. Budapester Mieterbewegung. Dokumentation [The Budapest tenants' movement. Documentation], unpublished research report.

Lőrincz, Ernő. *A munkaviszonyok szabályozása Magyarországon a kapitalizmus kezdeteitől az első világháború végéig 1840–1918* [Labor relations in Hungary from the beginnings of capitalism until the end of the First World War 1840–1918], Budapest: Akadémiai Kiadó, 1974.

Löwenfeld, Walter. "Die Statistik der direkten Steuern" [Statistics of direct taxation]. *Zeitschrift für Volkswirtschaft, Sozialpolitik und Verwaltung* 14 (1905): 299–320.

Magyar Hirlap, 18 (1908).

Magyar ipar, 19 (1898); 31 (1910).

Magyar közigazgatás, 5 (1887), 17 (1899), 33 (1905).

Magyar Statisztikai Évkönyv. Új folyam [Hungarian statististical yearbook. New series], vol. XVIII, 1910.

Magyar Törvénytár [Hungarian Corpus Juris].

Magyarországi rendeletek tára [Collection of Hungarian ordinances].

Mannová, Elena. "Charitable Societies and the Construction of Collective Identities," in: Moritz Csáky, Elena Mannová, eds. *Collective Identities in Central Europe in Modern Times*, Bratislava: Slovak Academy of Science, 1999. 197–216.

Marx-Jaskulski, Katrin. *Armut und Fürsorge auf dem Land. Vom Ende des 19. Jahrhunderts bis 1933* [Poverty and poor relief in the country-side. From the end of the 19th century to 1933]. Moderne Zeit. Neue Forschungen zur Gesellschafts- und Kulturgeschichte des 19. und 20. Jahrhunderts, vol. XVI, Göttingen: Wallstein Verlag, 2008.

Mairhuber, Ingrid. *Die Regulierung des Geschlechterverhältnisses im Sozialstaat Österreich* [The regulation of gender relations in the Austrian welfare state], Frankfurt/M. – Berlin – Berne – Bruxelles – New York – Vienna: Peter Lang, 2000.

Melinz, Gerhard, Susan Zimmermann. "Die aktive Stadt. Kommunale Politik zur Gestaltung städtischer Lebensbedingungen in Budapest, Prag und Wien (1867–1914)" [The Active City. Municipal Policy and the Shaping of Urban Living Conditions in Budapest, Prague and Vienna (1867–1914)], in: Gerhard Melinz, Susan Zimmermann, eds. *Wien, Prag, Budapest. Blütezeit der Habsburgermetropolen. Urbanisierung, Kommunalpolitik, gesellschaftliche Konflikte (1867–1918)* [*Vienna, Prague, Budapest. Heyday of the Habsburg Metropolises. Urbanization, Communal Policy and Social Conflict* (1867–1918)], Vienna: Promedia Verlag, 1996, 140–176, 263–276.

———. "Mit den Waffen der Sozialpolitik? Wohnungspolitischer Interventionismus in Österreich und Ungarn von 1890 bis in die 1930er Jahre" [With the weapons of social policy? Housing policy interventionism in Austria and Hungary from 1890 to the 1930s], in: Clemens Zimmermann, ed. *Europäische Wohnungspolitik in vergleichender Perspektive* [European housing policy in comparative perspective] (1900–1939), Stuttgart: Fraunhofer-IRB Verlag, 1997, 85–129.

Meyers Großes Konversations-Lexikon (1907), available at http://www.peter-hug.ch/lexikon/arbeiterschutzkonferenz?q=Arbeiterschutzkonferenz#H.18_0048.0540, 09/04/2009.

Mezey, Barna, ed. *A magyarországi cigánykérdés dokumentumokban 1422–1985* [The Hungarian Gypsy question in documents 1422–1985], Budapest: Kossuth, 1986.

Munkásbiztositás. Munkásbiztositási, munkásvédelmi és közgazdasági folyóirat 1 (1908), 2 (1909).

Munkásbiztositási Közlöny. A M. Kir. Állami Munkásbiztositási Hivatal hivatalos lapja 1 (1907), 2 (1908), 4 (1910), 5 (1911), 7 (1913), 8 (1914).

Munkásügyi Szemle. Közlemények a munkásbiztositás, a szociális egeszsegügy, a munkásvédelem, a munkaviszony és az idevonatkozó joggyakorlat köréből 1 (1910), 2 (1911), 3 (1912).

Nagy, Ferencz. "A községi illetőség" [Legal residence status]. *Magyar közigazgatás* 33, no. 27 (1905): 1 f.

Országgyűlési Képviselőház Jegyzőkönyvei [Minutes of the House of Parliamentary Representatives].

Országgyűlési Képviselőház Naplói [Chronicle of the House of Parliamentary Representatives].

Pallas Nagylexikon [Pallas Encyclopedia], 18 vols., Budapest: Pallas, 1893–1900.

Pap, Géza. "Törvény (1913. évi XXI. törvénycikk) a közveszélyes munkakerülőkről" [Law (21st Law of 1913) on the publicly dangerous work-shy]. *A munkanélküliség elleni küzdelem. A nemzetközi egyesület magyar osztályának közleményei*, no 1. (1913), 5–13.

Perneczky, Béla. *A gazdasági cselédek szolgálati viszonyai* [Conditions of service of agricultural servants], Budapest: Pátria, 1928.

Petrák, Katalin. *A szervezett munkásság küzdelme a korszerű társadalombiztosításért* [The fight of the organised workforce for modern social insurance], Budapest: Táncsics Kiadó, 1978.

Pik, Katalin. *A szociális munka története Magyarországon (1817–1990)* [The history of social work in Hungary (1817–1990)]. Budapest: Hilscher Rezső Szociálpolitikai Egyesület, 2001.

Pomogyi, László. *Cigánykérdés és cigányügyi igazgatás a polgári Magyarországon* [The Gypsy question and management of Gypsy affairs in bourgeois Hungary], Budapest, no publisher given, 1995.

——. *Szegényügy és községi illetőség a polgári Magyarországon* [Poverty policy and legal residence status in bourgeois Hungary], Budapest: Osiris, 2001.

Protokolle der Internationalen Arbeiterschutzkonferenz. Im amtlichen Auftrag [Minutes of the International Labor Protection Conference. Officially commissioned], Leipzig, 1890. Available at http://ia311333.us.archive.org/0/items/dieprotokolleder00confuoft/dieprotokolleder00confuoft.pdf, 10/04/2009.

Pruns, Herbert. "Soziale Sicherung im Bereich der Landwirtschaft. Versuch eines internationalen Vergleichs" [Social policy in the area of agriculture. An attempt at international comparison]. *Vierteljahresschrift für Sozial- und Wirtschaftsgeschichte* (1991), supplement no. 95: Hans Pohl, ed. Staatliche, städtische, betriebliche und kirchliche Sozialpolitik vom Mittealter bis zur Gegenwart [State, municipal, company and church social policy from the middle ages to the present], 295–357.

Reidegeld, Eckardt. *Staatliche Sozialpolitik in Deutschland. Historische Entwicklung und theoretische Analyse von den Ursprüngen bis 1918* [State social policy in Germany. Historical development and theoretical analysis from the beginnings to 1918], Opladen: Westdeutscher Verlag, 1996.

Richers, Julia. "Johanna Bischitz" in: Francisca de Haan, Krassimira Daskalova, Anna Loutfi, eds. *A Biographical Dictionary of Women's Movements and Feminisms: Central, Eastern and South Eastern Europe, 19th and 20th Centuries*, Budapest – New York: CEU Press, 2006, 58–61.

Ritter, Gerhard A. *Der Sozialstaat. Entstehung und Entwicklung im internationalen Vergleich* [The welfare state. Emergence and development in international comparison], Munich: Oldenbourg, 1991, 87–95.

Rodgers, Daniel T. *Atlantic Crossings. Social Politics in a Progressive Age*, Cambridge – London: Belknap Press, 1998.

Rodríguez-Lores, Juan, Gerhard Fehl, eds. *Die Kleinwohnungsfrage. Zu den Ursprüngen des sozialen Wohnbaus in Europa* [The question of small scale apartments. On the origins of social housing in Europe]. Stadt. Planung. Geschichte [City. Planning. History], vol. IXX, Hamburg: Christians, 1988.

Rokken, Ferenc. "A pesti kényszerítő dologház" [The Pest workhouse]. *História* 3 (1930): 82–87.

Rózsay, Jos. *Sanitätsbericht vom Jahre 1851 über das Zwangsarbeitshaus zu St. Rochus und die Armenversorgungsanstalt der königlichen Freistadt Pesth* [Sanitary report from 1851 on the workhouse of St. Rochus and poor relief institute of the royal city of Pesth], Pesth: Landerer u. Heckenast, 1852.

Sárdi, Gyula. *A Kaposvári kerületi betegsegélyező pénztár története 1894–1916* [History of the Kaposvár District Health Insurance Company 1894–1916], no place given: Önadózó Rt., 1996.

Schulpe, György. *Munkásügyi reformok. Államügyi, törvényhatósági és társadalmi szocializmus* [Reforms to workers' affairs. State, municipal and social socialism], 2 vols., Pozsony: Steiner Zsigmond, 1908.

Schmelhegger, Árpád. "Városépítés" [Building the city], in: *A negyvenéves Budapest. Értekezések a városi közigazgatás köréből. A Városi Szemle jubiláris száma* [Budapest forty years. Studies on municipal administration. *Városi Szemle* anniversary edition], [Budapest: Székesfővárosi Házinyomda, 1914], 378–437.

Schuler, Dezső. *A hajléktalanság kérdése a székesfővárosban* [The question of homelessness in the Capital City and Royal Seat of Budapest]. Statisztikai Közlemények, vol. LXXVI, no. 1, Budapest: Székesfővárosi Házinyomda, 1935.

Stubenrauch, Moriz von. *Statistische Darstellung des Vereinswesens im Kaiserthume Österreich* [Statistical presentation of societies in the Austrian Empire], Vienna: Kaiserlich-Königliche Hof- und Staatsdruckerei, 1857.

Szaplonczay, Mihály. *A toloncz-ügy közigazgatása. A tolonczügyre vonatkozó összes rendeletek és szabályok gyüjteménye és magyarázata* [The administration of relocation. Collection and explanation of all decrees and directives related to relocation], Budapest: Országos Központi Községi Nyomda, 1903.

Szeglethy, György. "A községi illetőség és a szegényügy országos rendezése" [Legal residence status and the countrywide regulation of poverty policy]. *Városok Lapja* 1 (1906): 2.

Szikra, Dorottya. "Az 1891. évi betegbiztosítási törvény végrehajtása" [The enforcement of the health insurance law of 1891]. *Aetas* 19, no. 1 (2004): 31–48.

Szociálpolitikai Szemle 3 (1913), 4 (1914).

Szterényi, Josef. *Die Arbeiterversicherung in Ungarn. Internationaler Arbeiterversicherungskongress, 7. Tagung, Wien, 17. bis 23. September 1905* [Labor insurance in Hungary. International labor insurance congress, Vienna, 17–23 September 1905], no place, publisher, year given.

Thiele, J.C.von. *Das Königreich Ungarn. Ein topographisch-historisch-statistisches Rundgemälde, das Ganze dieses Landes in mehr denn 12.400 Artikeln umfassend* [The Kingdom of Hungary. A topographical, historical and statistical overview, capturing the whole of the country in more than 12,400 articles], 6 vols., Kaschau, no publisher given, 1833.

Thirring, Gusztáv, ed. *A magyar városok statisztikai évkönyve* [Statistical yearbook of Hungarian cities], vol. I, 1912.

Törvényjavaslat az iparüzemekben alkalmazott nők éjjeli munkájának eltiltásáról [Legislative proposal for the prohibition of women's night work in industry], no place, publisher, year given.

Váradi, János. "A magyarországi cigány népesség számának alakulása 1850–1910" [The development of the Gypsy population 1850–1910]. *Regio. Kisebbség, Politika, Társadalom* 20, no. 4 (2009): 60–81.

Veits-Falk, Sabine. "Öffentliche Armenfürsorge in Österreich im 19. Jahrhundert" [Public poor relief in Austria in the 19th century], in: Prenninger, *"Mercy or Right"*, 2005, 31–44.

Werkner, Albert. *Der Kleinwohnungsbau in Budapest* [The construction of small apartments in Budapest], Weida: Thomas & Hubert, 1913.

Zimmermann, Susan. "Das Geschlecht der Fürsorge. Wohlfahrtspolitik in Budapest und Wien 1873–1914" [The gender of poor relief. Welfare policy in Budapest and Vienna 1873–1914]. *L'Homme. Zeitschrift für feministische Geschichtswissenschaft* 5, no. 2 (1994): 19–40.

———. "Frauenarbeit, soziale Politiken and die Umgestaltung von Geschlechterverhältnissen im Wien der Habsburgermonarchie" [Women's labor, social policies and the transformation of relations between the sexes in Vienna under the Habsburg Monarchy], in: Lisa Fischer, Emil Brix, eds. *Die Frauen der Wiener Moderne* [Women in modern Vienna], Vienna – Munich: Verlag für Geschichte und Politik, 1997, 34–52.

———. "Geschützte und ungeschützte Arbeitsverhältnisse von der Hochindustrialisierung bis zur Weltwirtschaftskrise. Österreich und Ungarn im Vergleich" [Protected and unprotected labor relations from the peak of industrialization to the great depression], in: Andrea Komlosy, Christof Parnreiter, Irene Stacher, Susan Zimmermann, eds. *Ungeregelt und unterbezahlt. Der informelle Sektor in der Weltwirtschaft* [Unregulated and underpaid. The informal sector in the world economy], Frankfurt/M.–Vienna: Brandes & Apsel, 1997, 87–115.

———. *Prächtige Armut. Fürsorge, Kinderschutz und Sozialreform in Budapest. Das "sozialpolitische Laboratorium" der Doppelmonarchie im Vergleich zu Wien 1873–*

1914 [Splendid poverty. Welfare, child protection and social reform in Budapest. The "socio-political laboratory" of the Dual Monarchy in comparison to Vienna 1873–1914]. Historische Forschungen. Im Auftrag der Historischen Kommission der Akademie der Wissenschaften und Literatur [Historical studies. On behalf of the historical commission of the Academy of Sciences and Literature], vol. XXI, Sigmaringen: Thorbecke, 1997.

———. "Making a Living from Disgrace". The Politics of Prostitution, Female Poverty and Urban Gender Codes in Budapest and Vienna, 1860s–1920s, in: Malcolm Gee, Tim Kirk, Jill Steward, eds. *The City in Central Europe: Culture and Society in Central Europe since 1800*, London: Ashgate, 1999, 175–195.

Index

Illustrations

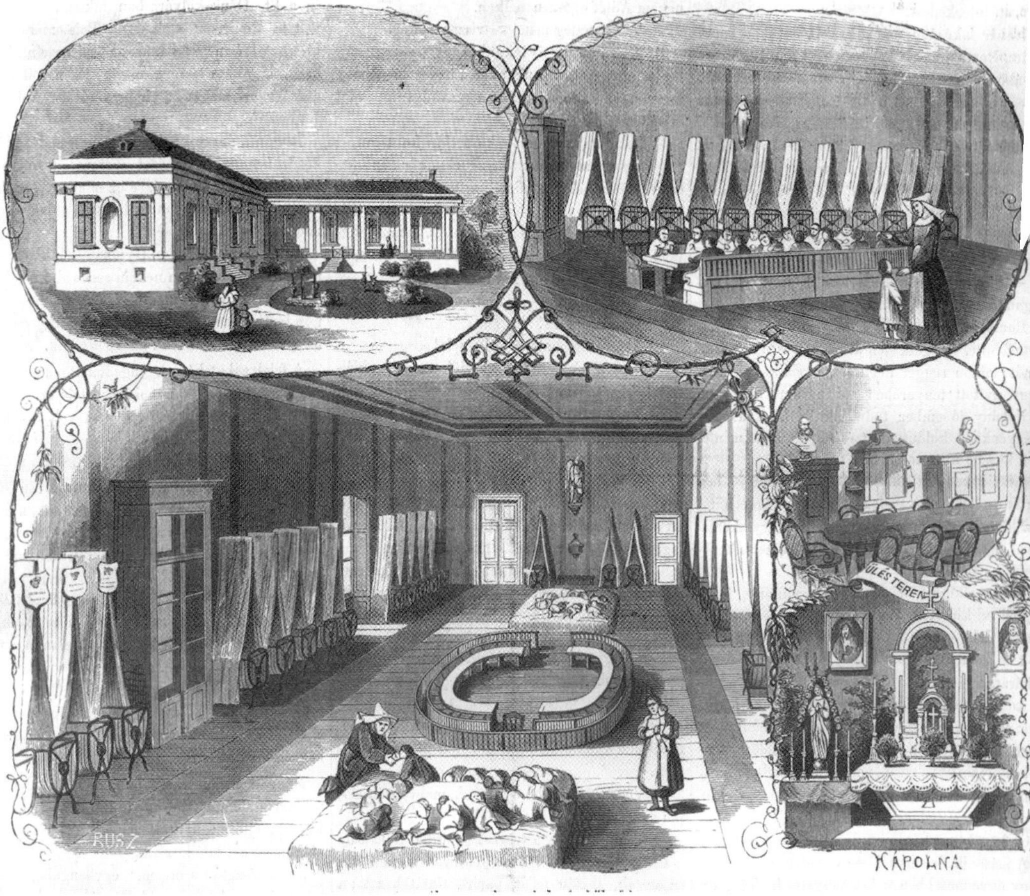

1. Rented facilities of the Budapest First Children's Asylum Association, 1871.

In the early period it was largely local actors, both private and public who engaged in welfare provision and almsgiving. Women's organizations, often established along denominational and ethnic lines, played an important role. Institutional welfare, including poorhouses, infirmaries and children's homes remained a significant feature of poverty policy throughout the period.

2. People's kitchen at the market in Buda, Budapest, 1874.

Since the 1870s the municipalities, small and large, were legally responsible for poor relief. Outdoor relief now developed into a more general feature of public assistance which, however, remained limited in scope and provided scarce benefits. In periods of economic depression and enhanced need, the authorities put special emphasis on immediate crisis intervention measures.

3. Nighttime razzia, Budapest, 1905.

Over the decades repression and especially the clearing of the public space from manifestations of poverty and need formed a key dimension of poverty policy. The criminalization of vagrancy, begging, and illegal prostitution were at the core of these policies. Different norms of decent behavior applied to poor women and men, with women being treated in an overtly sexualized manner.

4. The yard of the police prison for collecting relocatees, Budapest, 1908.

Internal migration and local responsibility for poor relief often resulted in forcible relocation of the poor to the legally responsible "home" municipality. The relocatees often could not even identify the often remote village or small town to which they legally belonged. Immediate return migration and renewed "vagrancy" was the order of the day.

5. Roma camp on the outskirts of Féltorony (Halbturn), Western Hungary, today Austria, 1909.

In the last years before World War I the pressure of repressive poor policy aimed at marginalized groups increased. New state legislation against the "work-shy" implicitly focused on the Roma while also mirroring the rising tension over the "social question" in the country. The Roma over the decades were always subject to specific repressive policies and social prejudice.

6. Crowd, assembled at the time of the distribution of 100,000 crowns bequeathed to the Jews of Pest by Baron Rothschild, 1911.

Welfare activities of denominational and other communities and individual actors continued to play a distinctive role in providing for the poor after the institutionalization of public assistance. The municipalities themselves sought to finance their related expenses through income from funds bequeathed from private donors or sponsored by particular revenue set aside for poverty policy.

7. The Budapest and Vienna mayors visiting the municipal bread factory, in front of one of the Budapest municipal housing projects, 1910.

From the turn of the century, new visions of "the social" and social reform emerged, especially in the fields of housing, child protection, and labor market policies. In part, state legislation enabled or supported these new beginnings, in part individual municipalities and especially the capital city of Budapest, where reformers had taken control of the municipal administration, took the lead.

8. Demonstration against rent usury, Budapest, 1910.

Militant tenants' activism and later a veritable rent-strike movement, supported but not dominated by the Social Democratic Party, played a significant role in bringing about the new public housing policy. Activities of the organized labor movement also played a role in new employment services developed on the national level and within the municipal unemployment policies in Budapest.

9. Boys playing cards in a park, Budapest, around 1905.

Around the turn of the century the Hungarian state identified children's misery and "abandonment" as one of the most burning social problems. Financed by a new state tax and the municipalities, a new childcare system was developed. A few years later attention shifted to child "neglect" and "delinquency", with more institutions of corrective education added to the system.

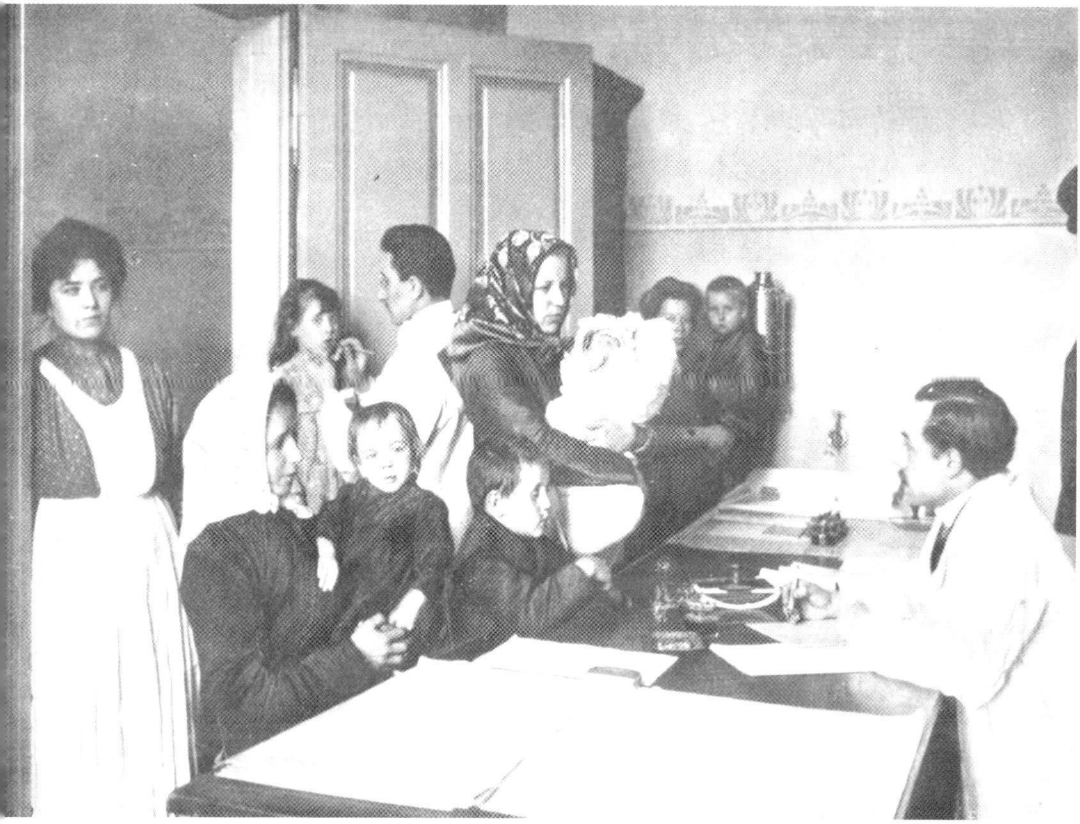

10. Children being admitted to the Central State Children's Home, Budapest, 1911.

Prioritizing foster care over family benefits, state childcare hoped to avoid conflation with old-style poor relief. Foster children were placed in Hungarian-dominated areas so as to promote Magyarization of the next generation. Widespread poverty and the generally low level of welfare made the system into what contemporaries perceived as a bottomless pit.

11. Workshop of the Hirmann Metalware Factory, Budapest, 1912.

Legislation aimed at protecting workers in trade and industry reached back into the middle of the 19th century. Labor protection setting minimum social standards at the workplace and in labor relations was often disregarded in practice. While minors were subject to special protection early on, gender-specific labor protection made inroads only in later decades.

12. Headquarters of the District Workers' Health and Accident Insurance Company, "an immaculate humanitarian institute, which has no equal in Hungary", Pozsony (Bratislava), today Slovakia, after 1906.

Workers' insurance provided for an unseen involvement of organized labor in expanding public social administration. Yet the political storm against the "red" insurance never died down, and heavy state supervision was introduced. Conflict in workers' insurance also erupted over incessant deficits and debt, and the relationship with the medical profession remained strained.

Quote taken from: *Illustrierter Führer durch Pozsony (Pressburg) und Umgebung* [Illustrated guide to Pozsony (Pressburg) and its surroundings] (Pressburg, no year given), 100.

13. Threshing, in Zsombolya (Jimbolia, Hatzfeld), today Romania, around 1910.

The strategic importance of the agrarian and agro-industrial workforce was mirrored in significant and partly original inventions in agrarian social policy involving a separate scheme of social insurance and rural housing policy. Yet this was combined with highly restrictive labor legislation and a bitter struggle over the boundary between agricultural and workers' insurance.

14. Building site for the new Palace of the Ministry of Finance, between 1901 and 1904.

Workers' insurance was so structured that it discriminated against informal and insecure as well as women's labor and labor organized within paternalistic legal frameworks. While a remarkable proportion of the overall workforce in trade and industry enjoyed insurance, the distance between urban and rural regions, and core as opposed to marginalized workers grew.

15. Charity ball in the capital city, 1875.

Even with, if unevenly, expanding poor relief and social policy as well as considerable efforts of social reform, social exclusion remained a dominant feature of Hungarian urban and rural society. The cleavage between the propertied and those benefiting from economic development on the one hand and the lower classes and the poor, on the other, was and remained vast.